D1826737

THE BOOK
IN THE
UNITED STATES
TODAY

THE BOOK
IN THE
UNITED STATES
TODAY

**Edited by
Gordon Graham
& Richard Abel**

TRANSACTION PUBLISHERS
New Brunswick (U.S.A.) and London (U.K.)

Copyright © 1996 by Whurr Publishers Ltd. as LOGOS, vol. 7., issue 1.

Printed in the United States of America in 1997 by agreement with
Whurr Publishers Ltd.

All rights reserved under International and Pan-American Copyright
Conventions. No part of this book may be reproduced or transmitted in any
form or by any means, electronic or mechanical, including photocopy, record-
ing, or any information storage and retrieval system, without prior permission
in writing from the publisher. All inquiries should be addressed to Transaction
Publishers, Rutgers—The State University, New Brunswick, New Jersey
08903.

This book is printed on acid-free paper that meets the American National
Standard for Permanence of Paper for Printed Library Materials.

Library of Congress Catalog Number: 97-6314
ISBN: 1-56000-972-1
Printed in the United States of America

Library of Congress Cataloging-in-Publication Data
The book in the United States today / edited by Gordon Graham and
Richard Abel.
    p.   cm.
  Originally published in 1996 as v. 7, issue 1 of Logos.
  ISBN 1-56000-972-1 (alk. paper)
    1. Publishers and publishing—United States—Congresses.
2. Booksellers and bookselling—United States—Congresses.
I. Abel, Richard, 1925–   . II. Logos (London, England)
Z471.B587   1997
070'.5'0973—dc21   97-6314
                                      CIP

Contents

Prolegomenon

Richard Abel

This book, originally published as an issue of LOGOS, grew out of a meeting of an international group of book trade hands held at a summer retreat in the Adirondacks. In the course of extended conversations turning on the international book trade and how LOGOS might most usefully and best relate to it, the observation was advanced that no broad-scale account and assessment of the commercial aspects of the US book trade – from publisher to library by way of book dealers and wholesalers – had been undertaken and broadly disseminated for some years. It was further observed that such a project would be of great utility not simply to readers in North America but elsewhere around the world. The latter not simply because the US trade is so large in both monetary terms and in its role as a major supplier of editorial content worldwide – principally books of entertainment – but also because it has tended to be a forerunner in many of the trends shaping the present structure of the trade in books – retail price-cutting, consolidation of publishing houses, superstores, online journals, etc. The seed to embark on such an undertaking was firmly planted before the sequence of meetings had run their course.

A small advisory group, including Mark Carroll, Dick Dougherty, Ivan Kats, Donald Lamm and Herb White, was formed to assist with those multifarious decisions and chores which the production of a genuinely sound and useful survey and assessment of so various a trade entails. The first matter demanding attention was, of course, the devising of the extent and nature of the contents required to make this a meaningful account and appraisal. This work, together with the tentative identification of the most suitable author for each article was, in substantial measure, completed before the group disbanded. So the seed was not simply sown, but germination was well advanced before the participants set out once again on their separate ways.

With this framework in hand, and the good offices of Lyman Newlin, whose continuing assistance is gratefully acknowledged, the recruiting of the contributors was undertaken. The criteria for suitable authors had been set to such an extraordinarily high mark by the advisory committee that there was substantial concern as to the likelihood of successfully inducing players of such stature in the trade to allocate, in already over-committed schedules, the time we knew would be needed to prepare a comprehensive and authoritative account of the sector of the trade each was being asked to write.

In the event, not only did each willingly agree, but more significantly provided, at the end of the day, papers which are truly outstanding accounts of the sectors which they addressed. Yes, unhappy circumstance compelled us to seek surrogates in a couple of instances – the most touching, but hardly a surrogate in light of a long-shared association, that of Betty Ballantine, who picked up the reins dropped upon the death of Ian.

LOGOS has long maintained the policy of seeking as authors those who not only are/have been active figures in the trade, but who, from that experience, are possessed of that reflective nature suited to distilling a coherent body of insights useful to others. All of the contributors not only possess these qualities in full measure, but virtually every one has taken his/her assignment so seriously as to have undertaken a substantial research effort to provide the reader with as sound an account and evaluation as time and informed effort can provide.

By drawing on such a wide spectrum of authors, the contents, taken as a whole, diverge in marked ways from an assessment made by a single author. Not only do the authors write from different professional backgrounds, but within these backgrounds, distinct and different postures are evident. Even so, a unifying thread can be observed in a greater or lesser concern of each contributor with respect to the impact of electronic technology on the world of books and journals. Indeed, the principal thrust of several turns on this perplexing and still far from resolved issue. This diversity of Weltanschauung and approach is one of the strengths of this colloquium, for it clearly reflects not only the broad reach of the book into the larger society and the great state of flux in which both the book and journal find themselves, but a healthy range of approaches which bode well for the continuing vitality of the book both as a cultural artifact and as one of the principal vehicles of cultural transmission.

So the reader will find discussion of the book cheek by jowl with discussion of the journal. Indeed, some publishers view them as of common or parallel importance, while librarians see the journal as a major source of their budgetary woes.

The Editors have tried to arrange a kind of sense of order on these singular and diverse papers. One concern has been to relate those papers which share, to some degree, as common a focus as such a varied lot of authorial viewpoints permits. The other has been to deliberately juxtapose contrasting contributions, in order to provide readers with frequent changes of pace and perception and to reflect the expansive variety and vitality of the key players.

The Editors are of the confirmed view that even readers well seasoned in the trade will come away from these papers with a wider and deeper understanding of "this curious trade" in which we are involved. But more importantly, we believe even the most skeptical will enjoy a substantially increased appreciation of what an extraordinary intellectual and moral enterprise we are all concerned with and the acute sense of responsibility for the continuing integrity of this marvelous patrimony brought to the enterprise by the best of its practitioners.

The Editors wish to acknowledge here our profound appreciation to the writers of the papers contained herein. Uniformly they have brought to the undertaking not only a wealth of experience in that sector of the US book world which they address, but a much appreciated sense of purpose in bringing to the reader the considered fruits of their service in the trade.

1

A Religious Country Reflected in Its Publishing Industry

Werner Mark Linz

When the British introduced book publishing to North America in the early years of the 17th century, the first books to be printed were the King James version of the Bible and other religious publications. This simply reflected the history of publishing in Europe, which from its beginning in 1456, when Gutenberg printed his Bible, was linked inexorably with religion. Religion-based publishing spread rapidly from Germany to England, France, Italy, the Netherlands and Spain. Those responsible for propagating the Christian faith speedily harnessed the power of the printing press to spread the word. The British were not the first to introduce publishing in North America. The Catholic Bishop of Mexico established a press in Mexico City in 1528 to produce religious books of all kinds in support of his church.

Today, religious publishing in the United States – Catholic, Protestant, Jewish and more – constitutes only between 5% and 10% of the American book market. But this is not a small business. At least 2,500 religious titles are published each year out of the annual total of around 50,000. The American public spends annually some $2bn on religious books, 6.6% of the total of nearly $30bn spent on all books.

A true and uncompromising definition of a religious book would be difficult, if not impossible, to come by. The publishing industry defines such a book for its own convenience as one with a religious theme. Yet

1

many popular novels, which it would not be accurate to call religious books, have religious themes. The problem of definition is complicated further by the fact that religious publishers issue some titles that have only a slight relation to religion and some that have none at all. Furthermore, the religious departments of large trade houses occasionally produce titles sold through regular trade channels and not, therefore, regarded as religious.

Religious publishers' lists fall into one or more of four categories:

1. Bibles, along with devotional manuals;
2. inspirational books written not for the clergy but for the layperson;
3. books directed to the theologian and professional clergy; and
4. textbooks used in religious educational programs.

Bibles and devotional manuals constitute a class by themselves because most of them are sure sellers and enjoy predictable sales year after year. When a new edition or translation of the Bible is commissioned, the project becomes a major undertaking for the publishing company, stretching over years and often times engendering large investments by the group sponsoring the project.

The sales of a successful Bible are often spectacular, with some editions running rapidly into millions and comparing with commercial bestsellers in profitability. An inspirational title written for the layperson, on the other hand, usually commands no more than a modest advance for the writer, with royalties conforming to acceptable textbook standards. Such a book usually gets off to a slow start, but once its sales are established, it can turn out to be a solid seller and may remain in print indefinitely. If the author of such a title is a well-known theologian or popular personality, launching the book may cost the publisher as much as would be spent on a strong trade book. Equally, religious textbooks, especially those that find wide use in adult and youth parish educational programs, may require major investments.

Serious theological books written for the clergy may be purchased by laypersons who have become interested in religious matters and want to study them at first hand, but generally such books have more limited sales records. Books for the clergy frequently require financial subsidies, but the other three categories of religious works – inspirational, theological and textbooks – can be self-sufficient, and even profitable.

*   *   *   *   *

The readership of a religious book varies according to the spiritual level of the reader and the area of interest that the book commands. Who the reader is – layperson, religious scholar or educator, church official or a member of the clergy – clearly affects his or her interest in each religious offering. Good reading for a religious leader may differ greatly from that of a member of the congregation.

Readers of religious books are not distributed evenly across the population of the US. One reason for this is that religious books are generally marketed outside of the trade mainstream. The hundred-odd religious book publishers – mostly private or denominational and covering a broad spectrum – use direct mail and book clubs extensively, with particular success in the Sun Belt of the South and Southwest and in parts of the West Coast.

There are also about 5,000 religious bookstores, which are particularly strong in the Northeast and Pacific States, where the proportion of religious book sales to other books far exceeds that in the rest of the country. The Southeastern states buy the fewest religious books in proportion to their population.

There are usually some (mostly old) religious titles available in regular retail bookstores, discount stores and even supermarkets. But because the bulk of the sales are usually made outside the general and chain bookstores, religious books seldom appear on bestseller lists, even when sales would have justified it. The exception is the Bible – a perennial bestseller, accounting for more than one out of five religious book sales.

Sales through Christian bookstores are approximately $600m (out of the total sales of religious books of $1.4bn). In addition, publishers achieve many of their sales through mail order solicitation, in some cases 50% or more. Because this method of marketing is not subject to the ups and downs of normal retail selling, religious books are not usually affected by recessions or economic slumps, but generally enjoy long shelf lives.

The mix of religious publishing is wide-ranging. It includes denominational and non-denominational presses, as well as secular and university presses, international agencies as well as local ecumenical agencies, and large trade publishers with religious departments.

By the very nature of the religious book, reprints, revisions and backlists have always been vital to book inventories, as readers have become more sophisticated in their tastes and have chosen more serious titles reflecting sound intellectual and solid theological backgrounds. In the 1980s, the percentage increase in unit sales of hardback and paperback religious books exceeded that in sales of general adult trade books and book clubs. As the century neared its final decade, the softcover book was just beginning to take over much of the place of the hardcover. The decline in unit sales of hardcover trade books during that same period was viewed as the response of younger readers to prices higher than they considered justified. However, this attitude did not seem to affect religious works, which remained lower in price than the average trade book.

In the '80s and '90s, the religious book industry has enjoyed a steady rise in the numbers of volumes sold as well as of titles published; also in popularity, readership and economic success. But the last fifty years have not seen constant progress. In ascertaining the worth of religious publishing as we approach the turn of the century, it is necessary to review the field since the years following World War II, when a high-water mark of religious book publishing was reached.

A harbinger of what was to come in religious publishing in the second half of the century was provided by the fiction market – at least for those who had the prescience to understand it. During the '40s, novels with religious themes followed one another with remarkable regularity and rapidity on the bestseller lists:

1941:	*The Keys of the Kingdom*, by A J Cronin
1943:	*The Song of Bernadette*, by Franz Werfel
1943-4-5:	*The Robe*, by Lloyd C Douglas
1944:	*The Razor's Edge*, by W Somerset Maugham
1946-7:	*The Miracle of the Bells*, by Russell Janney
1948-9:	*The Big Fisherman*, by Lloyd C Douglas
1950-1:	*The Cardinal*, by Henry Morton Robinson

During that same decade, other religious books were consistently garnering huge sales. Harry Emerson Fosdick's *The Man from*

Nazareth appeared as the Book-of-the-Month Club selection in 1949. E Stanley Jones's *Abundant Living*, one of three volumes of daily devotions, had a surprise sale of 750,000 copies.

Even theological studies zoomed to the top. With the publication of *Interpreter's Bible*, a twelve-volume set edited by George A Butrick, Catholic writers suddenly reached audiences far beyond the parameters of their faith. Four of the ten bestselling non-fiction titles of 1949 could be labelled religious: *The Seven Storey Mountain* by Thomas Merton; *The Greatest Story Ever Told* by Fulton Oursler; *Peace of Soul* by Fulton J Sheen; and *A Guide to Confident Living* by Norman Vincent Peale.

During the following ten years, religion-oriented titles could frequently be found among the top ten in both fiction and non-fiction. *A Man Called Peter* by Catherine Marshall; *This I Believe* by Edward P Morgan; and *The Power of Positive Thinking* by Norman Vincent Peale all appeared in 1952. That year was important for the first of two major events that had extraordinary religious significance for publishers in the decades following World War II: the publication and promotion of a brand-new translation of the King James version of the Bible by Thomas Nelson Publishers. The second major event was the convening of Vatican II by Pope John XXIII in 1962 and the resultant revolutionary changes in Catholic liturgy and Bible study. Both these events were instrumental in startling shifts in religious publishing that impelled many laypersons to buy more books with religious themes – and many also to cease buying them altogether.

The King James version of the Bible had been a steady bestseller since 1611. A major revision, known as the English Revised Version, had appeared in 1881 and had achieved an unexpectedly high sale of a million copies on the day of publication. American members of the translation committee had dropped out of the project and in 1901 published their own American Standard version. Fifty years later, many still saw difficulties in the American Standard's old-fashioned prose. The time was ripe for another attempt at a truly modern Bible. The Nelson interdenominational Revised Standard, published in varying shapes and sizes and ranging in price from $1.00 to $20.00 and higher, responded to this demand and was enormously successful.

So the '50s were a time of euphoria for religious publishing houses. In the nerve-racked '60s, much of it fell apart. No one knows for sure what caused it – the civil rights' struggle; the political dissension over the Vietnam War; the youth rebellion; the sexual revolution; or simply Vatican II and its revolutionary shift in liturgical and ecumenical activities. In any event, the '60s saw interest in truly religious publications first increase and then plummet abruptly.

In the Catholic sector of the industry, Pope John XXIII's loosening of the bonds of tradition, with its far-reaching effects in altering much of Catholic life, caused a temporary rise in lay theology, but sales of missals and prayer books plunged disastrously. Concurrent with this slump, ironically enough, there was increased interest in religion on the airwaves. Spearheaded by popular evangelists and Protestant fundamentalists, the broadcasting phenomenon, both on radio and television, continues to this day, and it has not all been bad news for publishers. Many of the evangelists of the air have stimulated the sales of popular religious books. Some publishers have looked askance at mass merchandising of books on the air and blamed the evangelists in part for the depression in their trade. Mass circulation of religious books, they claim, has diluted the true worth of all religious publications. Evangelists, they say, have replaced pastors. Scholars, they lament, have been ousted by entertainers.

In spite of these cries, hundreds of religious titles of good quality, written by authors of conscience and taste who never appeared on either radio or television, continued to be published. Protestant presses experienced a surge in sales. The evangelical revival was helping them instead of hurting them. The movement seemed to emphasize a return to basic values, with Bible study and private and public morality featured. The religious bookstore universe expanded dramatically in the '70s.

Among Protestants, what had once been called "fundamentalism" was now politely known as "evangelical" or sometimes simply "conservative" publishing. However, the term "fundamentalist" was heard more and more in the atmosphere of the '80s. While there was little agreement about the meaning of these labels, there was no doubt that the overall effect on publishing was beneficial. During the '70s and '80s, the religious publishing field developed its own bestseller lists, its own specialized stores and magazines – and even its own annual bookseller convention, run by the Christian Booksellers Association, complete with large annual meetings and trade exhibits. At the same time, the sectors in religious publishing became more pronounced, the largest group constituting denominational publishers. Many religious publishers represented no denomination at all. Some were conservative, some evangelical, some liberal, some ecumenical. Whatever their affiliations, their lists tended to reflect current controversy within each faith or tradition.

Both Protestant and Catholic faiths published a number of books centered on the charismatic movement – the type of Christianity that emphasizes personal religious experience and divinely inspired powers, as of healing, prophecy, the gift of tongues and the laying on of hands. Books like Hal Lindsey's *The Late Great Planet Earth* moved far beyond the traditional religious experience, expressing the assertion that soon all Christians would depart from the world to a better life, leaving Christ to establish a millennial reign on earth.

Books on popular theology proliferated: *Angels: God's Secret Agents* by Billy Graham; *If This Be Heresy* by James A Pike; *The Screwtape Letters* by C S Lewis; and inspirational books by Catherine Marshall, Dale Evans Rogers and Anita Bryant. Since the '70s, there were many titles concerning women's place in church and society, eg, *Women in the Pulpit: Is God an Equal Opportunity Employer?*

Scholarly works by American women theologians became especially influential and often very powerful, eg, *In Memory of Her* by Elisabeth Schussler-Pierlura.

Jewish religious publishing has also prospered in the last fifty years. Generally defined as "books about Jews written by Jews for Jewish readers", or, more simply, "books of Jewish interest", they are issued by publishers catering for Orthodox, Reform and Conservative Judaism, each house issuing its own Bibles, prayer books and liturgical texts as the basic instruments of the faith. By the '70s, there were two large houses specializing in Jewish religious education: the Union of American Hebrew Congregations, representing Reform Judaism, and the United Synagogues of America, representing Conservative Judaism. Both published textbooks for use in synagogue schools.

The religious departments of general booksellers soon showed some interest in the demand for Jewish books. Doubleday published a number of hardback titles for the Jewish market and Bantam Books followed with paperbacks. Bookazine, a general book distributor in New York, publishes the twice-yearly *Judaica Book News*, which has come to be regarded as a primary tool in the marketing of Jewish religious books.

* * * * *

Today, there are well over 50,000 religious titles in print in the US, the majority of them Christian. Religious publishing ranks sixth in title output among twenty-three publishing categories, which include fiction, biography, poetry, juveniles, reference, art, self-improvement, sports and hobbies, business and professional books.

While readers of religious subjects have become much more ecumenical in their preferences, the market has remained stratified. Many denominations prefer to support only their own distribution centers, thus putting a de facto limit on available publications. Most religious book clubs and direct mail operations have denominational or organizational ties that tend to limit dissemination of their titles. While college bookstores hold large selections of religious books, the average public library circulates only a small number of titles. Most secular bookstores still contain a few shelves of religious titles. Equally, the national reviewing media are dominated by secular books, and few religious titles are reviewed for the general public.

Nevertheless, as the 20th century draws to a close, the total market for religious books in the US is enormous. There are an estimated 50,000 church and synagogue libraries; more than 600 church-affiliated four-year colleges and universities; and over 300,000 churches and synagogues. Roman Catholics comprise the largest single Christian body, nearly 30% of the total population of 250 million Americans. Protestant breaks down into Baptist 20%; Methodist 10%; Lutheran 5%; Presbyterian 3%; Episcopalian and Pentecostal 2% each; and numerous other denominations totalling 15%. The balance of religious adherence includes Jewish 2%; Muslim 1%; and Buddhist 0.5%.

Books are more important in some denominations than in others. The interdenominational Church and Synagogue Library Association has analyzed the ranking of library subscribers and found that Presbyterians and Methodists have the highest proportions of book users, followed by Episcopalians, Lutherans, Baptists and Mennonites.

Population trends in the US – specifically increased longevity – tend to favor continued growth in the purchase of religious books. There is also a new and emerging group of readers in the twenty-five to forty-four age range, which increased by more than ten million in the '70s and '80s, and continues to escalate.

In the light of this, there should logically be a greater growth in the sale of paperback religious books, which still fail to reach significant numbers of readers. The reason is that access to religious books is limited to fewer than 6,000 specialized smaller bookstores, while general paperback bestsellers have the potential to be placed in as many as 60,000 retail outlets, served by more than 500 distributors nationwide.

While in the past some backlist religious titles have broken sales records, unfortunately this does not apply to new titles coming on the market every year (except for occasional religious or "new age" personality books). The essence of retailing any book is time and space utility: having the product when and where the costomer wants it. A book so favored, especially one that is low-priced, as most religious books are, will be seen, and hopefully bought, by the greatest number of readers. In terms of distribution, this means the ability to supply a minimum order for initial inventory and then to resupply the titles that move successfully in the shortest period of time. However, it takes several weeks for a publisher to process an ordinary order, and most wholesalers concentrate on brand new titles of general interest and proven backlist sellers, and still have to issue special orders to publishers for almost all classical and backlist religious titles.

The crux of the problem of retailing religious books is the reluctance of general booksellers to stock large assortments of them. This scarcity cannot be counterbalanced by heavy book club and mail order promotions. But there is one aspect of book distribution in which religious titles seem to perform better than the rest of the book business. Returns average between 10% and 20%, compared with 30% to 35% for general trade books and as much as 60% for mass-market paperbacks.

Although the general movement of the book industry is toward high unit sales of fewer titles, relatively few general trade books sell over 100,000 copies, and even fewer religious books sell over 50,000. But religious books do remain longer in print, and this enhances their chance of higher total sales, enabling their publishers to reduce unit costs and increase profits – even for the not-for-profit religious houses.

Overall, the stability and continuity among religious publishers – denominational or commercial – reflect the stability and continuity of a country where religion flourishes in many different ways. Americans continue to search for meaning and to give thanks for abundance spiritually and ethically – as individuals, families and communities to whom religious books have been central. Religious publishers, and publishers of religious books, continue to serve and survive or succeed in a market that has reflected underlying historical and societal events and trends in North America over the last fifty years. Through creative editorial programs and energetic marketing practices, this sector of American publishing will continue to reflect the spiritual development of the nation.

Chairman and Chief Executive Officer of the Continuum Publishing Group, which he established in New York together with the Crossroad Publishing Company in 1980, Werner Mark Linz has been at the center of religious publishing in the United States since he moved from Germany to New York in 1959. His first association was with Herder & Herder, where he held various executive positions until 1973, when he became President and Chief Executive of the Seabury Press. Linz received his education (humanistic studies, book publishing and business administration) in Cologne, Frankfurt and New York. Throughout his career he has been active in many publishing associations and committees.

2

Children's Books: 500 Million a Year. Where to Go from Here?

Charles E Gates

In the immediate post-World War II era, juvenile books were poor cousins in the relatively small hothouse book world which had been delineated in the '20s and '30s. The juvenile titles published by the major trade houses were directed mainly at the library market. They depended on series or chapter books, such as the Nancy Drew Mysteries, The Hardy Boys or the Tell Me Why Books, to make their juvenile departments profitable. Of course, authors like Dr Seuss or Beatrix Potter contributed in a major way to maintaining these somewhat exotic enclaves in the world of trade publishing.

I was introduced to the world of children's books in 1959. My mentor was Martin Levin [a contributor to this issue]. I was working for the distribution division of Curtis Publishing Company, publishers of the *Saturday Evening Post, Ladies' Home Journal* and *Holiday Magazine,* among many others. The role of Curtis Circulation was to get magazines (their own and others) quickly into the hands of the independent wholesalers (ie, those other than the American News Company), and onwards into retail outlets – newsstands, drugstores, etc. When the first mass-market paperbacks began to appear, many of their publishers [see Ballantine in this issue] turned to Curtis Circulation. That was how I became involved with the book trade.

Curtis and Grosset & Dunlap, the trade publisher, each owned 50%

of Wonder Books, a mass-market publisher of hardcover and softcover children's books. Martin Levin was the Sales Manager for Wonder Books and employed me to work with him in Los Angeles to introduce our line of inexpensive kids' books to supermarkets and drugstore chains in the Western states. In 1965, I moved to New York to become Sales Manager for Wonder Books, and eventually for Grosset & Dunlap.

Wonder Books' strongest competitor was Little Golden Books, which sold for 25¢. Wonder Story Books were more expensive – 29 ¢ each, but in our opinion were of superior construction. They were bound and sewn rather than stapled. Wonder Books also had a lot more to offer than Wonder Story Books, eg, a line of softcover, graded, school supplemental *Practice Workbooks* (39 ¢); *How and Why Books,* covering everything from science to history (50 ¢); *Treasure Coloring Books* (25 ¢); hardcover, controlled-vocabulary *Easy Readers* (50 ¢); *Read Alouds* – softcover fiction (39 ¢); and *SturdiBoard* books for babies (50 ¢).

These books sold in millions. They were designed to appeal to the busy mothers of toddlers and pre-schoolers. We placed them where they would be bought on impulse while shopping for the family's groceries. They were all priced so as not to dent the family budget. Practically all the sales were made in what was then the mass market – supermarket chains, variety stores, chains such as Woolworths and drugstore chains such as Walgreens.

Neither Little Golden Books nor Wonder Books could look to traditional and conventional outlets to market their publications, because their books were part of the post-war mass-market revolution aimed at non-traditional readers.

* * * * *

To understand the market environment for all regular books forty years ago, it is important to remember that there were no national bookstore chains. Independent booksellers dominated the market and tended to be Mom-and-Pop operations. If they provided for a juvenile section, and most did not, it was likely to be at the back of the store where a few bestselling titles were laid out. The major outlet for trade publishers was the department store. In many cases, the book department of a department store was the only show in town. The department store bookbuyer was usually not only an experienced book person, but wielded such great marketing power that publishers not infrequently consulted her over what should be published. Faith Brunson, at Rich's Department Store in Atlanta, was just such a bookbuyer. But sometimes the department store bookbuyer was the newest and least experienced on the staff, often responsible for several departments. I knew one who had to select women's handbags as well as books. Whatever their bona fides or experience, no department store buyer would ever dream of stocking a book at a list price of less than $1.00. That was how retail sales, not only of juvenile trade, but of adult trade books, were achieved in those days.

The ways in which we sought to reach these readers were reminiscent of the cosmetic business, in which the whims of major department store buyers can make or break a new lipstick or perfume. Such a buyer, working hand-in-hand with the publisher, could create a best-seller. Eighty per cent of a department store's sales come in the Christmas season. In anticipation of this high point, buyers were often ready to buy in whatever publishers suggested – especially if you were supporting such purchases with generous advertising allowances. Much of the negotiating for such deals occurred at the American Booksellers Association's annual convention, where publishers made elaborate presentations to department store buyers. One question the buyers always asked was: "How big is the print run?" Once they knew this, they were ready to decide how much of the run they were willing to buy. Needless to say, the "print run" was always adjusted on the spot, based on what publishers thought the market would bear.

Buyers' bonuses were based on sales. They hated to lose even a single-copy sale because a title had gone out of stock. However, their willingness to buy was frequently counter-balanced by their employers' strict budgeting systems, a constraint which made it particularly important for publishers to get orders confirmed either at the ABA or shortly thereafter. Immediately after Christmas, and before January inventories were taken, all unsold books would be returned. In my first years in publishing I was deeply shocked by the enormous percentages of returns. Our largest accounts ran credit balances from January until they placed their fall orders, after which the cycle repeated itself.

* * * * *

The small world of juvenile publishing was transformed in the mid-'60s when President Johnson's New Society program suddenly made millions of tax dollars available to the nation's libraries and schools for the purchase of "supplemental reading materials". The Johnson administration was determined to cure the "Why Johnny Can't Read" syndrome by means of government largesse. These funds, referred to as "Title 2" money (I never knew why) included a "use it or lose it" stipulation. Juvenile publishers found themselves inundated with orders. Sales managers of houses who were working on some kind of bonus plan suddenly were earning more than the presidents of their companies.

Publishers could sell almost anything they printed, provided it had a "library binding" and was non-fiction. A 50 ¢ *How and Why Book* could be sold for $5.00 – with a reinforced binding. Best of all (from the publishers' point of view), libraries and schools had not yet caught on to trade discounts. "Educational discounts" of 20% on titles already marked up in price over their trade editions (thanks to the "special binding") brought their publishers previously unheard of margins of profit.

Suddenly, long-neglected children's departments of major publishing houses were star performers. Publishers who had never had juvenile departments became eager to establish them. Overnight, more hardcover, non-fiction juveniles were being published in the US than ever before, including, inevitably, a lot of junk.

Naturally, it was too good to last. The decline of the program started in the mid-'70s under President Nixon and was completed in President Reagan's administration. Liz Gordon, Publisher of Disney Press, told me that Reagan said: "My school did not have a library. Look how I turned out." As government funds dried up, juvenile sales skidded. While a lot of people lost their jobs, the profit that juveniles had earned in these bonanza years convinced many publishers that it was too good a field of publishing to be abandoned. After all, juvenile departments were up and running, complete with editors and staff. What they needed was simply better sales.

Their salvation was the "baby boomer" parents. In my generation, parents paid their taxes and expected the schools to educate us without much more parental involvement. This did not mean that reading at home was not encouraged, but that was what the library was for. Anyway, the small West Texas town where I first fell in love with books and reading had neither a bookstore nor a department store. The local library was the only source of sustenance for my growing literary appetite.

The new generation, by contrast, had quietly and painfully learned that the schools were not always doing the best possible job of educating their children. Certainly, the better schools regularly turned out more college applicants than the poorer schools, but even the poorest school could provide a satisfactory education if the children were willing and the parents were ready to help. Parents began to animate their children's desire to learn by providing their own "head start" programs at home. All they needed were the materials. Parents began to demand good books for their children from infancy onwards. Once publishers came to recognize and appreciate this emerging market, and to start publishing for it, juvenile sales skyrocketed once again. The impulse of parental motivation started in the late '60s and facilitated a remarkable growth of juvenile publishing in the '80s. It remains the driving force today. Juvenile publishing grew by over 400% between 1980 and 1992. The last big spurt saw sales double from $500m in 1987 to $1bn in 1992.

*   *   *   *   *

Since 1992, sales have been relatively flat. It is estimated that in 1994 publishers' billing of children's books totalled about $1.2bn from sales of 526 million units. This was a decline of 1.1% from 1993. Fifteen publishers control about 89% of the market. Together they determine what kinds of books are made available to the public. Save for the enormous sale of movie and television tie-in books, initiated largely by Disney and Barney, the juvenile publishing scene is not much more diverse than it was back in 1959 – just much more expensive and much more novelty-driven. Little hardcover juvenile fiction is now published, and print runs of 5,000 copies or less last for two years, with libraries accounting for most of the purchases. Paperback fiction, on the other hand, is growing almost beyond belief. I wish I had bought stock in Scholastic when I first heard of the print runs of its Goosebump Series. Major sales in juvenile books today – with the exceptions of the *Babysitter's Club* and lines like the Goosebumps – are pretty much confined to the pre-school and early grade school markets.

However, there are solid sales to be made in up-market hardcover non-fiction for older children. Dorling Kindersley's output is a good example of this genre. Anthologies of older literature and childhood classics can also sell quite well, particularly as nostalgic gift purchases by those hoping their children – or grandchildren – will enjoy them as much as they did. There is also considerable evidence that there is a serious and growing collectors' market for good juvenile books. To my certain knowledge, any pop-up book automatically becomes a collectible, at a price several times its list price, as soon as it goes out of print.

How much the business has changed and yet remains the same can be revealed by perusing the 1994 *Red and Black* report from *Publishers Weekly,* listing the bestselling frontlist and backlist titles of all publishers. I never look at these figures without being depressed over the small number of titles selling, or at least reported as selling, more than 75,000 copies – with returns, I imagine in most cases, still to be accounted for. In 1994, only thirteen new titles sold over 200,000 copies. Seven of these were *Lion King* books. Three more were based on Disney movies and the thirteenth was a Barney book. Only Eric Carle's new board book version of *The Very Hungry Caterpillar,* and *The Christmas Bunny* made the top thirteen without television or movie tie-ins. Twenty-five titles sold over 100,000 and another twenty-one over 75,000. In all, thirty-one of the fifty-nine bestselling new hardcover books were based upon movies or television shows. Keeping in mind that hardcover juvenile book sales declined 1.1% in 1994, one wonders what would have happened without these media tie-ins? Such heavy dependence on the initiatives of the audio-visual media can only be depressing to the causes of social progress, literacy and culture.

On the other hand, paperback sales grew dramatically in 1994, when 130 new titles sold over 100,000 copies, compared with only ninety in 1993. Most of the credit goes to R L Stine, whose Goosebumps series captured thirteen of the fourteen top spots. In fact, series books dominated the list, with a total of eighty-one titles. Add another twenty for movie and TV tie-ins, and 101 of the 130 bestselling books are accounted for.

As with adult trade, backlist titles have always been the backbone of juvenile publishing. In 1994, there were seventy-five backlist hard-cover titles selling 100,000 copies or more and 106 selling 125,000 copies or more. But again, I must unhappily report, the titles dominating the backlist, like those forming the frontlist bestsellers, were tie-ins. The tremendous sales of tie-in books are a powerful indicator of the potential for all juvenile books – provided publishers produce what our audiences want.

There are lessons to be learned by juvenile publishers from publishers of adult books, who have done a wonderful job of creating "superstars" like Tom Clancy, John Grisham, Stephen King and so many others. Any book by one of these superstars becomes an automatic bestseller. Juvenile publishers should develop more juvenile stars, like Eric Carle, Jan Brett, David Carter, Dr Seuss and others, whose names, without any dependence on tie-ins, are guarantees of print runs and sales exceeding 200,000.

Who is going to develop these stars? The fifteen publishers who control 89% of the market are (in descending order):

Publisher		1994 ($m)
1.	Western Publishing	290
2.	Random House	120
3.	HarperCollins	93
4.	Simon & Schuster	90
5.	Scholastic	83
6.	Putnam	81
7.	Penguin USA	72
8.	Bantam Doubleday Dell	55
9.	Disney Publishing	45
10.	Hearst (Morrow/Avon)	41
11.	Dorling Kindersley	26
12.	Houghton Mifflin	24
13.	Harcourt Brace	20
14.	Little, Brown	20
15.	Henry Holt	10.2

That was the list in 1994. At the beginning of 1996, I would venture

to add: Publishers International in Chicago (producers of predominantly novelty soundbooks for the mass market); Candlewick (the US
division of Walker Books); Joshua Morris (the former packager
acquired by Reader's Digest); and Landoll (a mass-market publisher
with reported revenues of $50m +).

But the addition of these four imprints is unlikely, I predict, to
increase the number of major players. Mergers and acquisitions are
ever with us.

*   *   *   *   *

Meanwhile, every juvenile publisher, large or small, is having to
cope with changes in the pattern of distribution that have occurred in
the last few years. The Book Industry Study Group (BISG) analysis of
October 1995 reported that only 5% of juvenile books were purchased at independent bookstores and only 10% at book chains. The
highest percentage (30) are sold by discount houses, with book clubs a
distinct second at 17%. Where else do you go to buy children's books
today? Toy stores, food and drug stores, mail order catalogs, variety
stores, warehouse clubs and a lot of other places. This in contrast with
adult books, 50% of which are sold through chain and independent
bookstores. Although most children's book publishers with whom I
spoke believe that the percentage of sales through bookstores, both
independent and chain, was understated in the BISG report, all con-
ceded that the major share of their sales was made in the "other markets". BISG also reported that unit sales hover round the half billion
mark and show no signs of improving, although dollar sales are edg-
ing up, probably due to price increases. Two-thirds of the unit sales are
paperbacks.

I have difficulty in believing that only 10% of juvenile sales are
through chain bookstores. What, one wonders, in the light of the welcome that book lovers have given to the growth of the superstores [see
Horvath in this issue], accounts for the differential between juvenile
and adult book sales? I have a theory. Perhaps the wonderful displays
of children's books in superstores are simply overwhelming. After all,
most juvenile bookbuyers are shopping for someone else, and that
someone else is a child. Unless you have a specific title in mind, you
can be totally confused by the multitude of choices. Alas, the superstores have displaced many "children's only" bookstores. Their decline

is sad, since they were truly the children's publishers' best friends. Often they spotted trends long before the publishers did and created bestsellers by personal recommendations. It is possible that the buyers of children's books need help and guidance which the superstores, serving primarily the intellectual and cultural needs of adults, are unable to provide.

The October 1995 BISG report convinces me that juvenile books are now much more price-sensitive and much more impulse purchases than they ever were before. Consumers do not go to discount stores with the intention of buying juvenile books. The BISG report further reveals that over 56% of all unit sales of juvenile books were made at outlets normally offering discounts. If we add book clubs and book fairs – both of which provide incentives to purchase below the retail prices – the percentage of discounted sales jumps to eighty.

I am frequently told by publishers that it is difficult to sell a hardcover novelty book for over $12.95, unless it is really special or different. But a warehouse discount store will sell a $12.95 book for $7.80. A chain superstore will probably sell it for under $10.00. And you can be sure it will cost substantially less than the retail price at a toy chain such as Toys R Us. In such a price environment, it is easy to imagine a customer's reaction when he or she happens on a pop-up or thirty-two-page picture book at $18.95. In the vast majority of titles, the retail price is becoming only a benchmark from which the publishers calculate the trade discounts they can afford. These range from 40% to a high of 60%, the latter usually restricted to a large non-returnable sale. Even higher discounts are sometimes given for special "print quantities" sales. Retailers are free to charge whatever price suits them. With discount houses, chains and many other kinds of outlets all offering discounts to their customers, it is small wonder that the latter rebel when offered a book at the full price. At bottom, the retail list prices are a farce, and the consumers know it.

Who are these consumers? The BISG study tells us that mothers and grandparents still account for the great majority of juvenile purchases and that most books are bought as gifts. To reach more of these consumers, new marketing ideas in children's books are continually being developed. A recent example, not yet widely reported, is "display marketing". The few titles so far sold in this way have achieved very impressive unit sales. My own experience as a packager with our

"Mick Inkpen Inkpops" is an example. These are four little mini pop-ups retailing at $5.00 each. The original trade publisher, Bedrock Press, sold a little over 50,000 copies of each title. Then a display marketer called Reading's Fun sold 75,000 more copies of each. Our sale to Scholastic Book Fairs of the same titles sold another 35,000 of each. So, of the 160,000 copies sold of each title, 110,000 were sold in the special sales area. The alternative sales were much bigger than the trade sales. Where might this lead? We might sell, at best, five or six titles or series through these special sales, out of the approximately 100 titles we publish each year. Clearly, no publisher can depend upon sales to display marketers as the central thrust of the business, but equally clearly, we cannot possibly ignore the opportunities that these specialized marketers represent. Every publisher with whom I have spoken reports that special sales are becoming more and more important.

* * * * *

All of which leads back to the vexed question of why unit sales remain so persistently static. There has been much talk about CD-ROMs cutting into the juvenile book business. I don't buy that! Any parent who can afford to buy computer products can buy regular books. There is no sign that parents by the hundreds of thousands are simply turning their backs on books in a lemming-like stampede to CD-ROM. Personally, I have used dozens of CD-ROMs. Once you are over the novelty, in my opinion they are boring. But, unwilling to look only to my own response, I have tested them with children and have yet to find a child willing to undertake all of the activities on a CD-ROM before becoming bored. By contrast, how many times do children insist on having their favorite books read to them? Those whose faith in the book may be wavering have only to watch infants encountering magazines and books for the first time. First they are fascinated simply by turning the pages. Then fascination gives way to infatuation as they learn to recognize the images on the pages.

I have recently installed System 7.5 on my Macintosh by inserting another disk whenever instructed, always a nervous moment for a neophyte like me. As I did so, a stream of messages kept appearing on the screen telling me how I could solve any problem simply by asking for "on-screen help". This help consisted of instructing me to see pages

140 to 145 in my 300-page instruction book. These tomes required to explain computers are one reason why I don't think the computer will ever replace the printed page.

I do think children's videos are cutting into our sales. At one time, we juvenile book publishers had a price advantage against videos. Not any more. Our pop-up for Disney's *Lion King* has a suggested retail price of $12.95. The video, published just months after the theatrical release, bears a suggested price of $19.95, but anyone can get it, with all the discounts and coupon rebates, for as little as $9.95 – serious price competition for children's entertainment. As with the book, children will watch the video over and over again. But at the same time, the "Disneys" and "Barneys" have shown us that huge numbers of children's books can also be sold. All we have to do is publish the books that children and parents want, at prices they can afford, let them know that we have them and place them where they can easily be purchased.

I read recently that Philip Morris has an annual promotion and advertising budget of $3bn for Marlboro cigarettes – two-and-a-half times the *sales* of juvenile literature in the US. We ought to be able to grow our sales to equal the Marlboro ad budget. This modest goal could, in my judgment, be achieved by juvenile publishers, their editors and marketing people hand-in-hand with their authors. The children are on our side.

President and CEO of Intervisual Books, the leading packager of pop-up books, from 1992 to 1996, Charles Gates began his career in children's book publishing as the representative of Curtis Publishing Company in Los Angeles in 1957. In the intervening years he served as Sales Manager of Grosset & Dunlap, Vice-President and Director of Marketing of Ballantine Books and President and CEO of Price Stern Sloan.

3

US School Publishing: From Webster and McGuffey to the Internet

Cameron S Moseley

The publishing industry's school segment develops, produces and markets instructional materials and systems, both print and non-print, specifically designed for use as instructional aids by students and teachers in public and independent schools from pre-kindergarten through grade 12. To achieve and maintain success, school publishers – often referred to as "elhi" or "K-12" publishers – must provide a constant flow of soundly-conceived, up-to-date, properly-graded and attractive instructional materials and systems. Their products, reflecting the requirements and recommendations of various educational and governmental agencies, must meet extraordinarily variegated and constantly changing learning/teaching needs in many different disciplines at thirteen different grade levels in fifty different states as students progress from kindergarten through high school.

School publishers also must respond to educational trends, which often prove to be fads. Some remember, with particular pain, that the "new math" rapidly became old hat and that the heralded move to metrics is barely inching along. They also must react intelligently to incredibly rapid technological changes that are having powerful effects on the thoughts and actions of those concerned with the nature and quality of instructional materials used with children.

Pressures and complaints from advocacy groups of all persuasions, especially in the areas of social studies, literature and science, are a problem unique to school publishing. Some of these complaints are wholly justified, such as those beginning shortly after World War II about the disgraceful treatment, or lack of any treatment, that black Americans received in US schoolbooks. History textbooks rushed through production to meet Texas adoption deadlines did indeed contain hundreds of errors that had to be corrected before the books could be authorized for purchase. But the issues are not always so clear. Should *Huckleberry Finn* be banned because "nigger" appears so often in it? What may be said and shown in health textbooks about sexual practices, abortion, breast implants and AIDS; in science materials about creationism, nuclear power protests and toxic wastes; and in 1996 social studies books about Bosnia, Ireland, Israel, Palestine, Clinton, Gingrich and Dole? Should Columbus be portrayed as explorer-hero or despoiler-knave? Should selections about witches be dropped from middle-grade reading textbooks?

Although efforts are now being made to establish "national standards" in major curriculum areas, and curriculum similarities throughout all fifty states are greater than the differences, procedures for developing specific school curricula are decentralized. Procedures for selecting instructional materials range from individual teacher choice in most independent schools (secular and religious) and in some public schools, through "building level" and "district level" adoptions in twenty-eight "open territory" states, to state adoptions of varying complexity in twenty-two states.

Developing products to meet the instructional needs of such a diversified school universe and marketing them effectively and profitably present a challenge of large dimensions. School publishing is an extraordinarily complicated business, not easily comprehended by outsiders nor clearly understood by many insiders. And yet, from the inception of a publishing idea through the marketing of a completed product, it is essentially like all other kinds of publishing. The specifics of the "mix" are peculiar to school publishing, but the basic ingredients are the same.

Most persons outside of school publishing – including other kinds of publishers – have little conception of the importance of school publishing as part of the nation's educational system. Trade publishing gets most of the attention in the public press, where school publishing is mentioned only when schoolbooks are being attacked or when it is being prophesied that they will be displaced by electronic systems. Many publishing insiders appear to regard school publishing as easily comprehensible, essentially dull and something to be taken for granted. Dick Abel in his piece in *LOGOS* on "Measuring the Value of Books" devoted only 6% to school and to college textbooks, treated as a single category. The author was kind enough to say, however, that "On the whole the book community can take deep and genuine pride in this sector of the book trade."

In a sense, school publishers live in a limbo between their own industry and the community they serve. Although many of them come from the teaching profession and their business demands that they become immersed in school curricula, they are not regarded as full-fledged members of the education community. Probably because they are profit-oriented, they are seldom heard in high-level discussions of educational policy, although, according to A Bartlett Giamatti, former President of Yale University, speaking at a 1988 Council for Basic Education Seminar, school publishers "know as much about the curriculum as educators". Their influence is pervasive, but they are voices at the back door in US education.

*   *   *   *   *

US school publishing historically rests on the shoulders of two authors – Noah Webster and William Holmes McGuffey – and of publishers Truman and Smith. The first truly American school textbooks were Webster-conceived, Webster-produced spellers, readers and grammars published originally from 1783 through 1785. Webster's "Blue-Backed Spellers" achieved total sales estimated at 100 million copies. His dictionaries gave him worldwide fame. And, fighting successfully to protect his schoolbook copyrights, he became the acknowledged father of US copyright legislation. Truman and Smith, Cincinnati publishers, conceived the idea of graded reading selections, chosen and edited by William Holmes McGuffey, language professor and educator. McGuffey's seven "Eclectic Readers" sold about 122 million copies in various editions from 1836 to 1920. Webster's spellers and McGuffey's readers began a tradition of teacher/ scholar/author/editor/publisher partnership that continues to be characteristic of the highest standards of US school publishing.

US school publishers at various stages have worked either too closely or not closely enough with one another. In the late 19th and early 20th centuries, a group of interrelated companies known as the "Book Trust" were creating a schoolbook monopoly. After this illegal trust had finally been busted, US school publishing became increasingly and fiercely competitive. Dozens of small, privately-owned companies were competing for the tiny share of the school dollar spent on textbooks. In 1942, twenty-eight of these companies finally agreed among themselves to form the American Textbook Publishers Institute (ATPI). College publishers became eligible for membership a year later. Although not stated in the ATPI's high-minded objectives, a primary purpose of the organization was to develop reliable industry statistics. By the late 1950s, so many producers of non-print educational materials wished to join the ATPI, and so many ATPI members were themselves producing such materials, that in 1962, the name was changed to the American Educational Publishers Institute (AEPI). In 1970, the trade-book-focused American Book Publishers Council and the AEPI merged into the Association of American Publishers (AAP). The AAP's School Division can trace its lineage directly back to the formation of the ATPI in 1942.

In the ATPI's first annual industry survey, issued in 1946, "elhi textbook" sales for 1945 were reported as $53.7 million. The term "elhi textbook" now included not only basal textbooks, usually clothbound, but also many other "printed materials of instruction", many of them correlated with basal textbooks but many others "stand-alone" products – workbooks, test booklets, supplementary textbooks, text editions of traditional and modern classics, literature collections, educational periodicals and teachers' guides. Because of advances in printing technology beginning in the 1930s, basal textbooks, particularly in the elementary grades, were becoming increasingly colorful, more sophisticated in graphic design, better illustrated – and bulkier.

Sales to schools in 1995 of all types of materials and systems (but excluding hardware) used for instruction probably exceeded $5bn, about half of which was approximately equivalent to 1945's "elhi textbooks". While sales have risen astronomically in fifty years, the num-

How the School Publishing Scene has Changed

1942	1995
The twenty-eight ATPI Charter Members	Eight *parent corporations and the thirteen major basal school publishers

The Bobbs-Merrill Company	Harcourt General
Follett Publishing Company	*Harcourt Brace* (K–8)
Ginn and Company	*Holt,* Rinehart and *Winston* (6–12)
The Gregg Publishing Company	*Houghton Mifflin*
Harcourt Brace & Company	*Houghton Mifflin* School (K–8)
Harper & Brothers	*Heath* (K–12)
Henry Holt & Company, Inc	McDougal Littell (6–12)
D C Heath & Company	McGraw-Hill Companies
Houghton Mifflin Company	*Macmillan*/McGraw-Hill School (K–8)
	Glencoe (6–12)
Laidlaw Brothers	News Corporation
Lyons & Carnahan	*Scott, Foresman* (K–12)
The Macmillan Company	Pearson
McCormick Mathers Publishing Co	Addison-Wesley Longman (K–12)
Charles E Merrill Co, Inc	Scholastic
Newson & Company	Instructional Publishing
Noble & Noble Publishing Inc	Group (K–8)
	Thomson
Rand McNally & Company	South-Western/ITP School (6–12)
Row, Peterson & Company	Viacom
William H Sadlier, Inc	*Silver Burdett/Ginn* (K–8)
Benj. H Sanborn & Co	Prentice Hall School (6–12)
Scott Foresman & Company	
Silver Burdett Company	
The Southern Publishing Company	The nine surviving imprints out of
The Steck Company	the original twenty-eight are shown in italics above.
Webster Publishing Company	
John Wiley & Sons, Inc	
The John C Winston Company	
World Book Company	

*Among the eight, only Houghton Mifflin remains a parent company devoted entirely to publishing.
Since the above list was compiled, News Corporation has sold Scott, Foresman to Pearson, and the future of the Heath imprint is uncertain.

ber of major publishers has gone down. Most sales classified as "elhi text" in 1995 were generated by thirteen divisions of eight corporations – Harcourt General, Houghton Mifflin, McGraw-Hill, News Corporation, Pearson, Scholastic, Thomson and Viacom. Among these thirteen only nine names from the original list of twenty-eight ATPI charter members can be found.

Does $5bn seem like a large figure? It seems much smaller when compared with $3bn spent annually in the US on bottled water, $3.4bn on bananas, $4.3bn on greeting cards, $9bn on pizzas and $9bn on funeral caskets and related services. It shrinks even further when expressed as about 2% of total annual expenditures on US schools. For all instructional materials and systems in all subjects and in all grades, US schools now spend only about $100 per student annually.

The school publishers of 1942 would be amazed by the range and variety of products, print and non-print, offered in 1996 by the members of AAP's School Division, and by their increasing involvement in electronically-focused publishing. They would be particularly bemused to learn that a portion of industry revenues is derived from the computer-software segments of "integrated learning systems" (ILS), and that many products of members of the Software Publishers Association (SPA) must be considered in compiling industry statistics. Words like "content provider" and "edutainment" would puzzle them, and they would be appalled by the predictions of some electronic apostles that connections to the Internet will, early in the 21st century, replace school textbooks altogether. They would not be astonished, however, to learn that compiling accurate statistics for expenditures on instructional materials has become even more difficult than it was in 1945.

School publishing products today can be divided into four major categories:

1. Multi-component core curriculum programs for the early and middle grades usually consisting of basal textbooks and an array of correlated materials in various media (eg, K-5 reading, K-8 mathematics).
2. Subject-centered core curriculum programs for the middle and upper grades, usually consisting of a basal textbook in a specific subject (eg, world geography, biology, US history) plus correlated materials in various media.

3. Supplementary materials in any and all media, ranging through all grades and curriculum areas, and sometimes used as core curriculum programs (eg, manipulative materials for K-5 mathematics instruction, a paperback book on world religions aimed at middle-grade students, a computer-software program for typing instruction, a CD-ROM on Abraham Lincoln for upper-grade history and literature students).
4. The instructional-content portions of ILS designed to teach language arts and mathematics skills in the early and middle grades.

Schools also purchase for instructional use a variety of products designed for other publishing markets – eg, trade books, reference books, general interest periodicals, video cassettes, CD-ROMs and computer games. Recent emphasis on a "whole-language" approach to reading instruction, stressing "real books" (ie, not textbooks), has increased the use of trade books to replace, or supplement, textbooks. Schools also have access to a variety of curriculum materials distributed without charge, or at minimum cost, by corporations as forms of advertising or public relations. Ethical questions about using such materials began receiving special attention when Whittle Communications in 1992 offered news-related TV programs to schools without charge, provided that students watching these programs also watched two minutes of advertising. Standardized and other objective tests, once treated as part of school publishing, are now regarded as a separate business. Of the $5bn estimated to have been spent by schools in 1995 on instructional materials, about $1bn probably was spent on products designed for other markets and on testing instruments.

* * * * *

Basal textbooks, despite their well-publicized limitations in comparison with other media, remain the keystone of US school publishing. Usually clothbound, they are designed as instructional aids to be placed in the hands of students, most frequently in school settings under the supervision of teachers, who customarily receive help from heavily annotated "wrap-around" teachers' editions. A well-designed school textbook is intended as a guide to the study of a subject, not a complete course and not a reference book. A major purpose is to lead students beyond its contents to other learning resources and experiences, including other textbooks with different points of view.

Misunderstandings about these points are at the root of many adverse criticisms of school textbooks. Designed to withstand many years of heavy use, basal school textbooks usually are issued on loan to public school students. They conform with rigorous manufacturing standards developed by a joint committee of state textbook directors, school publishers and manufacturers, and are expected to last many years. In most independent schools, however, students buy their textbooks every year and, as with college textbooks, frequently sell them to the next generation of students.

As they review curricula and courses of study and attempt to decipher educational trends in planning new core curriculum programs, school publishers assemble data from sources available to all, such as enrollment projections, state and large-city adoption schedules, reports of educational assessments, policy statements and recommendations by governmental and educational groups. They also listen carefully to reports from field representatives, conduct intensive market research (eg, focus groups, questionnaires, field tests of portions of programs), analyze competitors' present products and "guesstimate" new ones in preparation, and confer continually with educators at all levels in schools and at educational conventions. They depend heavily on in-house judgments by experienced editors, marketing persons and seasoned executives. The crux of all these efforts is attempting to distinguish accurately among what opinion leaders say schools *should* buy, what educators *say* they will buy and what schools actually *will* buy with available funds. When asked why educational products are not tested and validated in advance of publication, school publishers generally will reply that their activities are a seamless web of research, development and market testing. They will point out that, although small portions of programs can be field-tested in advance, it is manifestly impossible for an entire multiple-component program (eg, reading K-5) conceived in 1996 to be tested and validated in controlled classroom situations in advance of 1999 publication. In the words of Paul F Brandwein, author, educator and publisher, "The first edition is the trial edition."

The authors, consultants and advisers listed on major school programs generally include school teachers, supervisors, college professors and technical experts. But since the ability to write clearly and appealingly about a particular subject at a specific grade level is rare, much of the actual writing of instructional materials is done by in-house editors and free lance writer/editor professionals. At all levels, school publishers often turn to outside "educational developers" to produce portions of programs, and sometimes entire programs, to meet adoption deadlines without the expense of staffing up internally. In the decades immediately following the launching of the first Sputnik in 1957, instructional materials developed by a number of government-funded and other non-profit curriculum groups were published commercially after competitive bidding by school publishers. The best of these, in foreign languages, mathematics and science, had considerable influence, mainly favorable, on education and school publishing.

Outside authors and advisers receive either royalties on net sales, usually for one edition only, or flat fees. Since more and more work on major core curriculum programs is being done inside publishing houses, royalty and fee payments are becoming a smaller and smaller percentage of the cost of products sold, ranging from 1% to 4% on lower-grade programs up to 5% and 6% on upper-grade textbooks. Authors of supplementary materials whose work requires little or no in-house editing, however, sometimes earn royalties up to 15%.

Any basal or supplementary product designed to be purchased in multiple copies for per-student use is sold to schools at a wholesale net price that remains the same regardless of how many copies are purchased. There are no quantity discounts. Large customers, however, receive special benefits in the form of trial sets, extra desk copies, exchange allowances when new adoptions replace older books, additional consultant service and business entertainment. The larger the adoption, the larger the extra benefits.

By publishing industry standards, the capital investment required to produce a multi-component core curriculum program for the lower grades is very high – eg, up to $50m for a K-5 reading series. Millions of copies must be sold in order to recoup such an investment within two or three years. Publishers of such massive programs usually can maintain satisfactory growth and profits only by publishing in so many curriculum areas that disappointing results in one or two can be counterbalanced by success in others. Today, a core curriculum publisher achieving annual net profits in the 7% to 10% range is considered highly successful. One of the major attractions of supplementary-materials publishing is that initial capital investments for each product are far lower and potential profit percentages much higher.

Marketing methods vary according to the kind of product (basal or supplementary) and adoption procedures (open territory or state adoption). Strong combinations of direct selling, mail promotion, telemarketing, journal advertising and exhibit attendance are required to market core curriculum programs in all regions, and particularly in major state adoptions. To enable prospects to examine materials at their leisure, school publishers must furnish at no charge examination copies of basal textbooks and correlated items. The cost of free materials is second only to salaries in the marketing of core curriculum programs.

"Stand-alone" supplementary products (ie, unrelated to core curriculum programs) require different development and marketing strategies and tactics. This has led to the formation of hundreds of smaller companies producing supplementary materials in various media and of supplementary-materials divisions in five larger companies, such as the SRA Supplementary Group (McGraw-Hill) and Great Source (Houghton Mifflin). Supplementary publishers can move faster than basal publishers in trends-responsive product development. In marketing they rely less on direct selling and free materials, more on mail promotion, telemarketing, exhibit attendance and on-approval sampling/ordering. And they concentrate on open territory states.

In open territory states and in many state adoption areas, instructional materials are purchased directly from publishers. In several states, however, state-adopted materials must be ordered through state-approved "depositories", usually privately-owned companies handling the products of several publishers, but sometimes a publisher-owned facility. Depositories, established in the Southeast, Southwest and West when transportation and communications in those areas were poor, are publisher-expensive anachronisms that are being phased out. Virtually unknown to the general public, they received grim publicity in 1963 when the bullet that killed President Kennedy was fired from an upper floor of the now-defunct Texas School Depository.

* * * * *

Long-term success in school publishing, supplementary as well as basal, depends not only on intellectual ability, business competence and adequate financial resources, but also on patience and continuity, combined with a desire to produce high-quality products that will provide real help to students and teachers. It is a seasonal business. Most school orders are placed from June through September. Most payments are received from September through December. Marketing expenses, however, are particularly heavy from September through May and development expenditures and inventory purchases continue through all twelve months. Owners and executives who do not understand these characteristics, who add too many rungs to the decision-making ladder and who demand short-term adjustments to improve earnings ratios can create serious problems for dedicated school publishers. Major changes in corporate ownership and management and the breathtaking speed of technological change have exacerbated these problems.

Technological changes and the increasing diversity of the student population are having profound effects on the products and processes of school publishing. The system of state adoptions that, whatever its shortcomings, has been a stabilizing influence on school publishers' planning for nearly a century now appears to be eroding. California, Florida and Texas are following Georgia's lead in broadening the definition of textbook to include instructional materials in all media. A little-known new company astonished the industry, and probably themselves, a few years ago by winning about 35% of a major Texas science adoption with optical disks. Yet, though some observers predict that all the states will be open territory early in the 21st century, school publishers must continue to base much of their planning on published state adoption schedules.

School publishers always have attempted to cope sensibly with technological change, beginning with "audiovisual" aids and other nonprint products after World War II, "programmed instruction" and "computer-assisted instruction" in the '50s and '60s, then video cassettes and disks, computer software, electronic books and CD-ROMs. "Interactive multimedia" and connections to the Internet are the latest buzzwords. The problems of inventory control, greater in school publishing than in any other industry segment, led school publishers in the 1960s to embrace computers and to begin to understand their potential. In the past two decades, computer systems have transformed the production process. School publishers now have pre-press control of the "look of a book", no matter how complicated, almost until it goes on press. Many supplementary items are produced almost entirely in-house through advances in "desktop publishing".

Some technophile futurists now predict that, first, interactive multi-media products and, then, connections to the Internet will soon sup-plant printed-and-bound textbooks and all other instructional materials as well. But how multimedia publishing and Internet connections can be harnessed efficiently for schools at affordable prices has not yet been explained satisfactorily to most educators and school publishers. A recent *New York Times* feature article included an estimate that it would require nearly $50bn to provide enough computers to enable all classrooms in the US to have adequate connections to the Internet. No predictions were made, however, concerning who would prepare appropriate materials for these connections, nor what they would cost, nor who would pay for them.

*   *   *   *   *

Many adversarial critics describe a book, especially a textbook, as linear, rigid and confining. They fail to acknowledge that a textbook is portable, durable and relatively inexpensive. It allows the student read-er, with the aid of table of contents, index and glossary, to flip back and forth easily and at will, providing complete browsability. On every page it encourages the student to take advantage of the incredibly diverse information sources now available. It compels the reader to interact continuously with words and illustrations. Furthermore, since words represent sounds; since words and pictures are comprehended through a remarkable optical device (the eye); and since pages are attached to a hinge, a textbook is actually an audio-visual hardware device with built-in software, requiring no power source except the hands and eyes of the user. Its battery life is unlimited.

Electronic materials and systems, however, certainly can take over the burdens of color, graphics and information overload that have out-run the natural capacities of a textbook. As a result, schoolbooks of the future, customized in various ways to fit specific curriculum require-ments, may look more like Wentworth's *Elements of Plane and Solid Geometry* (Ginn and Heath, 1879) or Truman J Moon's pioneering *Biology for Beginners* (Henry Holt, 1921) than the cumbersome monsters that US school children are now lugging from home to locker to classroom and back home again. It would take five copies of either Wentworth or Moon to match the poundage of a 1996 high school geometry or biology textbook.

Examining Wentworth's 1879 geometry textbook is particularly instructive. Combining "plane and solid" in one volume is acceptably modern. The user is told that "important changes are not sufficient to prevent the simultaneous use of the old and new editions in the same class" – a selling point as relevant now as it was then. Back-matter "testimonials" claim it "had been introduced into sixty-four colleges and nearly 400 preparatory schools" – another familiar selling point. Measuring 5" × 7" and weighing 1.2 pounds, it can be held easily in one hand. The "introduction price" is $1.00.

Wentworth's geometry textbook looks to the future in other ways. It was published in 1879 by Boston-based Ginn and Heath, which split into Ginn & Company and D C Heath shortly after the book was published. In the 1960s, Ginn was acquired by Xerox, and Heath by Raytheon. Today, Ginn, along with Silver Burdett, is a division of Simon & Schuster's elementary education group, with Viacom as the parent company. In late 1995, Heath was purchased by Houghton Mifflin, and its imprint may soon disappear.

Although the future of school textbooks seems somewhat cloudy, the weather ahead in school publishing generally is fair. School enrollments are projected to increase by about one million students a year for the next five years and beyond. There always will be children and there always will be schools. Schools will of necessity buy new instructional materials every year. Curriculum trends can be discerned and evaluated. Whatever role the Internet may assume, and whatever world wide webs we weave, school publishers will still be needed to develop valid instructional content that can be marketed to schools effectively and profitably.

After twenty-four years with Harcourt Brace, in the course of which he filled a wide range of roles from school/college sales representative to corporate director, Cameron Moseley was a founder of Moseley Associates Inc, who, under his leadership, have been successful management consultants to the US publishing industry since 1971. Among many services to the publishing industry, he originated the "universal ownership label", which has appeared in virtually every school text-book printed in the past twenty-four years. A Phi Beta Kappa Yale graduate, Moseley is the author of numerous professional articles, books and papers.

Bibliography

Bates, Emmert W; Hagar, Hubert A: Loveland, Gilbert; *Textbooks in Education;* The American Textbook Publishers Institute, 1949

Buckley, Leonard Ralph; "Textbooks", *Encyclopaedia Britannica* Volume 21, 1969

Cole, John Y (Editor); "Television, the Book, and the Classroom", A Seminar cosponsored by the Center for the Book in the Library of Congress, Library of Congress, 1978

Dessauer, John; *Book Publishing* : A Basic Introduction, New Expanded Edition, The Continuum Publishing Company, 1989

Goldstein, Paul; *Changing the American Schoolbook* , Lexington Books, D C Heath and Company, 1978

Moseley, Cameron S: "Saints and Cynics: The Learning Materials Industry in an EPIE-Centered Universe". A report to the School Division of the Association of American Publishers on validation practices and attitudes toward validation, with recommendations concerning industry action. 1973.

Moseley, Cameron S; "How School Textbook Publishers View the Information Age", National Council for the Social Studies, Bulletin No 83, Spring 1989

Reid, James M; *An Adventure in Textbooks* , R R Bowker Company, 1969

Tyson-Bernstein, Harriet; *A Conspiracy of Good Intentions* : America's Textbook Fiasco, The Council for Basic Education, 1988

Also: Various issues of *Publishers Weekly,* Bowker; *LOGOS* : The Journal of the World Book Community (Editor Gordon Graham); *BP Report* ; *Educational Marketer; Electronic Education Report; Multimedia Business Report* (SIMBA Information, Inc). Various annual surveys; ATPI, AEPI, AAP, BISG 1993, 1994, 1995 issues of *The Moseley Report*

4

The New World of the American
Public Library

Mary R Somerville

Community activities center, community information center, formal education support center, independent learning center, popular materials library, pre-schoolers' door to learning, reference library, research center.....

Collectively, American public libraries today encompass all of these roles (listed in 1989 by the American Library Association), though most libraries focus on a few key areas. Larger urban systems or aggregates of many neighborhood libraries may almost do all of them, offering research at the Main Library, providing popular materials and community activities at a branch serving elders, and an emphasis on learning from cradle to grave in a neighborhood facility filled with recent immigrants.

This greater goal of the public library goes back to its roots in democracy, underpinning the public's right to know, learn and enjoy at an institution accessible to rich and poor alike. In the beginning, there were no tax-supported American public libraries, just private collections for the élite. Ben Franklin's subscription library, or gentlemen's reading club, represented a step towards popular access, but the first tax-supported public libraries were few and far between, starting in Boston.

Then, during the late 19th and early 20th centuries, Scottish

Carnegie dollars sowed the seeds for a new American library revolution. All told, Carnegie constructed 1,679 of the eventual 15,481 public library buildings across America (George M Eberhart, *Whole Library Handbook 2,* American Library Association, Chicago, 1995).

Some library systems, such as Philadelphia (Pennsylvania) and Louisville (Kentucky), incorporated the word "Free" into their titles, emphasizing democratic egalitarianism. Similarly, reading rooms from New York to Cleveland became centers for acculturation of newly arrived citizens and their children. The spirit of the Statue of Liberty – "Give me your tired, your poor" – provided American public libraries with a fervent mission: lifelong education of the masses.

Sometime between the 1950s and the 1970s, another major shift occurred, and it was about time, since a 1948 Michigan study indicated that only a tiny fraction of the population was using public libraries in the immediate post-war era. Libraries needed to respond to the demands of a more eclectic, leisure society, one that enjoyed reading for its own sake. Collections reflected the new stateside affluence, as well as an increasing demand for information. How-to-do-it books on everything from home carpentry to building a compost heap flourished.

Formats changed, too, with paperbacks emerging triumphant. Librarians who clung to the status quo dubbed new leisure-time collections ephemeral, characteristic of the bourgeoisie. Librarians who accepted the new populism created Popular Reading Centers of westerns, romances and pot-boilers. At the same time, children's librarians bent on hooking the TV generation added comics, hi-low reading, even *Nancy Drew.* Judy Bloom's *Deenie* supplanted *Rebecca of Sunnybrook Farm,* as Dr Seuss levelled *Dick and Jane.* On the adult side, Danielle Steel replaced Daphne du Maurier and *The Bridges of Madison County* far outsold *Lady Chatterley's Lover.* Even the leisure-time shift, however, seemed glacial when compared with what was to come.

In the '80s and '90s, the slow-turning world speeded up, careening relentlessly forward towards a Brave New Real-Time World. As America's public libraries responded to this digital revolution, the computer replaced hand-charging; books sat side by side with CDs, computer screens, books-on-cassette and videos. Instantaneous global information left yesterday's standing order reference annuals in the dust. Meanwhile, a new nation of immigrants, resisting English-only assimilation, demanded collections in the languages of their cultures. Swelling crowds flocked to library doors, defying the myth of a non-reading public.

Paradoxically, while there were more users, formats and languages to purchase, available dollars did not keep pace with demand. America's tax-supported, free public libraries faced a tax revolt, while local budgets increasingly went for police, fire and garbage. Librarians and trustees learned to do more with less, to market library services, to speak less softly while carrying the big political sticks of increased library usage and the public's right to know. At the same time, library supporters lobbied for state and federal dollars, also raising corporate funds to supplement local taxes.

Even so, the future seemed uncertain. Some said the American public library would go the way of the dinosaur, to be replaced by a combination of the bookstore and interactive TV. Cassandras were everywhere apparent, despite evidence to the contrary of libraries' increasing gate counts and growing numbers of registered borrowers. Library doomsday prophets lacked a clear understanding of the public library's mission, its historic significance – and its phoenix-like ability to transcend hard times.

The American public library has rolled with the punches, transcending the ancient role of passive preserver and repository of dusty tomes, while answering the newer challenges of the coffeehouse/bookstore, the video store and the computer service provider. Professionally staffed, the library offers friendly, informed assistance to students and those unfamiliar with the library and information retrieval. To scholars, public officials and savvy business types, it offers personalized service and unique collections on everything from urban renewal and local history to Latin American business trends.

Public libraries also abound in sites. At a time when neighborhoods celebrate cultural and demographic uniqueness, marketing means reaching people where they are and with what they want. McDonald's knows this. So do public libraries. Sixteen thousand outlets make library books more accessible than Big Macs to most of the people almost all of the time.

*   *   *   *   *

And especially children. In the '70s, it was fashionable to downplay library services to children. Emphasis was on what was known as "the total population". Theoretically, the American public library reached all citizens equally, from cradle to grave. In actuality, the market segment was much narrower. Theater owners and cereal companies grasped this concept because they understood marketing. Many public library directors didn't. Because children were politically powerless, services to them often were overlooked or downplayed, until a strong children's librarian or parent advocate spoke out.

The best directors, conversely, knew that the library's most frequent customers were and continue to be children. Currently, children and youth, especially students, generate one-third to one-half of public library usage. *Whole Library Handbook 2* (ALA, 1995, p4) notes that three out of four children ages three to eight use the public library.

Since the 1980s, children's services in public libraries have flourished for the following reasons:

- More former children's librarians, usually women, have risen to positions of power.
- Children's librarians and youth advocates have become more active in the higher echelons of the American Library Association, where they influence national policy and learn new advocacy skills to take back home.
- LSCA (Library Services and Construction Act) federal funding has offered concrete support for creative and innovative programs for children, especially the disadvantaged.

Those serving the very young had a true sense of mission: If they could promulgate youth reading and learning, they'd change the world. Programs and services included:

- Preschool story time, toddler (two-three-year-old) and Lap-Sit programs for parents and child care-givers; storytelling festivals and special events designed to attract school-age children and young adults.
- Outreach to HeadStart and Title XX day care centers, including the loan of books, tapes and flannel board materials; training of day care workers; storytelling outreach to such centers, using children's librarians and senior volunteers.
- Outreach to well baby clinics, migrant worker camps and other places where children congregate, but may be beyond traditional library service.

- Summer Reading programs with aggressive marketing campaigns and concrete incentives such as skating rink passes designed to reach urban reluctant readers.
- Cooperation with schools, parks and agencies serving children to get youth reading and learning, via storytelling outreach to children and booktalking outreach to young adults, as well as through library homework centers for students of all ages.

Young Adult services continue to receive strong emphasis, despite staff cuts eliminating YA positions in many libraries. For example, Chicago Public Library's Male Mentoring/Read-Aloud Program, which matches high school role models with elementary school boys, reinforces the importance of reading.

* * * * *

While vigorously promoting early literacy through youth programs and services, libraries have also tackled mounting adult illiteracy. Since democracy requires an educated citizenry, illiteracy represents a major national hurdle, especially in the light of the need to compete in an increasingly sophisticated global economy. A national survey by the US Department of Education (September 1993) indicated that forty million adult Americans can't read or write beyond third grade level.

In Dade County, Florida, hundreds of citizens seek reading assistance each year from Miami-Dade Public Library through Project LEAD (Literacy for Every Adult in Dade), a free service that provides basic reading and writing instruction to those who are unwilling or unable to participate in school-based learning. Students are tutored individually, advancing at their own pace in an atmosphere of encouragement and respect.

Literacy resource centers, identified as "Lifelong Learning/Easy-to-Read Books for Adults", support library literacy efforts with collections of books, videos and audio tapes for check-out. Personal computers dedicated to literacy software are located in many libraries.

In addition to extending a helping hand to achieve literacy, libraries from Los Angeles to Miami are also helping to acculturate new immigrants and prepare them for American citizenship. Formal classes on English as a Second Language, on studying for the citizenship exam and on obtaining information about government services such as Social Security help inform recent immigrants. Where citizenship registration occurs, library staff are present with registration forms, bibliographies and information fliers in several languages, reaching out to embrace a new wave of customers.

Libraries also seek to serve seniors and people with disabilities. Older citizens use the library less frequently because they may lack transportation or become physically immobilized. The Americans with Disabilities Act (ADA) has impacted library planning, covering every aspect of facilities development from signage and computer table height to bathrooms. Programs and services also now reflect the special needs of people with disabilities. The Miami-Dade Public Library System, for example, currently provides:

- *Talking Books Service* to patrons who can't use regular print materials due to visual or physical disability. This program also provides books and magazines on cassette and disk, and in Braille along with free playback equipment. Computers and optical scanners "read" for blind patrons, translating print into voice, computer disk, large print and Braille formats.
- *Deaf Services* features library materials of interest to the deaf or hearing-impaired, as well as for family members and professionals who work with the deaf. Video cassettes for children and adults feature closed captioning and Sign Language, as well as information about deaf culture. Video decoders are available on loan and Assisted Listening Devices can be used at library programs.
- *Connections Books-by-Mail Service* sends books, cassettes and videos directly to patrons who are physically unable to come to the library due to age, disability or lack of transportation. Deposit Collections reach institutions serving the deaf in retirement residences, senior centers and nursing homes.

* * * * *

While public libraries must all offer citizens, including people with disabilities, access to computer and audio-visual presentations, our stock in trade continues to be the book. Branch libraries offer book discussion clubs, author lectures and book signings. Non-fiction happenings include lectures on history, biography, ethics, sports and hobbies.

Book displays accompany these events, which are engineered to promote library usage.

Marketing materials bookstore-style, face-out, has become a *fait accompli* in many libraries. Display opportunities now exist throughout many library buildings, not just in a few entrance exhibits. Que Bronson of Montgomery County, Maryland has pioneered this technique, which increases circulation and contributes to overall library attractiveness.

Many large public libraries also offer art, historical and cultural exhibits, incorporating both in-house collections and traveling exhibitions. Smithsonian Museum exhibits have featured protest posters from the old Soviet Union and World War II posters from America. The National Endowment for the Humanities (NEH) has funded many vital exhibitions, accompanying them with panel discussions by historians and journalists.

The Library of Congress's Centers for the Book likewise bring programs and exhibits to public libraries. Broward County (Florida) Public Library's Jean Trebbi suggested and implemented the first regional Center, of which there are now thirty. The Florida Center for the Book has hosted exhibits such as the "Language of the Land" literary maps project.

Preserving the past, whether through exhibitions or rare book collections, is still a part of modern public library life. While most libraries collect and preserve local history, some major public libraries possess outstanding regional collections. For example, it is almost impossible to find a book on the westward expansion of the US that does not credit the Western History Department of Denver (Colorado) Public Library.

The Burton Historical Collection, Detroit (Michigan) Public Library, constitutes another excellent resource for regional studies, including adjacent Canada. The Detroit Public Library also houses the National Automotive History Collection. The Free Library of Philadelphia has an outstanding special collection of children's literature, including original illustrations, manuscripts and typescripts.

The Nebraska Heritage Collection, located in Lincoln City Libraries, features first-edition and non-English publications of Plains writers John G Neihardt, Loren Eiseley, Willa Cather, Mari Sandoz, Wright Morris, Bess Streeter Aldrich and Weldon Kees.

The science fiction collection at the Dallas Public Library (Texas) was formed around the personal library and archives of author Brian Aldiss. In the area of Black Studies, the New York Public Library's Schomburg Collection represents a world resource. Other outstanding New York Public Library special collections include the Oriental Division, performing arts and private and special press books. The Rare Books and Manuscripts Division places special emphasis on early Americana. The only surviving copy of the Barcelona printing of *The Columbus Letter,* written to Luis de Santangel by Pedro Posa in 1493, resides here.

Rare books and special collections in America's public libraries covering every possible subject, from whaling at the Providence Public Library (Rhode Island) to folklore at the Cleveland (Ohio) Public Library, remain rich resources for professional and vocational researchers and scholars.

* * * * *

While preserving the past, America's public libraries must also address the present. Modern America is a nation of readers, but also one of viewers and listeners. Television possesses tremendous pull; video stores abound. In response to demand, some libraries have attempted to duplicate video store offerings by focusing on feature films. Others have chosen to feature cultural and informational videos, as well as book-based videos for children.

Extremely popular with adults, especially commuters, are books on cassette, spanning titles from Chaucer's *Canterbury Tales* to biographies of major personalities like General Colin Powell. Cassette book packages for children, such as *The Cat in the Hat,* are equally popular as early learning tools. Sound recordings in CD and audio cassette formats are also popular.

One problem with audio-visual formats is their susceptibility to theft. Security devices have helped prevent loss, but AV materials still disappear in larger numbers than books, suggesting both their popularity and their perceived street value.

America's larger public libraries are linked to the Internet, at least in headquarters libraries. When smaller libraries achieve linkage, they experience a quantum leap in reference service, both in terms of real-time information and in access to extensive resources. Regional networks such as SEFLIN (Southeast Florida Library Information

Network) have created Free-Nets of local government and community information, as well as a menu of Internet offerings and access to E-Mail.

The State of Maryland has created Sailor, a Gopher network. Similarly, the State of Utah is providing linkage with the World Wide Web. Miami-Dade, too, has recently made the Web available at its Coral Gables Branch, and the Free-Net accessible at larger libraries. Plans are for systemwide expansion of Internet accessibility.

Dial-up to digitized resources means a whole new ball game. In the process of building a new Main Library, Kenneth Dowlin, Director of the San Francisco Public Library, is incorporating technology into every aspect of planning and construction. Three staff members are digitizing collections, including early film footage of San Francisco and local history print resources. Dowlin envisions a children's encyclopedia as well as Home Pages on specific subjects, such as African-American History, enabling the citizen to focus on his or her unique individual interests in a manner that will seem transparent when using electronic resources. Public libraries like San Francisco are key on-ramps to the Information Superhighway, and are leading the way to citizen access.

Citizen access today is a serious fiscal challenge. Americans want to have their cake and eat it. Library customers clamor for electronic information, traditional book collections – and lower taxes. Monies shrink and costs increase, but library customers expect a library building on every corner and service round-the-clock. Electronic kiosks and citizen dial-up access from home or office to online library catalogs and information databases promise some relief. Such instantaneous computer retrieval mimics banks' automated teller machines.

Mere machines, however, can't do it all. Citizens require friendly librarians and clean, well-lit library buildings with expansive open hours. While automation promises the library without walls, citizens covet more walls. The recent construction of three eye-catching, new, big-city main libraries in Denver (Colorado) Phoenix (Arizona) and San Antonio (Texas), and the success of thirty-eight out of fifty-three bond issues for public library building projects held in 1994, (Richard B Hall, "The Vote Is In", *Library Journal,* June 15, 1995 pp 40-45) are evidence that libraries still need buildings

Once they are built, garnering long-term operational funding is the greater challenge; paying for heating, air-conditioning, roofing, staffing and continuing collection support beyond the bricks-and-mortar stage can be difficult. Operating levies can help. For example, Miami-Dade passed a ten-year collection and automation bond issue, the Book Trust, in 1988.

Federal and state dollars must also play their part. The US government's Library Services and Construction Act (LSCA) has helped public libraries introduce innovative services such as family literacy programs, and to strengthen collections. Renamed the Library Services and Technology Act (LSTA), it promises to place new emphasis on technology. Similarly, Georgia's state lottery funds support library technology and Florida's State Aid matches local tax dollars with critical monies.

Public library funding strategies are many-layered. To help close the gap in dollars, library foundations have sprung up from Louisville (Kentucky) to Los Angeles (California) and Friends of the Library have helped supplement lagging tax support. Planned giving campaigns through library foundations have become increasingly popular.

Many libraries, eg, Baltimore County (Maryland), have altered the traditional free public library concept and are assessing user fees. Citizens purchase Baltimore County's WOW Card for value-added services such as computer print-outs, thereby saving the library system a projected $200,000 -$400,000 yearly.

But history can't repeat itself in the form of subscription libraries. Children, young adults, adults, people with disabilities, citizens in towns, cities, countrysides, small business owners, students, new citizens, leisure readers, connoisseurs of art and rare books, multimedia and new technologies all require that America's public libraries continue to flourish and that sufficient funding be found. Andrew and Andrea Carnegies must come forth across the country to help preserve and strengthen collections, to help expand services and programs and to enable building of more on-ramps to the Information Superhighway for all people, thereby truly helping Americans discover new worlds.

Director of the Miami (Florida) Dade Public Library System, Mary Somerville served as President of the American Library Association (ALA) for the 1996/97 term. She has been a member of the ALA since

1974, having started her career as a clerk librarian in children's services. She has held posts in public library administration in Kentucky, Nebraska and Florida, has served the ALA in many capacities and won numerous awards. Somerville has bachelor and master's degrees in English literature and a master's degree in library science.

5

Independent Bookselling:
A Frontline Dispatch

William J Kramer

The central question is simple: What is the fate of independent booksellers in the age of superstores? The answer is complicated.

To begin with, we have to agree who the combatants are. What is an independent? A single store only? Do multiple outlets qualify? Is it a matter of size? Some of the largest bookstores in the country are independents. The Library Ltd in St Louis measures 53,000 square feet. How are university-owned and/or-connected stores to be categorized? The Harvard Coop has long been a major retailer as well as bookseller, and if you apply some of the same measures to the Coop as to Barnes & Noble – size, capital source, market orientation – it may be hard to tell the difference between them. What is a bookstore these days anyway? How many books do you have to sell to qualify? What proportion of space must be devoted to books? Are the B & N bookstores in Stop 'n Shop grocery stores to be counted? Sam's Clubs?

My definition of independents is those stores that are *not* classified as "national accounts" by publishers; are locally-owned and -operated; and have a different raison d'être than the "corporate" stores. In other words, independents are everybody except the chains, who, by the way, are not always identified by their corporate banners – the top four chains (B & N, Borders, Crown and Books-a-Million) operate under sixteen different trade names. Other characteristics, such as central buying and shipping, sales volume and physical size, I deem irrelevant to this essay.

I am an independent. I own Sidney Kramer Books and Kramerbooks & afterwords, both of Washington, DC. Sidney Kramer Books is a specialized bookstore (a "niche" store, in the new vernacular), concentrating on "the business of Washington" – politics, economics, area studies, business management, military affairs. Sidney Kramer Books has a presence in multiple markets: retail, direct mail, institutional and school. Kramerbooks & afterwords is one of the original bookstore/cafes. It opened in 1976 as a general bookshop and an eclectic, full-menu/full-bar cafe. I can modestly say that this store has had an enormous influence on bookselling in the past twenty years, showing just how successful a bookstore as "entertainment" can be.

It would be possible, and, indeed, a great temptation, to devote this space to a jeremiad. Instead, I have used this opportunity to speak at length with a variety of players in the game – editorial directors, sales and marketing directors, house and commission sales reps, credit managers and other booksellers. I have also reread relevant material from *Publishers Weekly* (PW) and *The American Bookseller* (AB), in an effort first, to educate myself, and second, to bring multiple perspectives to this quick portrait of the new retailing landscape, the most obvious feature of which is the looming bulk of the superstores.

The issues, as framed by Carol Horne of Harvard Bookstore, are three: Does the superstore chain strategy make sense? Can the independents compete? What will happen to books, and therefore bookstores, on the so-called information highway of the future?

* * * * *

A few statistics:

- The Book Industry Study Group (BISG) reported publisher sales in 1994 of $18.3 bn and estimated 1995 sales at $19.6 bn.
- Of the 1994 total, probably $13-$15 bn was directed through retail outlets of one kind or another.
- Chain store sales were $3.6 bn in 1994 (27% of the retail book market), up from $3.1 bn (23%) in 1993.
- Independents accounted for 19% of the retail book market in 1994, down from 24% in 1993. (Their share was 32.5% in 1991.)

- 1994 profit margins at the chains varied from a significant loss at Crown (6.3% of sales) to a healthy 4.7% at Books-a-Million. As a group, chains reported a 0.6% margin.
- Independent bookstore net profit was also down, according to the American Booksellers Association Abacus survey. Independents averaged a 1.53% margin in 1993.

Book industry statistics are somewhat confusing. BISG counts differently from *PW*, which counts differently from the Department of Commerce. Nonetheless, these few numbers give some idea of what's at stake. We're talking about a book market that has more than doubled in the past decade. It is big business now.

But the bottom lines are thin, even for the chains. Will the capital driving superstore growth, which comes from outside the retail book trade (as it did in the '60s and '70s when it fueled the growth of mall bookstores) be satisfied with these meager rewards? There is nothing in the history of the retail book trade, or in the current numbers, to suggest that these rewards will increase.

According to Alberto Vitale, Chairman, President, and CEO of Random House, scale can outweigh percentages. In an interview with *AB* in June 1995, he said: "Percentages are significant, but not always. It's the dollars that count – how many dollars you can produce at the end of the day. Two percent of a million dollars is a lot more than 2% of a hundred thousand dollars. And it's pretty obvious that 2% of two billion dollars is a lot of dollars." In response to a question about Random House's publishing culture, he remarked: "My policy certainly has been to never interfere with the culture of various imprints. However, I have worked to instill a sensitivity to the fact that, at the end of the day, this is a business. I don't want any handouts. We have to earn our keep and reward our capital, to have the means and resources to continue to experiment and to get into new businesses.... The minute you put your hand out, you're not independent." If Mr Vitale is right, the chains are going to be content with these low margins, but does anyone out there believe that Mr. Vitale – or Si Newhouse [owner of Random House] – would consider 2% an adequate profit margin at any sales level?

Vitale's point about absolute dollars is confirmed by the superstores, who are pursuing a two-pronged strategy: first, to create new dollars by expanding the pie and, second, to grab market share by cannibalizing from anyone and everyone. Len Riggio, B & N's CEO, says that B & N does not have a policy of cannibalizing sales from other stores, but he also said, shortly after author Russell Banks suggested publicly that chains were the wave of the future, that B & N plans to expand from its current 11% market share to "no more" than 20%. Just a mere doubling.

All industry figures confirm that the total pie is growing, but that the share held by the independents is shrinking. Profits on this shrinking share are being eroded by discounting, and since the easy sales are being creamed off by mass merchandisers (at virtually no profit), the sales must come from slower moving titles, which by any definition are more expensive to produce.

Vitale's statement on Random House's publishing culture raises a significant, long-term question for both chains and independents. Can either of them, with these razor-thin margins, "reward their capital" sufficiently "to continue to experiment"? Whatever one thinks of 2% of a million dollars, it does not represent available cash; it's all tied up in inventory, especially when a store is undercapitalized. And will 2% of a billion, even if it's in real dollars, satisfy the financial markets?

* * * * *

How do publishers see the warring sides? The credit manager of one major trade publisher remarks that the chains are at present well-heeled enough to pay their bills on time, but, he added, weekly calls are necessary to make certain they do pay on time, don't skip invoices or come up with surprise shortages months after receipt. The senior management of this company also calls book chain accounts regularly to make certain that the check is in the mail. Sounds like a company gearing up to cope with certain trouble ahead, if you ask me.

The marketing director of a mid-size publisher/distributor already sees cracks forming in the capital structure of the chains, with some already pushing terms to the limit (testing their clout? or running into cashflow problems?) and occasionally going on hold.

Both these publisher observers are grim in their assessment of the financial future for many of the independents, acknowledging tighter reins on credit, closer inspection of retailers' operations and a general caution well justified by a steady flow of closings and bankruptcies. Even those who express optimism about the future of independent bookselling suggest that the publishers will be searching for new outlets – non-traditional vendors such as diving equipment shops, kitchenware stores, sports stores or pet suppliers – for as much of their list as they appropriately can. As the pressure for new cash flow grows, opportunities will not be ceded to the existing corps of retailers. Paying the bills is not the only issue. Many observers have concerns about the structure and competence of the chains' buying staffs and the motivation of their lower echelon employees.

Publishers' sales reps and sales managers report that the buying systems in the chains are clumsy and bureaucratic, and that the quality of buyers is spotty. Experienced buyers with historical knowledge of the industry have been replaced by youngsters, who, smart though they may be, have no accumulated knowledge on which to base decisions. They are prone to make buying decisions based on marketing factors, not the merits of each work.

Publishers wonder, too, how multi-million dollar inventories at hundreds of outlets can be adequately maintained over a long period, even with high quality of sales data. If the right books aren't in the store to begin with (and they all agree this can happen even with 120,000 titles in stock), then they won't ever turn up in the sales reports. According to a senior sales executive of a major university press, the chains stock only a very few scholarly or professional titles – the ones they are willing to "get behind". The rest are skipped. "They can't, and they won't, hand-sell."

* * * * *

"The death of the independent bookstores has been predicted almost as long as the death of the novel," says Jonathan Yardley, *Washington Post* book reviewer. Like Yardley, most of the industry-watchers believe that independent bookselling (not necessarily all of today's independent booksellers) will survive; that, for one reason or another, the pendulum currently swinging towards gigantism will swing back....one day. There will be a thinning out of the ranks of independents, runs the theory. The survival of the fittest will be accompanied by all-out war among the superstores, the failure of multiple superstore locations and the abandonment by the chains of secondary markets (as is happening now with hundreds of stores, especially in regional malls). "Independents," says our credit man, "have to be ready to jump back into the fray and pick up the pieces."

The financial survival of the independents will hinge, in part, on the success of efforts to eliminate the vestiges of discriminatory discount and promotional policies by the publishing industry. The big chains were given a tremendous boost in their drive to market dominance with "off-the-schedule" support – sometimes enthusiastic, sometimes reluctant – by the publishers. Chains received allegedly illegal support: preferential discounts, promotional reimbursements, payment for placement in catalogs or within stores, payment for the appearance of books on bestseller lists and so on. A suit relating to some of these practices, brought with the financial help of the American Booksellers Association (ABA), has been settled by a group of defending publishers. New suits are also being brought. The ABA filed an action against Random House in January 1996.

Meanwhile, independents, like the small mammals of the late Jurassic, will have to forage among the dangerous footfalls of the giants. Let's examine how.

By general agreement among my sources, independents have at least the potential to beat the chains on several levels:

1. knowing the customer and hand-selling books;
2. knowing and relating intimately to the community;
3. reacting swiftly to new ideas; and
4. providing varied environments and services.

These are all areas in which the chains suffer from structural, philosophical, managerial or financial constraints. In addition, chains suffer from: high fixed overheads, which can seriously affect the bottom line in a downturn; rigid central buying policies, which cannot truly respond to local needs, hard as the chains may try; a lack of serious involvement by store staffs, a situation Borders has tried to overcome with generous profit-sharing plans; and the debilitating effects of "homogenization" at all levels. Large entities must necessarily smooth the differences between stores and regions. Personnel decisions, salaries, customer relations policies, etc all have to be standardized.

This tends to eliminate the "edges" which give competitive advantage.

On the other side, chains have great strengths: capital ability, marketing clout and the tremendous inertia of a general trend in retailing toward bigness. Discounting is often perceived as important in the growth of chains, but not as the critical element in the survival of independents. Most independents, and many publishers, see the erosion of confidence in "list prices" and the accompanying cynicism of consumers towards full-price vendors, mostly independents, as a highly destructive force in the industry. Discounting slows the turn of midlist titles, destroys backlists and supports the tendency, to which publishers are too often prone, toward category, as opposed to content, publishing. Even bestselling author Stephen King has expressed concern "about the effect that price-cutters are having on American popular culture, and God knows, the American popular culture is debased enough."

Knowing the customer

It was a bromide of 1980s' bookselling that the independent had to find a "niche", a space between the bestsellers and the sidelines to shelter the store from the storms of discounting and mass merchandising. Every observer with whom I spoke noted that this is even more true today, although even a specialty may not be sufficient protection. Recent days have seen the closing of independents who concentrated on literature, science fiction, mysteries, children's books and art books. Nonetheless, virtually all the book people consulted and every article perused agreed that you had better have a category-killer if you want to maintain your market presence. As Tom Peters put it in an AB interview in May 1994: "My hypothesis about retailing— whether the issue is the Gap versus Wal-Mart, Banana Republic versus Wal-Mart, or whether it's the Mom-and-Pop shop versus the Banana Republic—is that in the face of intelligent, sophisticated, general-purpose merchandisers, it is almost suicidal to believe that you can exist as a tiny general-purpose merchandiser unless you happen to be in a small town."

In my own experience, any new competition hurts, even if not aimed at my specialties, simply because it takes away browsers. A customer who shopped my store once a week may drop to once every two weeks. Bookbuyers have no more "disposable time" than others. The time for book browsing may well not increase, even as the supply of interesting stores to browse does.

As to hand-selling, I think the brouhaha over Russell Banks illustrates just how passionate independents are on the issue. The anger at Banks was so quick and strong because Banks is "one of ours". Independent booksellers had made Banks a success, and like a ship-jumping professional athlete, Banks was all too ready to cast his lot with the team that could pay him the most. I can't imagine the same outrage directed at Sidney Sheldon under similar circumstances.

Adam Bellow, Editorial Director of The Free Press, could have been talking about many independent booksellers, when, in our conversation, he said of his own publishing program, "We don't have a market, but a readership." Bellow speaks directly to our mutual concerns in decrying the pervasiveness of the "marketing mentality" in publishing, the transformation of publishers and editors into marketing directors, and the dehumanizing impact of marketing: its application of behavioral psychology to generate stimulus and response in the "subject", in this case the hapless bookbuyer. Booksellers who become just marketers lose connection to their customers and will, like the publishers themselves, become category-driven, not content-driven. Bellow again: "The logic of publishing today is that you can't publish something that hasn't been done before. If we are leaders, not followers, we are penalized."

Knowing your community

The ability to take that hand-selling model and grow it to community proportions is a critical skill in today's market. I am told that the community relations job in a Borders store ranks in authority and salary only behind the store manager.

Many who proffer advice in the retail book field confirm this:

- Jay Conrad Levinson (author of *Guerrilla Marketing* , *AB*, February 1994): "The first weapon is called relationships, and it encourages you to stop thinking in terms of making sales and start thinking in terms of making relationships."
- Richard Cross and Janet Smith (authors of *Customer Bonding: The Five Point System for Maximizing Customer Loyalty*): "There are five

ascending priorities in establishing customer loyalty: awareness, identity, relationship, community, and advocacy" (*PW*, April 24,1995).
- Faith Popcorn (author of *Clicking*, *AB*, July 1995): "…. there's a new
crossover where the bookstore becomes more of a library–a lifestyle
library, you might say–an information provider, a friendly, central
place, a place to meet people, pick up people. "

I certainly believe that the success of Kramerbooks & afterwords is
a direct outgrowth of our intuition in 1976 that the bookstore/cafe was
just such a place. The store has woven itself intimately into the fabric
of the community. People have life experiences there, not just consumer
experiences. When James Naisbitt (*Megatrends*) was featured in
People Magazine, he asked that his picture be taken at Kramerbooks,
for that was where he met and courted his wife. Therapists in the
Washington area often tell me: "Oh, you're the Kramer from
Kramerbooks? You know, so many of my patients (started, ended) a
relationship there. The place appears in their dreams all the time."

The techniques of community outreach are many and varied: food,
drink, author appearances, book circles, loyalty programs in the form of
discount cards, cross-promotions with other retailers, community
event-hosting, newsletters, sponsorship of local sports teams, and more,
but the objective is the same, to make the bookstore more than just a
place of retail transactions. As Faith Popcorn put it, "If I simply wanted a book, I don't need that retailer. But that's not why people are going
in and buying. They're buying experience."

Swift reaction

Tom Peters (*AB*, 5/94) puts it like this: "The problem…is the
requirement in these fast-changing times to throw out a lot of the baby
along with the bath water and to constantly move forward to reinvent
yourself, redefine yourself." And, "The whole key to me is that the definition of the chain is 'cookie cutter'. And the definition of the one big
advantage that the independent bookseller has is that he or she doesn't
want to work for one of those damn chains, which suggests that they're
a little bit independent of spirit to begin with and they have the flexibility to reconfigure the store and to trot over to LearningSmith and
steal five ideas by noon and implement them by four o'clock."

Of course, to be swift requires that you be energetic. To be energetic you have to have some reserves, both human and financial. Will independents have enough of either? I was struck, as I researched this piece, by the observation that the unusually successful are unusually endowed with great energy. They don't need much sleep; they live and breathe their work; they spend (as reported of the wonderful and wonderfully successful Joyce Meskis in *Sales & Marketing Magazine*) 60 to 100 hours a week at the business; they are often either unmarried or with grown children. How many of us can do that? Must the cost of keeping our businesses alive be the total loss of any other life?

Varied environments

Peters again: "The notion that Barnes & Noble will go on to dominate the world is pure bullshit. And the bigger they get, and the more they buy up, the less interesting they get. Borders and Barnes & Noble have copied two or three interesting little things from good independent booksellers...And suddenly, we're panicked because, my God, look, they can have chairs in their stores too. To which my response is: If the only damned difference between Barnes & Noble and your independent bookstore is that you have a leather chair and they use fake leather...then God help you. Close the doors tomorrow. Unless I don't understand anything about corporate America, the ability of Barnes & Noble to capture the spirit of a Bookshop Santa Cruz is approximately zero."

Unfortunately, the ability of many existing independent bookstores to capture – or finance – the spirit of Bookshop Santa Cruz is, if not zero, at least dangerously close to it.

To be sure, independents are at some levels less constrained. What happens in one store doesn't have to be copied in another. Nonetheless, the revolution that Tom Peters outlined at the New England Booksellers Association trade show last spring, where he urged independents to "empower clerks, nurture inconsistency and inculcate randomness, change, variations, and unpredictability", (*PW*, April 24, 1995) may sound invigorating, but as any bookseller who has gone through the gut-wrenching process of business realignment in the past few years knows, it is difficult – no, impossible – to live at the edge all the time. Humans cannot function for extended stretches on a war-foot-ing. As Carol Horne reports, many booksellers of her acquaintance are losing heart and getting tired. "It's no fun anymore" is a refrain often heard.

Restructuring your business may be exciting for a while, but there comes a time when you need calm waters. If the reality is that independent booksellers have entered a long period during which they must constantly reinvent themselves, then the toll will be heavy indeed. And, returning to the million-dollar question, where will the profits come from over the long haul? The jury is out on both these issues, for most independents

* * * * *

Finally, the electronic onset. CD-ROM. The Internet. Books-on-demand. The sky is full of portents. Are kids reading? What is to become of literacy? Virtually all the folks I spoke with observed, through their own lens, the same phenomenon: the dumbing down of books. Not across the board, and certainly not in specific instances. The flow of good writing, solid historical research, profound thinking has not stopped, but the common assessment is that the environment in which these works of quality appear has deteriorated. Jonathan Yardley, a "reader of publishers' catalogs for thirty years", notes the disappearance of midlist titles and the transfer of serious publishing away from the commercial firms to small independent presses. "It's all glitter and glitz."

Michael Denneny, a senior editor at Crown, told an American Association of University Presses (AAUP) meeting last summer that the future of quality non-fiction and literary fiction is in doubt at large houses, given the pressure for every book to sell in substantial five figures. "Therefore when you present your books, you have to lie, and they know you're lying; so you only try to do it maybe once a year, and then you have to have a big commercial book to cover it." (*PW*, July 10, 1995)

Denneny went on to note the opportunities this situation offers university presses. Yes, but...university presses are in much the same boat. A university press sales director notes that the really strong titles continue to do as well as before, but books just below the top echelon are performing less well, putting extreme pressure on the entire university press program. "The library market is gone and the independents are running leaner inventories. As a result, the books we do publish have to be more expensive to cover the costs."

Those involved in academic and scholarly publishing see a future of smaller press runs, higher prices, greater direct competition among the houses for the consumer's dollar and the growth of alternative means of production and distribution.

Even the sales director of one of the largest trade houses sees these trends impacting trade publishing, especially in the arena of new media. "We're being aggressive in developing 'digital content.' It's happening. And it's all competition for my customers' (the bookstores') time and money."

Adam Bellow is troubled by a larger issue. "The underlying question is the health of the reading public. They have to want to read. Then, and only then, can we address *how* to get books to them." Bellow sees a serious lack of commitment to primary, secondary and college educational support policies at the state and federal levels. "This affects everyone. It goes well beyond the boundaries of our business." Bellow links it to larger forces in play. "My instinct is that we are in a deconstructive stage of public life and of institutions of public authority. In this broad crisis, the media, including publishers, are viewed with suspicion. The more that publishers succumb to the bureaucratic impulse, which includes the culture of bigness, the more our industry will suffer."

Faith Popcorn sees the same trends with a different eye. "I think people over forty have a lot of reverence for the written word, and it's been beaten into us how wonderful it is. Young kids have no attachment to it at all. As a matter of fact, they are learning words on computers."

Bookstores are just learning how to navigate in cyberspace. It may be too soon to know whether the Internet will be a critical element in business terms, but one thing is clear already: Bookstores will have to compete for every dollar with the manufacturers. It's a wide-open market today, and booksellers have no more claim on the business than the publishers. Indeed, scores of publishers, including virtually all of the majors, have already created their own Internet "home pages", on which they are offering direct sales to consumers, bypassing both wholesalers and retailers. Marshall Smith, the guru of leading-edge bookselling, takes a more upbeat view from his perch at his new retail environment, Cybersmith. In response to an AB question on the future of bookselling, he says, "Doesn't the business keep growing? Don't we sell more books every year? It's conceivable that books will be on hand-held computers, but the print can only be so small before it's a problem. So a hand-held computer probably isn't the right format. Maybe something bigger. But if that happens, so what? It's the words that are the important thing.....In my mind, the newest way of learning or understanding or satisfying curiosity is incremental to what was there before. It doesn't replace the old way; it just adds on."

I count myself among Faith Popcorn's "over forties". I can't conceive of a reading experience more satisfying than holding a well-printed book. I'm not seduced (yet) by the siren call of digital content. I'd rather ski a mountain and go home to a good book than surf the net. But, but, but... It's our job to get beyond our personal limitations, no? If the 20th century was a golden time for personal bookselling, then it may well be true that the 21st will see the dawn of impersonal book-selling: "Whatever you want, we can make it.... instantly....with a few keystrokes." We could be the new Peter Zengers – printers, publishers and booksellers all in one – reunited, unexpectedly, by the new culture we all fear.

After graduating from Oberlin College, where he was Editor-in-Chief of the newspaper, Bill Kramer returned to Washington to enter the family business begun in 1946 by his father, Sidney Kramer (d 1961). Within a few years, he opened new book retailing and whole-saling businesses – scholarly remainders, a book and record store combination, and, in 1976, Kramerbooks and afterwords, a book-store/cafe. Over the years, Kramer has been author (a guidebook to Washington written with his wife and published by Random House), author's agent and board member for local and national bookselling organizations.

6

The Rise of the Book Chain Superstore

Stephen Horvath

The retail book business in the United States is diverse and highly competitive, and, as the following figures show, its pattern is changing:

	1993	1994
Chain bookstores	23%	27%
Independents	24%	19%
Book clubs and mail order	20%	22%
Discount/warehouse stores	13%	14%
Used book stores	5%	4%
Food/drug stores	5%	4%
All other	10%	10%

There is every indication that chain bookstores will continue to increase their market share. Chains are not new, but a lot of new things have happened in the chain segment of the industry over the last ten years. Like many other bookbuyers, I have observed these changes from the customer's point of view. My vantage point, until 1988, was Boston, Massachusetts. As an avid reader and compulsive bookstore browser, I was well-served there by a number of independent bookstores – Harvard Bookstore and Wordsworth in Cambridge, Boston University Bookstore in Kenmore Square, and Brookline Booksmith.

They were all good places to browse, with inviting (albeit somewhat pedestrian) displays, with all the current books and with a good backlist selection. These stores were suited to the serious reader. Their stock selection was made by a knowledgeable "book person", not by a computer. You might have had to canvass more than one shop in order to find out what you were after, but that was a pleasure, not an inconvenience.

There were chain bookstores in the Boston vicinity in these years, confined mostly to shopping malls. The one exception was a multi-storey Barnes & Noble downtown. To my mind, such stores were for discounted bestsellers (or books published with such aspirations) and children's books. Serious readers did not go to malls to shop for books.

In 1988, we moved to Thousand Oaks, California. The bookstore landscape changed dramatically – for the worse. We found ourselves in a town of 75,000, well above average in education and affluence, but without a single decent bookshop. What was there – sterile, cramped Walden and B Dalton mall stores – did nothing to excite the book lover's soul. The nearest independent, a shop called Book Soup, was thirty miles away in West Hollywood.

Our next move, to Palo Alto, part of the Bay Area anchored by San Francisco, San Jose and Oakland, brought us back into good bookstore country. Palo Alto, a university town, had the same quality of bookshops as Boston/Cambridge. But in the forty miles between Palo Alto and San Francisco – an area known as the Peninsula – there was nothing but Walden and Dalton in a mall.

Not any more. With the coming of a new kind of chain bookstore – the superstore – starting in late 1991, the sophisticated Peninsula book-buyer today has little to complain about. Where before there was a desert, there are now three Barnes & Nobles, one Crown and a Borders store opened in Palo Alto in early 1996. All of these are large, attractively laid out, well-stocked and well-staffed emporiums, some with cafes added. This revolution in the Bay Area is representative of what has occurred in almost every major metropolitan area in the US. If the plans of the largest players are realized, it will soon be happening in medium-sized cities and towns as well.

Where did this bookselling *blitzkrieg* come from? What is the current state of the game? Where is it going?

*   *   *   *   *

Over the past twenty years, the bookstore business has experienced a series of changes centered on expansion, mass merchandising, discounting, uniformity of presentation and concentration on high-volume titles. Major developments in this evolution have included:

1. regional chains, a few of which (B Dalton and Barnes & Noble) were precursors of today's mega-chains;
2. consolidation, merger and expansion among the chains;
3. location in shopping malls, eventually resulting in most major malls having both B Dalton and Walden Books as tenants;
4. deep discounting of bestsellers; and
5. the coming of the book superstore, pioneered by Borders and aggressively joined by Barnes & Noble.

The superstore phenomenon has proceeded by means of a serial saturation of selected markets. This has brought intensified competition based on price, selection, service and 100-hours-a-week store operation. Superstore appeal has been enhanced by the creation of pleasant browsing environments, events for adults and children, large periodical offerings, music – and coffee. The typical superstore comprises at least 10,000 square feet of floor space and a minimum of 100,000 book titles on hand.

The outcome of these developments is a retail book industry in which national chains are becoming predominant. Independent bookstores are struggling. In 1994, the leading chains increased their sales by 16% over the previous year, while total bookstore sales were up only 5%. Not only are the independents being crowded out, but within the chains there have been numerous store closings, as the old mall sites have lost business to the superstores.

As of the end of 1995, there were four major bookstore chains:

	1994 ($m)	1995 ($m)	Increase %
Barnes & Noble (including B Dalton, Doubleday and Scribners)	1,337	1,623	21
Borders (including Walden)	1,370	1,511	10
Crown	275	305	11
Books-a-Million	123	172	40
Total	3,105	3,611	16

These four major chains are today jockeying for locations and dominance in local markets across the country. Ironically, the chain concept originated in widely scattered independent stores – Powell's of Portland, Oregon; The Tattered Cover of Denver, Colorado; and the original Borders store of Ann Arbor, Michigan. These pioneers offered larger selections of books; were more inviting to the casual browser; and emphasized customer service by a helpful and knowledgeable staff, people who knew and loved books. They were the innovators, but visionaries were needed to recognize the applicability of the concept to the national market and to take on the risks of making it happen.

The first thrust came from the Borders brothers, Tom and Lewis. Their first shop had succeeded in Ann Arbor, a major university town; the second, opened in suburban Detroit in 1985, was a test of whether this kind of bookshop could thrive outside an academic setting. It succeeded, beyond all expectations. The brothers then expanded into other Midwest and Northeast locations, as fast as their capital resources would allow. These first two stores were the laboratories in which the superstore concept was refined and improved over the rest of the decade.

The Borders brothers' success stimulated another visionary, Len Riggio of Barnes & Noble. He expanded the existing Barnes & Noble stores in a similar way, but faster and more aggressively than Borders had been able to do. In late 1992, Borders was acquired by the merchandising giant Kmart, which provided the capital necessary to accelerate expansion, and the battle was joined. When Crown and Books-A-Million arrived, the game was already in progress. Now there are more than 500 superstores (about 300 Barnes & Noble, 100+ Borders, 70 Crown and more than 40 Books-A-Million). More than a hundred new superstores were opened in 1995.

*   *   *   *   *

These bookselling enterprises can be studied from three points of view – as a business, as seen by the customers and as seen by the employees (of whom I am one).

The Business

Viewed from the top down, the industry is currently at a stage where profitability is a secondary pursuit. First priorities are growth and the contest for market share. For their most recent fiscal year, Barnes & Noble had a net income of $25m on sales of $1.62bn – a profit margin of just 1.5%. In 1994, the Borders Group had revenues of $1.5bn and a net income of $21m – 1.4% of sales. Statistics for the four major chains, quoted in *Publishers Weekly* of July 10, 1995, showed a loss of 1% for 1993 and a profit margin of only 0.6% for 1994. Plainly, the business is not, at least for now, an engine of economic surplus.

To a large extent, the modest profits reflect the dynamics of the four strata which compose each of the four competitors: mature traditional stores; obsolete traditional stores; maturing superstores; and recently opened superstores. The mature traditional stores (typically located in malls) are achieving minimum growth at best, but they are the indispensable "cash cows" for the rest of the operations. When the cash flow falters in such stores, the companies close them down and swallow short-term write-offs. Barnes & Noble has closed about 100 B Dalton stores over the past few years; Borders has written off $97m as a result of closing 114 Walden stores. To replace these, maturing superstores (those in operation for two years or more) are beginning to contribute profits, albeit slowly and unevenly. On the other hand, the new superstores are a cash drain. Start-up costs vary from $1.5m to $2m per store. It takes a year or more for revenues to reach full potential. Meanwhile, the meter is running.

These figures illustrate the contrasting financial effects of stratification:

	Sales ($ million)		No of stores	
	1993	*1994*	*1993*	*1994*
Borders				
Borders superstores	225	425	44	85
Waldenbooks	*1,146*	*1,086*	1,159	1,102
Total	1,371	1,511		
Barnes & Noble				
B & N superstores	600e	958	200e	268
B Dalton	*737e*	*665*	750e	698
Total	1,337	1,623		
e = estimate				

As these figures show, the number of new superstores rose dramatically from 1993 to 1994, while the number of traditionals was marginally reduced and the average superstore income was much higher than that of the traditionals.

The cost structure of superstores is fairly simple. There are only three major expense categories: the cost of merchandise (65% to 70% of sales); rent, which can vary widely depending on location; and staff costs for management and hourly personnel (8% to 10% of sales). Rent per square foot of space more or less dictates the sales required for profitability and staff levels are geared to planned revenue.

Distribution is effected from regional warehouses – Borders, for example, has four. A small amount of stock is received directly at stores from publishers or wholesalers. Finally, there are the centralized functions, such as purchasing and stock allocation, store planning and development, computer systems, inventory control, merchandising policy (for nation-wide consistency) and company management. Independent bookstores must also execute these functions, but the chains realize large economies of scale and a real competitive advantage.

The chains' differing strategies emphasize a variety of competitive factors:

Location

Each chain has a mix of "flagship" city locations, suburban sites and stores in smaller towns. Barnes & Noble is highly visible in Manhattan, while Borders has pre-empted Chicago and downtown San Francisco. Large-scale shopping malls are out; strip malls are in. Intent on speedy saturation of metropolitan markets with multiple stores, B & N and Borders put a premium on grabbing choice locations first.

Facilities

Borders stores tend to be larger (partly because of music departments and cafes) and their buildings are more impressive. B & N and Crown are more uniform in design. They favor boxy shells with high ceilings and glass all around.

Advertising

B & N is highly visible, with national ads in the *New York Times* and other leading papers. Crown also advertises extensively, emphasizing low prices. Borders approaches advertising with caution.

Price

Crown is seen as the deepest discounter, partly because the titles it discounts represent a larger proportion of their inventory. Slow-moving titles are ordered in small quantities. All the chains give deep discounts (30% to 40%) on bestsellers, a practice which the independents loudly lament, since it cuts into their most profitable business. While Crown and B & N give 20% on all hardcovers, Borders gives only 10%. Crown discounts paperbacks by 10%; B & N and Borders give no discount on paperbacks. My own view is that pricing attracts customers to the store, but all the other features of the superstore are what really drive the business.

Inventory

While Borders stocks each store in depth (backroom overstocks are often sufficient to open a medium-sized independent store), B & N leans towards a "just in time" strategy. Almost the entire B & N inventory is displayed on the shop floor. At a B & N store where I worked, the policy was to clear the backroom of books at least once a week. Borders attempts to maximize the amount of stock purchased directly from publishers to maximize discount. However, publishers give slower service than wholesale distributors, so orders have to be proportionately larger. B & N is more nimble, using a combination of publisher orders for initial quantities and distributor orders for rush replenishment. This means lower average discount, offset by lower inventory costs and fewer returns.

Service

The customers' service needs are expressed in three questions: Do you have this book? If you do, can you please find it for me? If you don't, can you get it? Borders does well on the first question because of the depth of its inventory. Borders also scores well on the second question because it spends more on its hourly staff. B & N is best for special orders, especially in getting them quickly.

Merchandising

All four chains are very good at this. They know how to lay out shop floors to make them attractive to customers. Crown and B & N are more uniform; Borders is a little quirky.

Amenities

Borders is known for providing cafes and music departments. B & N is catching up in coffee (in partnership with Starbucks), but soft-pedals any plans to add music. Crown has no frills.

Other Media

Borders has taken the lead in stocking software, computer games and videos, which, curiously, are generally found in the music department.

The Customer

When I first saw a Barnes & Noble superstore, there seemed to be an intelligence behind it; someone who had a list of what bookbuyers would like to have and then created the organization and stores to deliver it all. On the list were things not previously available at the typical independent bookstore: discounts, not only on bestsellers but on all hardcovers; more breadth (more authors and more subject areas); and more depth (better backlist and authors' more obscure titles); and ambience – clean, well-lit places with expensive-looking fixtures.

A major ingredient in the superstore recipe is service. Such an assertion is bound to raise hackles among devotees of the independents, who contend that superstores are impersonal places which don't care about serving customers in the ways to which the old, local, independent (all of these words have become value-laden) booksellers are devoted. There was a lot of lip service paid to helping customers before the coming of the superstores. The new breed of store spends time and money training its staff to deliver customer service and implements the principle in specific concrete ways, such as information desks.

Superstores can only prosper by doing better what independent stores have long done. For example, they have to offer more desirable remainders and more of them; enticing displays; and special orders if a title is not on hand. I still patronize my local bookstore (Kepler's in Menlo Park), a very good bookshop, voted National Independent Bookstore of the Year a few years ago. However, their policy on special orders was: 1) you had to pay $3 for the privilege; 2) there were no discounts on these; and 3) you were obligated to take the book when it arrived. With an exception or variation here or there, the superstores impose none of these penalties on special orders.

Superstores have also brought bookbuying customers some benefits they probably didn't know they wanted. For example, the store I work in is open more than a hundred hours a week. When customers ask me about hours, their response is invariably pleasant surprise. In San Francisco, we are open until midnight Thursday through Saturday, in a section of the city without much night life. It's virtually impossible to clear the store of customers until ten or fifteen minutes *after* "closing". Then there's the coffee. There's nothing new about this. As far back as the '70s, attempts were made to combine books and sustenance in so-called bookstore cafes. Generally, these early endeavors were coffee shops attached to modest or inferior bookstores, where the books were decorative, almost ancillary. Superstores start by making the best possible bookstores and add coffee as a complement. Coffee is intended to generate traffic, not profit. The same applies to readings and signings, performances, participatory happenings for children (the Barnes & Noble store in San Jose has a mini-stage for kids' events; our Borders store has a small amphitheatre in our children's department). All such amenities existed before the superstore came along, but in isolated instances. Now they are a chain-wide phenomenon. Borders stores have full-time "Community Relations Coordinators".

You know something new has happened by the number of times customers arrive at the cash register saying, "I didn't really mean to buy so much. I came in to get a gift for my husband, but I just could-n't stop." Good superstores are merchandising packages which make it possible for the customer to be sold by the books.

As I said at the beginning of this piece, I am able to look at super-stores as a customer. My experience as a publisher, dealing with the hard economics of the print run, made me fear that in the future the trade book would be highly vulnerable to a vicious circle of declining readership, higher costs of materials and labor, lower print runs and increasing prices. If literacy continues to decline; if multimedia and video games continue to divert; if all the many magnets to discre-tionary time and income continue to multiply, new hardcover trade titles, I used to fear, can only diminish in number and soar in price. The new stores have restored my optimism. They provide the trade book with access to the widest possible audience, giving it a chance to flour-ish and sustain itself at a time when trends – economic, cultural, tech-nological – are not favorable.

I recognize that the relationship between the chain stores and the independents is an emotional issue, if ever there was one. It is too often posed as either/or, an economic war superimposed on a previously gentlemanly trade in which the clout of the chains is destined to over-whelm the meagre resources of the stand-alones. This simplistic view ignores the benefits of competition which should make all parties – independents, the smaller chain stores, the superstores – better at sat-isfying their customers. One reason why bookbuyers have not in the past been aware of what they wanted was that they weren't presented with choices. With the advent of the new stores, choices abound and customers are voting their choices with their dollars. Independents are getting better. The need to survive is an effective discipline. Good as they were, Kepler's, my local independent, has instituted a number of improvements in the past two years. Would these have occurred in the absence of superstore competition? Perhaps. I can be less equivocal about who benefits from these changes, for surely it is the customer.

I believe that competition stimulated by the superstores is expand-ing the total market, not cannibalizing it. Making readers excited about going to a bookstore; expanding the awareness of bookbuyers of the magnificent variety of books available; bringing a new generation to a place where books are inviting – all of this can only be for the good.

The Employees

I entered the retail book industry at the age of fifty, an exploratory move rather than part of a career plan. It has been challenging, interesting and rewarding. There are aspects of retail bookselling which discourage young people and make for a high rate of staff turnover. Maturity enables a longer perspective, fewer illusions and the ability to focus on the intrinsic satisfaction of the work.

What does the assistant manager of a superstore do? I have personal responsibility for inventory management, which involves receiving and sorting incoming stock, processing returns, the integrity of on-hand data in the computer, selective ordering of books (especially local interest titles) and direction of the annual physical inventory. Secondly, I have responsibility for the section of the store which covers history, the social sciences, religion, philosophy and audio books – a department where I am assisted by five booksellers, who do most of the shelving and arranging. Thirdly, I oversee the floor for two to four hours a day, making sure all areas are properly staffed, making change for cashiers and processing cash receipts and, on some days, running the programs and doing the housekeeping chores necessary to open or close the store, duties I share with other managers. Finally, and most importantly, I serve customers.

The job of a bookseller is physically demanding. It's a big store. Books are heavy. Your feet are always reminding you how little time you spend sitting down. Hours are irregular. Days run from 4 pm to 1 am or 11 am to 8 pm. I get Tuesdays and Saturdays off. After twenty-seven years of Monday to Friday, with all colleagues on the same schedule, it's quite an adjustment. The store is open twice as long as anyone's working week.

In relation to their level of education or the pay they could earn elsewhere, just about everyone in the store is underpaid. Much of the work involves tidying up after customers, who seem intent on dismantling everything we build up (it's called browsing). But there are psychic rewards. We are doing something we believe in, something we are committed to doing well. We aim to be the best bookstore in the country and on good days we feel that goal is within reach. We all love books and/or music and are proud to provide the kind of shopping experience we ourselves look for. We get a consistent message from the Borders organization that we are valuable. High employee turnover is a fact of life, in spite of our enthusiasm for bringing books and people together. Borders takes an enlightened approach to this problem – emphasizing staff training, development, promotion and good communication. Besides reducing turnover, these policies motivate staff to deliver the exceptional customer service a superstore aims to provide.

*   *   *   *   *

How does the rise of the chain superstore affect publishers? In general, I think publishers and, by extension, authors prosper whenever readers are well-served. Do chains, because of their size, affect what publishers publish? I don't think this is true, but if it were, it would more likely affect specialty publishers and university presses, for whom inclusion in the superstores' offerings can be a jackpot. I doubt if superstores have any influence over the Simon & Schusters, whose size allows them to exercise an equal and countervailing power.

The primary importance of the book chain superstore is in the quality and volume of *resources* – marketing, financial, technical, physical and human – devoted to bookselling. It has made shopping for books a more rewarding experience, giving books a better chance to succeed in the marketplace, without, however, as yet, commensurate profits for the retailers.

What of the future? How will technology affect the distribution and sale of books? What about new media (computer software, compact disks, multimedia)? Of course there will be change – that's a given. But books, music and coffee have been around for a long time and they seem to satisfy basic needs and beget widespread customer loyalty. Silicon chips and dancing electrons are not going to change that.

I believe that independent stores can compete with superstores, but only if they are committed to continual improvement. But it's a highly competitive business and it is doubtful if all the current players in the game can prosper, or even survive. Even if the number of players is reduced, the massive resources deployed will have to be justified by the profits if companies' stockholders are to be satisfied. As I write, there are reports of financial difficulties experienced by Crown. Borders is no longer part of Kmart, so all of the major companies are at the moment independent, and, relatively, are small entities. The rules or conditions of the game could be drastically altered by takeovers, friendly mergers – or the demands of the bankers. I think the worst outcome would be the triumph of a single chain – a too dominant link in the connection between writer and reader. The most likely scenario is two or three major chains operating in an environment with fewer, but stronger, local independents. For both the publishers and the readers, that would be a propitious outcome.

After twenty years in the publishing business, during which he worked for a US educational publisher, for an international STM publisher and as a publisher of academic and professional journals, Steve Horvath entered bookselling. His first job was with Barnes & Noble. He is now Assistant Manager of the Borders Superstore in San Francisco. Horvath holds AB and MBA degrees from Dartmouth College.

7

Wholesalers Burgeon on Speed and Service

Steven J Mason

Only in the past twenty years has book wholesaling in the United States established itself as a major part of the fabric of book distribution. Until the 1970s, wholesaling was largely confined to small regional operations providing their customers with a narrow selection ranging from 1,000 to 5,000 titles. Since then, the business has grown by more than 3,000% to the point where, lacking wholesalers, the US publishing industry would be hard pressed to meet the needs of its book-consuming population. About 22% of all book sales in the US pass through wholesalers and jobbers.

The driving forces behind this growth have been the rapid expansion of B Dalton and WaldenBooks stores in the malls during the '80s and the emergence of superstores and multimedia stores in the '90s. The opening of many new public library branches has also contributed to this growth. Before this happened, wholesalers could only offer their customers, most of whom lived in or near their cities, quick fulfillment. Not infrequently wholesalers' customers would visit their warehouses to select books. Today, by contrast, some wholesalers have multiple distribution centers located throughout the US and stock several hundred thousand titles, with a one-day delivery service. Most wholesalers have also opened up their international markets and can deliver to customers in other countries in less than a week.

Publishers have traditionally undervalued wholesalers' services. After all, they have their own sales forces and distribution centers. Who needs an intermediary? Since publishers control the timing of the lay-down of new titles, they claim that delivery speed is not that critical for the bookstore. Publishers were also understandably reluctant to concede the deeper discounts typically offered to wholesalers.

Book wholesalers, however, have proved over the past twenty years that they are more than intermediaries. By providing additional services to booksellers, they have attracted business despite publisher resistance. These services include, for example, toll-free telephone and electronic ordering, immediate stock verification, next-day fulfillment, high fill-rates of 90% or more, multiple distribution centers, freight programs providing faster service at lower cost – all this on top of inventories larger both in depth of titles and breadth of numbers of copies.

The widespread acceptance of book wholesalers has been aided by the fact that they have been responsible for most of the innovation and technical advances in book distribution. In the early '70s, wholesalers began listing their inventory of titles, together with stock status, on microfiche. By the mid-'70s, they were able to confirm to their customers which titles could be shipped by return, as a result of major investments in computer-based inventory control systems. Wholesalers were the first to provide economic ordering via personal computers in bookstores and libraries. Pub Net, the publishers' electronic ordering system, was a direct response by the publishing community designed to offer electronic ordering services competitive to those provided by wholesalers.

Progressively, wholesalers won the confidence of their bookseller customers by being more than mere book suppliers. Some of the merchandising services offered by wholesalers today include:

1. *Inventory information on CD-ROM*, including stock status;
2. *Marketing information*, including schedules of book reviews, major media appearances, bestseller information, new title information and monthly new title catalogs covering hundreds of new titles from virtually all publishers;
3. Periodic *specialty and category catalogs*;
4. *Point-of-purchase material*; and

5. *Recommended inventories* for new stores that can be   packaged by subject categories.

As publishers have increased the output of new titles to roughly 50,000 each year, and as retail bookstores have increased the breadth of their inventory from the traditional 13,000 titles in the mid-'80s to more than 100,000 titles in some superstores today, the scope for wholesaling has become even greater. Many retailers have realized that they cannot afford to carry the depth of inventory that they need if they have to rely on publishers to re-supply them at a speed to satisfy their customers. Even the most efficient publishers typically can take from two to three weeks to supply re-orders. By contrast, bookstores are able to re-order daily from wholesalers, a process facilitated by computerized point-of-sale systems, and they can expect to receive nine out of ten books they order in one or two days. Retailers have come to understand that if they don't have a book on the shelf when a customer is looking for it, they have probably lost the sale. The marginally better discounts offered by publishers are not enough to compensate for the difference between two days and two weeks. On balance, most booksellers find that customer satisfaction, profitability and cash flow are better served by using wholesalers than ordering direct.

Discounts, of course, vary from publisher to publisher and wholesaler to wholesaler. Broadly speaking, retail booksellers can purchase from publishers at discounts in the area of 45%, while wholesalers receive around 50% from publishers. Wholesale discounts to booksellers range from 40% to 42%, varying with quantity. Free freight policies above a certain number of books can effectively increase wholesaler discounts by 2% to 4%.

As bookstores' inventory has broadened, they have had to face the administrative difficulties of ordering from hundreds, or perhaps thousands, of publishers. To indirect costs of time and administration must also be added the freight for shipping small quantities from many publishers. Re-orders to wholesalers can be consolidated into a single order, in many cases electronically, and result in just one shipment and a single statement. In the superstores, sheer volume of sales, combined with the need to re-order frequently, would overwhelm a manager who did not rely heavily on wholesalers.

Of course, no bookstore, not even the largest superstore, can stock every book that its customers might desire. But in such instances, speed of delivery can often secure the order. Many wholesalers provide their inventory information on CD-ROM, so that booksellers can check the availability of a desired title on the spot and promise delivery of special orders to their customers with confidence. Such orders can represent as much as 30% of sales for some booksellers. I suspect we have all observed customers walk out of a retail store in disgust when informed that a special order will take more than a month.

Publishers, on their part, have come to understand that they are likely to sell more of their deep backlist by placing books in wholesalers' warehouses than by having them tucked away in their distribution centers. In some cases, the wholesaler is the only place where the book can be found, since it is not unknown that books listed as in print may no longer be in the publishers' inventory. It is possible to trace in publishers' attitudes to wholesalers an encouraging graduation from disdain or simple tolerance to active cooperation.

*   *   *   *   *

As an example of wholesaler service, my firm, Ingram Book Company, carries 290,000 titles in inventory. We have recently offered bookstores our PROFiche Software which details the stock status of every title that we carry. With this software, a bookseller can hit one key on an in-store computer, which will automatically dial an 800 number. That number connects the bookseller (or librarian) directly into an Ingram computer and gives instant stocking information on any title in the database. Thus booksellers can virtually guarantee a book's availability while actually talking to their customers.

Not all book outlets are bookstores. Warehouse clubs, mass merchants, computer specialty stores and multimedia stores also sell books. The needs of these new outlets have generated wholesalers who specialize in categories such as religious, medical or computer books, or independent press books, or textbooks or children's books. Some of the earliest wholesalers started by being specialists, not in product, but in markets, such as academic, public and school libraries, and have developed programs and services specifically tailored to these markets. Over the years, these wholesalers have developed approval programs

for academic libraries, leasing programs for public libraries and continuation and standing order programs for all classes of libraries. Some
wholesalers have been asked to provide new title services for libraries.
Beset by budget reductions, librarians have asked wholesalers to
increase their responsibilities for acquiring books and provide processing and cataloguing services so that, when the books are received,
they are ready to be placed on library shelves for immediate circulation
without further processing by library staff.

The growth in book wholesaling over the last twenty years has led
to the formation of the American Wholesale Booksellers Association
(AWBA). Founded in 1984, it currently has fifty members located
throughout the country. Representing a diverse membership, of all
sizes and with all types of inventory and specialization, AWBA aims to
educate both retail bookstores and publishers into a higher appreciation
of the constructive role of the wholesale sector; and also to develop
and advance industry standards.

Today, the relationship between wholesalers and publishers can be
described as a very positive partnership. Getting books into the hands
of bookbuyers quickly and efficiently must come close behind publishing good books as an industry goal. Logistically, it has to be more
efficient for a wholesaler to consolidate small quantities of many publishers' titles into a single shipment to a customer than for many publishers to make multiple small shipments to the same customer. The
retailer's five-book order becomes a fifty-book order from the wholesaler. What would be a petty order for a publisher becomes an economic quantity for a wholesaler, shipping books from a dozen different publishers. Specialty wholesalers are particularly appreciated by
publishers because they reach markets that they could not reach with
their own sales forces.

The growing confidence on the part of publishers is also bolstered
by information feedback from wholesalers, which helps publishers to
make better informed reprint decisions. Publishers can now get information from wholesalers not only about which titles are selling in particular classes of stores but also how much inventory of these titles
such stores have on hand. As a result, there is no reason for a publisher today to take a reprint decision based only on his own sales information and inventory position. By knowing what inventory of a title is

still on the shelves of retail stores, publishers can make wiser decisions, which will both reduce returns and the need to remainder excess
stock.

The future of wholesaling, like other parts of the book business, has
been questioned by some on the grounds that the electronic formats
will automatically replace the book. People have speculated since the
advent of radio that new technology of some kind would replace the
book. Electronic "books" are available already in the academic market
and trends indicate that these non-print formats will spread to other
types of book. However, movies, television, video cassettes, music
CDs, audio cassettes and micro computer software have all burgeoned
without slowing the growth of book publishing and bookselling. I
doubt that people will want to take their computers to the beach or to
bed when they want to read. So it appears virtually self-evident to me
that neither books nor book wholesalers are about to disappear into
some kind of cyber-haze. A more likely scenario is that the electronic
firms will seek ways to use the established book distribution channels.

Already, most wholesalers stock spoken audio as part of their regular inventory and supply audio cassettes in the same way as books.
This makes sense as new titles are now quite often published in book
and cassette form at the same time. Wholesalers will have no problem
in stocking books in any multimedia format – provided there is a
demand. Several book wholesalers already provide multimedia titles.
This is simply a logical extension of their services. Who will be better
positioned, if books become available in electronic formats, to bring
together the thousands of titles published by thousands of publishers
and distribute them to thousands of accounts? Wholesalers, as the
established liaison between publishers and booksellers, will provide
"the book" whatever its format.

In the near future, I believe wholesalers will continue to lead the
book industry in technological advances. For example, bookstores can
expect advance shipping notification, delivered electronically, to
enable them to reduce even further the time taken for incoming books
to reach their shelves. Or again, by license plating cartons of books,
wholesalers will enable retailers or libraries to wand a bar code,
instantly entering the books contained therein into their own inventory systems – or into their online public access catalogs.

The only thing that might put wholesalers in jeopardy is a failure to lead the book industry in terms of innovation and technology. Those of us in the book business who bring together hundreds of thousands of titles have perhaps a rosier view of the future of the book – and of their own future – than their colleagues who see them in smaller quantities.

After qualifying as an attorney, with a BA degree from Louisiana State University and a JD degree from Loyola University Law School, Steven Mason joined the Ingram Corporation. He became Vice President, General Counsel and Secretary in 1979. After seven years as President of Ingram Book Company, Mason assumed the posts of Vice Chairman of that company and President of Ingram Library Services Inc and Ingram International.

8

The Internationalization of the US Book Trade: The World's Rediscovery of America

Richard Abel

It can be argued, in my view fallaciously, that, since the founding of the first colonies, the United States has enjoyed and supported an internationally oriented book trade. Those so arguing point to the successive waves of immigration and the national literatures and literary languages introduced into this "new land" on the crest of each. By the early 18th century, the narrow band of civilization, stretched precariously along the Western Atlantic shore, was a linguistic tapestry incorporating not only the principal European languages but transliterations of some native American languages. Here could be found books – mostly Bibles and religious tracts of one kind or another – not only in English but in French, German, Spanish, Polish, Yiddish, Algonquian, Swedish, Iroquois, Dutch, and on and on. Some of these publications were produced by local publishers, printers or booksellers, but the vast bulk were imported from the home countries of the settlers and mainly from the British Isles. In those days, there were probably a wider array and selection of books in a great variety of languages available in New York than in London.

But this cosmopolitanism was more apparent than real. This vast assortment of literary goods was precisely that: a disparate and unconsolidated mix of texts reflecting the local folkways and traditions of the settlers – plus, of course, the classic works of the great Western European cultural tradition. Many of the colonists were not only extraordinarily learned and thoughtful but good linguists. But if we leave this coherent and commonly shared canon aside, the stock-in-trade of early North American booksellers reflected parochial interests of distinct contingents of immigrants. There was a curious, even anomalous, juxtaposition of the remarkably cosmopolitan and the stolidly parochial.

Those few books published in North America were not exported substantially back to the fatherlands. Despite the occasional protest by patriots incensed by what they saw as the second-class status of the New World, reflected in the massive one-way traffic of knowledge and ideas, most members of the early US book trade were perfectly content to devote their energy and resources to the cultivation of their domestic markets.

This complacent parochialism persisted for more than two centuries. Bookstores displayed imported books; pirated reprints of bestselling authors, particularly from the UK; translations, mostly in English from the principal European languages; and, of course, reprints or translations of the Western European cultural canon. Despite the steady development of a distinct North American voice manifested in a rapidly burgeoning literature, the traffic in books, and hence in ideas, knowledge and culture, remained largely a one-way street from the Old World to the New until, incredibly, as late as the beginning of World War II. The total value of the exports of US books in 1941 amounted to roughly $5m (about 3% of the domestic sales), and of this, half was shipped across the world's most transparent border to Canada. Only six years earlier had the value of books exported from the US finally exceeded the value of those imported.

*   *   *   *   *

Parochialism came to a dramatic end with the refashioning of virtually all of the established structures of the world – including the intellectual and cultural – following World War II and its convoluted aftermath. North America found itself after the war, somewhat unwillingly and grudgingly, at the center of the world stage, not only politically and economically, but also in terms of its dominance of the disjunct realms of the world's intellectual undertakings and its popular fashions and folkways. Quite astonishingly, for the next generation, the US was to lead the world in the anomalous omnium-gatherum of science, technology and medicine as well as popular custom – the latter what an acute and plain-spoken observer styled as "... the law of one description of fools and fashion as the other."

Two of the consequences of World War II for the US book and US publishing grew out of the so-called GI editions. These were cheaply manufactured, lightweight paperback books produced for free distribution to the men and women in the US military forces during the war. Ranging from mysteries and westerns to classics, these editions had a double impact. They not only helped to develop a book market among servicemen and women when they returned to civilian life, but also a nearly worldwide market for cheap books with US content, since US military personnel largely disposed of their GI books, when they had finished reading them, by handing them over to the civilian populations in the countries through which they marched [see Ballantine in this issue]. And, secondly, this widespread acceptance of US books opened the eyes of US publishers first to a domestic market which they had not recognized and then to an international market created by the exigencies of war.

Another thread in the internationalizing of the US book trade was the evolution of the US college textbook, largely the invention of the US academic establishment and some enterprising publishers. The collecting together in a coherent and integrated package of the principles and concepts developed to roughly the date of writing in a particular subject area at a specific level of prior preparation has long been, and continues to be, a powerful educational recipe. While its antecedents were lecture notes written down and subsequently published by scholars or students, the US college textbook became, and remains, a remarkable instrument to convey the accumulated knowledge of mankind. Its pedagogic methodology has increasingly been employed in institutions of higher learning around the world, displacing the traditional lecture and/or tutoring methodologies formerly widespread, not just in the UK and Europe, but in the Islamic, Indian and Chinese traditions. Thanks to the prominent role US educational institutions and publishing organizations played in the development of the textbook, US college publishers were well positioned to provide textbooks not only for the rebuilding of educational establishments devastated by World War II, but for the expansion of access to higher education, often an imitation of the US model, which took place around the world in the second half of the century [see Worth in this issue].

Much of the new work being done in the sciences was published in the form of advance-level textbooks. As a consequence, the largest and most prominent scientific textbook publishers, such as McGraw-Hill, John Wiley or Prentice Hall, were among the first to look abroad to expand their markets. The rise in exports realized by firms like these led to the establishment of overseas outlets with book-stocking and marketing agencies, and progressively of overseas offices, which the larger houses substituted for agencies. These offices in due course took on lives of their own, evolving into full-fledged local publishing units, even exporting some of their titles back to their parent companies for sale in the US.

This overseas expansion, both of US textbooks and scholarly monographs, was powerfully impelled by the post-war needs of the devastated countries of Europe and Asia. The information and knowledge needed to rebuild demolished or badly dislocated economies; to heal ravaged social structures; to re-establish shattered educational institutions; to meet the demands of the post-war young for tertiary education; to reconfirm, if not positively reformulate, the foundation of a civil society – all of this was readily and efficiently available from a US whose publishing institutions and infrastructure were largely unscathed by war.

In short, the rapid post-war internationalization of the US book trade was more the creature of overseas demand than of the market-building initiative of US publishers, who, mainly for gain, but in some measure out of compassion, were responding to the needs of a badly wasted world.

*   *   *   *   *

Post-war growth in US research led to a vast increase in the number of scholarly books published not just in the sciences but in social sciences and humanities. Initially, much of the increased output appeared under the imprints of established houses, particularly the large textbook publishers. But soon, entirely new publishing firms were established, dedicated to the dissemination of this vast scholarly outpouring.

Names such as Academic Press, Interscience (subsequently acquired by John Wiley) and Plenum – all of these three, as it happens, established by European immigrant publishers – readily come to mind. These newcomers were well aware of the virtues not only of building export markets but of finding in these markets monographs by local scholars which could be sold in the US.

Other scholarly US publishers, university presses, small trade houses and scholarly societies, watching the successful internationalization of their larger colleagues, soon started to move beyond their traditional and rather desultory cultivation of co-publishing arrangements with their European counterparts. To serve the export ambitions of these houses, overseas marketing groups were established to sell in world markets with catalogs, direct mail and, most importantly, field representatives. The largest and best known of these firms were Feffer & Simons and the Henry M Snyder Company. The most fondly remembered must certainly be the legendary European book salesman, the articulate, amusing and learned Ben Russak.

The book marketing and stocking agencies established by US publishers in Europe, Africa and Oceania, mainly in the '60s, have proved more durable than these export marketing groups. They very often represent not only their principals' interests but also those of publishers too small to contemplate opening their own overseas offices. The independent agencies in export markets have sometimes proved too successful for their own good and have been replaced by branch offices.

The worldwide success of the US college textbook was bolstered by the introduction of low-price reprints. In the '50s, it was quickly apparent that there was a huge market among students, particularly in Asia, if US textbooks could be offered at prices geared to their purchasing power. The first US reprint, printed in Japan in 1956, Paul Samuelson's *Economics* reduced the price by 75%. Total sales in Asia went from less than 1,000 a year to 25,000. This was the first of hundreds of such textbooks which were ultimately offered as international editions throughout the world except in North America.

The sale of US books abroad was very much in the interests of the US Government, which instituted programs in the '50s and '60s aimed either at supplying free books or subsidizing their supply at reduced prices. The US Agency for International Development purchased many textbooks, and in the '60s a program under Public Law 480, designed to convert excess foreign currencies from food support programs,was instrumental in subsidizing low-cost reprints. Also in the '50s and '60s, the Informational Media Guaranty Program enabled American books to be supplied without credit risks in markets which had been denied imported books by shortage of foreign exchange. This not only afforded immediate revenues to US exporting publishers, but also seeded these markets with American books in advance of their British, French and other competitors, who did not enjoy equivalent support from their governments. From the Marshall Plan onwards, the US government was a powerful ally of the US book. Even the Cold War became a positive factor in assisting US book exports because the US government was anxious to get books into the hands of individuals in communist countries and into markets in the developing world which the USSR was cultivating with low-price books.

Generous funding of academic and research libraries around the world, including the establishment of totally new libraries, was another factor which facilitated the internationalization of the US book. This growth in library demand led to the formation or, in several cases, the repositioning of specialized book dealers in the US. Of these, my former firm, Richard Abel and Company, now Blackwell North America, was probably the most aggressive. Approval plans, cataloging facilities and turn-key library services were among the value-added services developed by this new generation of library suppliers. The thousands of library collections which were established across the globe, many of them larger than all but a handful of the great libraries of the 19th and earlier centuries, may prove to be one of the finest and most fruitful monuments of the 20th century book industry.

The powerful computer-based systems set up by these international library suppliers were and remain classic examples of the economic consequences of capital investment, for they sharply multiplied the productivity of dealers' staffs, and this in turn led to competition for increased market share. Two or three of these dealers equipped themselves to furnish libraries anywhere in the world with books published anywhere in the world. Despite resistance by some publishers worldwide, this internationalization of the book market led to the near dissolution of the centuries-old convention of exclusive territorial rights at local marked-up prices, as well as to a further weakening of the agency system already undermined by the setting up of overseas offices by publishers.

*   *   *   *   *

While US paperback publishers (notably Pocket Books, Bantam and the New American Library) had been quick off the mark to exploit international markets in the '50s, they had been restricted somewhat by the understanding between US and UK trade publishers known as the Traditional Markets Agreement, which had existed since 1947. Under this Agreement, British trade publishers retained the Commonwealth markets, with the exception of Canada. This meant that the rights to sell both hardcover and paperback editions of US trade books in the English-speaking world outside of North America were not available (a restriction which some export jobbers notoriously ignored). The Traditional Markets Agreement also meant that the international business of US hardcover trade publishing was limited, since the Commonwealth rights of the most saleable titles were sold to British trade publishers (who in turn sold the North American rights of their books to US trade publishers).

This situation came to an end in 1976, when the US Justice Department brought a case against a group of US publishers and the British Publishers Association. The agreement was dissolved by a consent decree, which was the signal for US hardcover trade publishers to retain, if they wished, the world rights to their titles, both in hardcover and in paperback. The entry of the hardcover trade publishers into the international markets thus did not become serious until the late '70s, after which leading US trade publishers such as Simon & Schuster or Random House established themselves in London and acquired British imprints, following in reverse the example set by British publishers such as Penguin, who had acquired Viking or Macmillan, who had long owned St Martins Press.

By the '80s, the world English language edition became practical, and those US trade publishers who wished could assail the entire world market. The international activity in trade books prior to that time had consisted almost entirely of the sale of rights, in which the Frankfurt Book Fair, in its role as the great annual in-gathering of the world's book trade, played a significant part. In the '50s and '60s, Frankfurt was mainly concerned with the German-language book trade and the international interests of scholarly and scientific publishers. By no coincidence, the annual meeting of the STM publishers group, formed in 1968 as a branch of the International Publishers Association, is held each year in Frankfurt at the time of the Fair.

US trade publishers venturing to the Fair for the first time (as much out of curiosity and/or the opportunity to travel to Europe on expense accounts as in search of business) soon discovered its potential as a fertile field to develop co-publishing projects which had previously been beyond them. Full-color art books and massively illustrated encyclopedias for lay audiences required the printing of enormous numbers of copies, far in excess of those which could be sold in a single country. Frankfurt soon became the meeting ground upon which the details of hundreds of such international co-editions were hammered out, some involving twenty-five or thirty partners. Such co-publishing replaced the sale of territorial rights between different countries with the same language.

The other principal activity stimulated at Frankfurt was the sale and purchase of translation rights. Thousands of translation agreements are either initiated or concluded at Frankfurt. The greatest beneficiaries of this blossoming of international transfers of literature and text were, and remain today, the reading publics of those countries whose publishers most vigorously work the Fair and subsequently the relationships developed and nurtured there. The sale of rights from English into other languages had traditionally been the major activity, but many important books reached the American public only because US publishers had the enterprise to purchase English language rights.

The progressive acceptance of the Frankfurt Book Fair by US trade publishers was followed by a more spectacular, gaudy kind of performance. That part of the US book trade devoted to the publishing and selling of entertainment, even of the most questionable kind, had never been reticent in the promotion of its "products" (favorite term in mass entertainment circles), but until the '60s had largely concerned itself with the US domestic market, where the ever-growing population offered scope beyond the dreams of publishers in other countries. Hollywood had led the way by "product-testing" its films in Europe, and had quickly learned that, with but minor modification in the conventional formulae which had served it well with domestic audiences, its products could play as well in London, Paris, Bonn or Stockholm as in DesMoines.

Books had attracted the mass entertainment industry for another reason. The latest of the au courant management theories had encouraged the rising ranks of financial managers in major US corporations to expand by acquiring "synergistic" firms. One of the results of this doctrine was the acquisition of a number of trade book publishers by entertainment and media corporations, a movement which boomed in the '60s and waned in the '70s [see Levin in this issue]. Managers of what had been small businesses centered round one or two founding figures suddenly found they had access to enormous financial resources. The book-as-mass-entertainment types soon began bidding wars for long-term contracts with literary agents,who were fronting for authors seeking to capture the fleeting allegiance of mass audiences. The sums of money involved in these preemptive games quickly exceeded any reasonable expectation from domestic sales of hardcover, paper and subsidiary rights. So the bright and beautiful of the literary set arrived in Frankfurt to seek further scope to justify excessive advances. The old reliable sale of co-editions and translation rights was augmented by frenzied literary auctions on an international scale, involving cliff-hanging conference calls, wee-morning-hour readings to meet auction deadlines and late-evening- party intrigues. Spectacular stuff – but not native to the book business. Auctions were of course pioneered by literary agents, some of whom were not unaware that auctions exercise and stimulate greed, vanity and the instinct for battle. Thus US mass popular entertainments in the form of fiction and non-fiction books became a dominant product in the major markets and languages of the world.

*   *   *   *   *

In the mid-'70s, the great post-war overseas push by US publishers, aided by US governmental support programs, and also the international expansion of US library dealers in scholarly and scientific books, came to a virtual standstill. The world economy had turned sour. Library funding around the world was dramatically reduced. In the face of reduced profits, international departments were retrenched and overseas activities curbed. This did not please the media conglomerates who not only had failed to find significant synergistic corporate uplift from their book publishing acquisitions, but had learned that the book trade was simply unable to generate the levels of profit and return to which they were accustomed. Their solution was to sell. Soon any number of publishing imprints were in the hands of acquisition and merger brokers, and the US book trade was not simply in the throes of another of its periodic down-turns but of another more or less radical restructuring.

But the move into world markets was irreversible. Twenty-five years of multifarious international activity had jolted the US book trade out of its perdurable, complacent provincialism. While managements continued to be preoccupied with economics of the domestic scene, many of the trade's foremost practitioners had at last come to understand that there was, in fact, a larger world out there in which they could sell US books which, by design or chance, spoke to international audiences. (And the traffic was running both ways, to the benefit of US readers.)

But all was not clear sailing for the US book abroad. There was a mounting resentment on the part of the governments and media of other countries, and also of their publishers and booksellers, of the increasing place that US books had found in the world marketplace. This presence has never seemed, and still does not seem, as large to US publishers as it does to those on the receiving end. Resistance to the US book has been particularly bitter in Canada, where many maintain that it has stifled the growth of Canadian publishing. But not only in Canada, loud laments about the loss of control of key national cultural components; about the erosion of national standards and sensibilities under the influence of the synthetic US mass popular ethos in the form of books; about the acquisition of venerable publishing imprints by US interests became staple fare in the book trade and news media. There remains, to this day, a fairly widespread dislike and distrust of the incursion of the US book into the literary ambit of other countries. While some of this disaffection is a corollary of criticism of the US's international political and economic role, a significant fraction can be attributed to the growth of US book exports.

Some of the great publishing corporations of Europe, however, saw the success of the US book more as an opportunity than a threat. Colonization could be mutual. European scientific publishers such as Springer and Elsevier had established branches in the US in the '60s. By the '80s, European, predominantly British, ownership of US publishing companies had become significant and covered all branches of the trade. Venturing by small steps analogous to those taken by US publishers abroad – first, the use of marketing and distribution agencies and the sale and purchase of co-editions; then, the opening of US sales offices; and, finally, full-fledged publishing offices integrated with the US publishing industry – dozens of European houses set up shop and purchased compatible US publishing companies. The US book trade has not been inhospitable to these incursions. Most observers see them simply as part of the continuing evolution of the international book trade and as but one sector in the internationalization of the world economy. While this new form of immigration waned in the face of the economic down-turn of the mid-'70s, as did the expansion of the US book trade overseas, these were temporary vicissitudes. The important fact remains that the internationalization of the US book trade had become by 1980 a heavily travelled two-way highway.

*   *   *   *   *

By the early '80s, the world had reacquired a more affable and encouraging mien. The process of the internationalization of the world book trade, of and in which the US was now an integral part and an active player, shared in this renewed vigor. The last half of the '70s had been marked by extensive within-country consolidation through acquisitions and mergers in the principal book publishing nations. These consolidations created corporations of a size previously unattained in the book trade. In the US, some of the consolidation grew out of another round of acquisitions as publishing imprints were put on the block by their conglomerate owners. These large firms possessed the financial muscle once again to venture boldly into the international marketplace, and they did it with considerable resolve and energy. The '80s saw more purchases of overseas imprints by large US publishers than did the "go-go" '70s. Some quite startling prices were paid, betraying the eagerness of US publishing executives to establish their companies firmly in the UK, Continental Europe and also in Australia and New Zealand. Further expansion in Canada was impeded by the Canadian requirement that 50% of any acquired company should be sold into Canadian hands. And there were some withdrawals from South Africa because of apartheid.

Acquisitions of US houses by UK and Continental European firms (not to mention Canada's Thomson International and Australia's News Corporation) also accelerated in the '80s [see Levin in this issue]. Again, the voice of the chauvinists could be heard in the land, but this time on the Western shores of the Atlantic. As is common when jingoistic games are played by book trade and book media figures, the winners were the readers. Internationalization of the book trade can only broaden and deepen the communication channels through which the best of the minds from around the world may enter the global marketplace of ideas. The happy result, at least for the serious reader, is access to an ever-wider array of the world's finest authors. Alas, this also has its dark side. US readers, having accustomed themselves to domestic literary trash, must now find their way through the rubbish generated in other parts of the world as well.

Virtually every overseas subsidiary office, whether established abroad by US publishers or in the US by foreign publishers, had, by the mid-'80s, a mandate to acquire companies and publish books locally. Within a matter of years, most of these subsidiaries were publishers in their own rights, selling more of their own publications than those of their parent houses. As foreign-owned houses become domestic, the intellectual rewards of internationalization are less than they could be. The wider international issues are often narrowed down by an ill-defined set of national mores and practices.

However, this ability to acquire protective coloration shows how the major publishing firms of the world today, whether publishing serious books or entertainments, have evolved into true multinationals, capable of publishing books written anywhere around the globe and then of successfully marketing them wherever they can be sold. In such firms, corporate decision-making has also become largely multinational. Management in such firms has so well mastered and understood much of the sense of the international marketplace that it is able to accommodate national mores within its policies.

Much of the pioneering work in the development of truly multinational publishing was done by US firms. Some, particularly our cousins in the UK, may object to this conclusion, pointing to both the long UK history of overseas branches and the fact that the export of UK-published books is between 30% and 40% of the total, while that of the US industry is below 10%. However, this UK export trade is rooted in history, first of the Empire and then of the Commonwealth.

The many successful UK-based multinational publishers have now largely shed the imperial approach in favor of the US model. This is not to say that, in making the transition from one model to another, they were not very careful about preserving the relationships and advantages of the earlier model. It is only to say that they adjusted their policies and practices to a multi-centered, as opposed to a single-centered environment. American and British publishers, inevitable rivals for the world's English-language markets, have learned much from each other.

*   *   *   *   *

Despite the enormous growth of sales of US books in the international markets, in 1994 they represented less than 8% of total sales by the US publishing industry – $1.7bn out of $21.9bn. Despite sustained Canadian efforts to reduce the flow of US books, our northern neighbor still accounts for nearly 50% of US book exports. US book imports at $1.1bn, or 5.4% of total domestic sales of $20.2bn, look comparable with the export figures, but the import numbers are deceptive because they partly reflect the import of essentially domestic books printed abroad. Canadians can take some comfort from the import figures, since they provide slightly more than 50% of them.

All of these figures, however, are understatements because they represent only finished books known or, in the case of small shipments, computed, to have moved across US borders. They do not reflect the huge trade in selling and buying publishing rights, in co-publishing and in royalties paid to authors across international borders. It has been fairly reliably estimated that both export and import numbers can be increased by 50%. The US publishing community probably received income in every form of export transactions connected with books of roughly $2.5bn and paid roughly $1.7bn for imports.

What will be the shape of US participation in the international trade in books in the next few years? The top twenty book publishers in the US, who generate 84% of the total book business [see Levin in this issue] tend also to be the largest publishers internationally. So the future of the international book trade is largely in their hands and those of their counterparts in other countries. The marketing strength and enormous financial resources of these companies permit them to make the long-term investments required to play the international game. This trend will continue, since small publishers who are forced for successional or tax reasons to sell, find the large companies their most likely buyers. Moreover, some of the corporate growth will come in the form of mergers, as Reed and Elsevier exemplified three years ago. One way or another, the international business in the future will be dominated by the big players.

On the other hand, small publishers have proliferated in the last few years and, I predict, will continue to do so because the very large firms will increasingly be forced to limit their lists to titles which sell enough copies to justify their overheads. As a consequence, an increasing number of first-rate manuscripts of high quality will be saleable only in small quantities and will find their place among the growing band of small houses. Few of these will have the resources to establish overseas offices. The international market for their lists will, therefore, depend in substantial measure on the old, reliable practices of agenting or seeking out co-edition partners. A combination of the jet aircraft and electronic networks will enable an ambitious few to sell world markets directly.

So the international book world a decade from now will not change much in structure or strategy, but operationally will sport many of the bells and whistles now being touted by the electronic hucksters, themselves a product, not a cause, of the world's increasing internationalization. The overall effect and virtue will be the widening of access to the world's information, knowledge and culture by the reader – a kind of marvelous outcome foreseen only by a handful of dreamers and by Adam Smith and his disciples.

Dick Abel graduated in Medieval History from Reed College, Portland, Oregon, where he still lives, more than forty years ago. After graduate work in the same field at the University of California, he became a bookseller, establishing in 1960 his eponymous company which became a major supplier of books to academic and research libraries in the United States and around the world. This company is now Blackwell North America. Since the mid-1970s, Abel has been an independent publisher, his principal interest being Timber Press, founded in 1977, which publishes books on horticulture and plant sciences. He also started Amadeus Press in 1985, to publish books on music.

Note

I wish to thank Bill Lofquist, the man at the US Department of Commerce who has been supplying not just statistical data but generously offering good advice and wise counsel in their use to all and sundry connected with the book trade for years, for all his help with the numbers used here and what implications they might have for tracing the growth of US participation in the international book trade.

9

The Paperback Conquest of America

Betty Ballantine

The genesis of what has come to be known as the paperback revolution in the United States can be traced to 1939, when, impervious to the imminence of war, two men, one in the US and the other in the UK, were preparing an assault on what they believed was an untapped market in the US for low-cost books. The US initiative, headed by Robert de Graff, resulted in the launch of a major paperbound book imprint called Pocket Books, under the aegis of Simon & Schuster. The British initiative was in the mind of Ian Ballantine, who had written – only the year before – his graduate thesis on low-cost book publishing and was in line for the job of bringing the famous British paperbacks, Penguin Books, into the US. The American Penguin venture was a modest operation compared with Pocket Books. Still, Penguins were internationally known and prestigious, and Allen Lane, who had founded the house in the UK in 1936, was eager to breach the US market.

In the face of what was about to happen over the next six years, both projects were a form of business insanity. Yet the visions were both right in the long term. America in 1939 was a wilderness so far as distribution of popular books was concerned, with literate readers crying out to be fed. Americans read magazines and for books relied on small local lending libraries.

Ian and Betty Ballantine were married the day before they sailed for the US in June 1939. The entire staff of Penguin Books America consisted of them and one stock boy. The concept was simple. Spot the demand and import as many, or as few, copies of each title as it seemed to warrant. Within two months of the launch,war broke out in Europe and shipments of up to 50,000 books at a time were being lost to German submarines. Moreover, the 1,500-odd bookstores in the US which were regarded as good credit risks did not all rush to buy the new British product. Many believed that paperbacks would compete with the more lucrative sales of domestic hardcover books. Still, there was a sufficient welcome to keep the business afloat, especially in college and university towns, where there was much enthusiasm for titles like Susan Stebbing's *Thinking to Some Purpose.* People with special interests discovered titles like Arnold Haskell's *Ballet* and others that were mainstays of the Penguin non-fiction list.

As the war progressed, there was strong US interest in works like Harold Nicolson's *Why Britain Is at War.* Penguin's political Specials provided information unobtainable otherwise. However, the physical quality of the books began to deteriorate, due to wartime shortages in the UK. Eventually, it would become impossible to sell British-made books in the US.

Pocket Books, uninhibited by material or financial restrictions, within two years established a well-deserved reputation for varied editorial content, albeit on the light side. A wide range of well-tested titles was readily available from hardcover publishers willing to release reprint rights in titles that had long since ceased to sell at the normal hardbound price (then $2.00 to $2.50).

More importantly, Pocket Books was reaching an ever-increasing market through drugstores, chains and other non-book outlets. The determined readership that had been sustained by a network of small lending libraries housed in candy and tobacco stores grasped eagerly at the new format, priced at a handy 25¢ apiece.

It was not long before Penguin and Pocket Books stimulated competitive start-ups, notably Pyramid and Avon, the latter of whom named its new line "pocket size" books, an imitation from which it was eventually dissuaded.

After Pearl Harbor in December 1941, the US book trade, like the rest of business and industry, was changed virtually overnight. Paper quotas were almost immediately imposed. All book publishers were confined to the parameters of their pre-war production. Pocket Books, which had expanded considerably before war broke out, was assigned a reasonable quota, although later it would feel the wartime pinch in fairly drastic terms. Penguin, forced into US production by the exigencies of wartime shipping and paper shortages in the UK, had only a small quota. But its entire American output up to that point had been dedicated to war books, and the Ballantines had formed close relationships with the military. Forming an official alliance with the *Infantry Journal,* they now published originals as well as reprints, including many titles edited and designed to be used by army personnel to replace the incredibly outdated manuals extant at the war's outbreak. Several of these were among the first visually oriented works to appear in paper covers. The price was still 25¢ and they were lapped up by a public eager for any information they could get on what their boys were doing and why. Successful titles included *How to Shoot the US Army Rifle, Psychology for the Fighting Man, What's that Plane?* (an aircraft recognition manual) and *Tank Fighter Team.* Among successful titles that followed these military themes was John Steinbeck's *The Moon Is Down.*

Wartime conditions were good for book sales. Civilian travel was severely restricted, the rail system being dedicated to military movements. People stayed home and kept in touch with events by listening to the radio. Or they went to a weekly movie to watch war reports. But more and more they not only read books, but sent books to their boys in the field. Cheap lightweight paperbacks were ideal for this purpose.

The demand for books among the forces was enormous. The Council on Books in Wartime soon gave high priority to books that could be carried anywhere. A plan to provide reading matter to the millions of men and women in uniform was drawn up and implemented. Penguin Books became a full-fledged American product, with illustrated covers bearing no resemblance to Allen Lane's universally known bicolor Penguin design. Reprint rights to all kinds of books were virtually contributed by publishers to create the Armed Services Editions – a project with which Ian Ballantine, with his established connections to the army and his impressive list of war books published under the American Penguin imprint, was closely connected. Under the aegis of the Council on Books in Wartime, these Editions were bound and distributed as modular libraries every month to all units in the armed forces. Books, like bullets, were officially declared "expendable", a shrewd tactical maneuver which enabled the program of providing reading matter for the millions actively involved in the war to roar ahead. This would have an important effect.

* * * * *

As the war wound down, the returning service men and women, habituated to the easy access and casual use of books, expected to find them just as readily available in civilian life. Moreover, in post-war America, thousands upon thousands of men and women went to college or school under the GI Bill of Rights. These mature students, many of them married and building families while acquiring their college degrees, created reading families. Books became a familiar part of the "baby-boom generation".

There was a parallel phenomenon among those who had never left home. During World War II, reading became a popular addition to civilian stay-at-home entertainment. Pocket Books and Penguin, the leading paperback imprints, enjoyed an enormous surge in sales arising from the social changes stimulated by the exigencies of war. With the coming of peace and the lifting of wartime restrictions, Pocket Books was able to expand at a vast rate.

The experience of Penguin was not so happy. Between VE Day and VJ Day the Ballantines had sought to continue their program of war books. Allen Lane, however, had never been enthusiastic about editions produced under the Penguin name in the US during the war. In his view, they lamentably lacked the distinguished aura of the British line. Lane elected to close down the Penguin wartime programs and make other plans, a move which led to new horizons both for the Ballantines and another European expatriate who was to make a signal contribution to the development of the US paperback industry. Kurt Enoch was a refugee from Germany where, before the war, he had founded the Tauchnitz and Albatross paperback imprints. During the war he had joined the American Penguin as its production head. He and editor Victor Weybright initially maintained their relationship with Lane and Penguin, but after a couple of years broke away to found the New American Library.

Meanwhile, the handsome income that could be generated by the sale of reprint rights had not gone unnoticed by leading hardcover publishers such as Book-of-the-Month Club, Scribner, Random House, Harper and Little, Brown. They formed a kind of consortium to enter the paperback market through Grosset & Dunlap, a former hardcover reprinter. This move coincided with the departure of the Ballantines from Penguin. The couple were able to offer these new partners not only their wartime list and experience, but their distribution relationship with the Curtis Publishing Company, publishers of the *Ladies Home Journal,* the *Saturday Evening Post* and *Colliers,* and the most powerful national distributor of popular books and magazines in America. Ian Ballantine brought Curtis and the new book publishing consortium together to create Bantam Books.

Then, as now, distribution was the engine that drove the paperback publishing industry. Curtis did not have access to the newsstands, which were controlled by the American News Company. But it did have access to the so-called IDs – a network of independent regional magazine and newspaper distributors covering 100,000 outlets nationwide. These were mainly candy-cum-tobacconist-cum-magazine stores and small drugstores, to which Curtis distributed not only its own publications but a host of other magazines on which the ID wholesalers depended. Curtis had a force of 350 salesmen, five times larger than its nearest rival. With the help of fleets of truck drivers, it was able to deliver the 25¢ paperbound book to the neighborhoods of America.

Sales were large, but the margin for profits was tiny. Twenty-five cents per book was not much to divide between author, printer, hardcover publisher, paperbound reprinter, national distributor, wholesaler and retailer. The business needed big numbers at the point-of-sale, or it would not work. And even with big numbers, it worked only because of the magazine distribution structure, which, in turn, would not work then – and does not work now – without advertising revenue. The paperback rode to glory on the back of the magazine advertisers.

The result was a post-war publishing bonanza. Readers bought four to six titles at a time, and often once a month. The main problem was to keep the pipelines filled. A by-product of the magazine distribution system, unwelcome to book publishers, was that all merchandise was returnable for full credit. But at that stage there were no returns. Titles went back to press once, twice, three times. Print runs were 100,000 to 300,000 or more.

This was also the time of the first runaway million-copy seller: Dale Carnegie's placebo *How to Win Friends and Influence People,* published by Pocket Books. Dr Benjamin Spock, through *The Commonsense Book of Baby and Child Care,* influenced a whole generation of parents. *Life Begins at Forty* by Walter B Pitkin was another title offering inspirational guidance in the years of post-war euphoria. Pocket Books also did well with its series on Perry Mason, the fictional detective, and built a strong stake in the general fiction market.

Bantam took a different tack. With the backing of its hardcover partners and the marketing power of Curtis, Ian Ballantine was eager and able to explore new reaches of readership interest and alternative marketing techniques. Cover design was one of Ballantine's enthusiasms. Covers by Ben Stahl and others made Bantam books physically attractive. Ballantine himself designed the first display rack (called a "Mae West") to give every title full frontal display.

It rapidly became clear that different kinds of outlets required different handling. A newsshop selling tobacco, candy and newspapers did not sell the same books as a drugstore. Two newsshops in the same town might have different patterns of sale because of differing locations. By dividing outlets into categories, the publisher was able to measure rates of sales not only by subject, but by location. Samplings from each type of outlet in thirty major markets were monitored at ten-, twenty-, thirty- and forty-day intervals to establish rates of turnover by title. This not only facilitated a more efficient pattern of distribution, but enabled the publisher to go back to press promptly with a promising title. Reprints of a title showing rapid turnover could be produced within twenty days. Sampling also enabled the publisher to assess the shelf life of titles on display and predict accurately when an edition would sell out. Distribution was the nuts and bolts of both marketing and selling. Paperback publishers did no advertising, except in the backs of their own books. And even that came later.

As the paperback business boomed, more imprints were founded. The Kurt Enoch/Victor Weybright partnership, like the Ballantines' break with Penguin, sprang from their desire for autonomy. Their creation, the New American Library (NAL), with its motto "Good

Reading for the Millions", grew by leaps and bounds. Acutely tuned to the American market, the NAL Signet and Mentor titles proved to be both saleable and prestigious.

Brief chronology of US paperback imprints

1936   *Penguin Books* founded by Lane brothers in the UK
1939   *Penguin Marketing* established in the US by Ian Ballantine and John Lane
        Pocket Books founded by Robert DeGraff together with Richard Simon, Max Schuster and Leon Shimkin
1940   *Avon Books* founded by Joseph Meyers and Edna Williams
1942   *Dell* started by magazine publisher George Delacorte
        Dover Books founded by Hayward Sisker
1944   *Pocket Books* acquired by Marshall Field, a Chicago department store
1945   *Bantam Books* founded by Ian Ballantine with backing from Curtis Publishing and Grosset & Dunlap
        Penguin continues under management of Kurt Enoch and Victor Weybright
1947   *New American Library* founded by Kurt Enoch and Victor Weybright
        Popular Library founded by magazine publisher Ned Pines
1950   *Bantam* sets up Transworld Publishing in the UK
1952   Ian and Betty Ballantine found *Ballantine Books*
1953   *Anchor Books* launched by Doubleday, under Jacob Ebstein
1954   *Vintage Books* launched by Knopf
1955   Oscar Dystel named president of *Bantam Books*
        Fawcett Books begins publishing reprints
1957   *Pocket Books* acquired by Simon & Schuster
1961   *Pocket Books* goes public
1964   *Bantam* begins to sell directly to retail book trade and premium accounts
1966   *Pocket Books* re-acquired by Simon & Schuster
        New American Library acquired by Times Mirror
1968   *Bantam* sold to a conglomerate, National General
1971   *Bantam* taken public
        National General sells its holdings in *Bantam*
        Popular Library acquired by CBS
1972   *Warner Books* founded by acquisition of Paperback Library
1973   *Ballantine* acquired by Random House
1976   *Dell* acquired by Doubleday
1977   *Bantam* acquired by Doubleday
1977   *Fawcett* acquired by CBS

By the very late '40s, the three major paperback lines – Pocket Books, Bantam and the NAL – were being pursued by imprints such as Avon, Pyramid, Popular Library and Dell. Things were getting a mite crowded. Titles were not as easy to obtain as in the early days, and guarantees for authors were going up (although hardcover houses still kept half the take from reprint sales). Roughly in parallel, the sales of magazines had been dropping, and paperback income was becoming more important not only to national distributors but to IDs and retailers.

With the exception of several original war books published by the Ballantines at Penguin, until 1950 paperbacks had consisted entirely of reprints from hardcover editions, but in that year Gold Medal became the first paperback house to launch original works only. Its list was largely light fiction, presenting no real competition to the three majors. At Bantam, Ian Ballantine had been champing at the bit to try new authors; to publish in subjects not previously covered by paperback; to break the 25¢ price barrier; and to develop new marketing techniques. Bantam was extraordinarily profitable and the directors and company owners were reluctant to depart from a proven formula. Pushing the envelope of publishing, taking chances on the untried, are not popular in such a climate. By late 1951, Ballantine was in deep disagreement with the company's publishing policies, and early in 1952 he left Bantam. Once again, the real question was autonomy. He was determined that the next firm he would launch would be his own.

* * * * *

About that time, the universe of magazines began to suffer tremors ɪrom the onset of television. Book reading was not similarly threatened. National distributors wanted even more books to replace their lost magazine sales. So the early '50s saw the emergence of yet more paperback houses. Among them was Ballantine Books, launched on November 10, 1952. At first, Ballantine bolstered the capital resources of the firm by co-publishing with several hardcover publishers, notably Houghton Mifflin and Farrar, Straus & Giroux. The firm quickly acquired a reputation for innovation, which was to last for the next twenty-two years. "The recurrent themes in Ballantine science fiction," wrote Ken Davis in his book *Two-Bit Culture*, "– serious overcrowding of the earth, dread of nuclear catastrophe, a dwindling food supply, ecological insanity, excessive government control – were all part of a pattern of concerns that later emerged on the Ballantine list in the form of serious non-fiction..'' The house of Ballantine locked horns with current political issues (C Wright Mills's *Listen Yankee);* with the prison system (John Bartlow Martin's *Break Down the Walls);* with censorship and political harassment (Frank Donner's *The Un-Americans*); while Paul Ehrlich with *The Population Bomb* and Dr Guttmacher with his guide to birth control challenged traditional social and religious attitudes. These were only two of the literally hundreds of titles Ballantine published in an ongoing battle for the environment. This subject and the science fiction list, which included virtually all the top names in the field, had the most continuing impact on publishing, at least in terms of sales, although it would take the critics twenty years to recognize that science fiction literature boasted some of the best minds and finest writing talents in the world. Moreover, the company policy of paying its authors all the royalty, both paperback and hard-cover, attracted both well-known novelists like Gore Vidal and first novelists such as William Manchester. And this policy would have major impact on successful paperback houses much later.

While Ballantine and others were building their lists and creating a plethora of titles, all was not well on the distribution front. Returns, which in the early '50s were regarded with alarm because they could be as much as 10% of what had been shipped, rose to 20% and showed no signs of receding. This one factor did more to affect the retail price of paperbacks than any other. Dedicated paperback readers found themselves paying 75¢, 95¢, $1.25 and upwards. This did not deter the fast-growing paperback industry from providing an ever wider cross section of reading for their public, including not only classics, but the best writers of the day in every field. Dell, which had started out as a standard romance, mystery and Western publisher, soon joined the three lead houses and also embarked on a series of original books called Dell First Editions. By now seven or eight houses were involved in competing for worthwhile authors.

Ballantine hit the rocks when its distributor defected as the result of an internal power play. In the ensuing financial crisis, the company was kept alive largely by the trust of its authors and the patience of its print-ers and hardcover publishers, who were its principal creditors. Ironically, Ballantine Books was able to reap some benefit from its reduced list. By maintaining its editorial standards and careful placement of books, it was able to stave off the ever-looming problem of returns. During the '60s, the works of J R R Tolkien became a cornerstone of the Ballantine list, a development initiated when the company combated a pirated edition of Tolkien's epic *The Lord of the Rings*.

*   *   *   *   *

By now the price barrier was truly broken. Paperbound editions such as the Ballantine Sierra Club series (environmental works in full color) were sold at $3.95 and $4.95 and standard texts were in the $2.00 to $3.00 range. In less than twenty years, paperbound publishing had become really big business and intensely competitive. Auctions with high-bid guarantees became commonplace. Under such conditions, the entry of paperback publishers into hardcover publishing was inevitable, since being the publisher of both editions gave them a considerable royalty earning edge.

Science fiction again led the way. At Ballantine Books, acquired in 1973 by RCA, Betty Ballantine persuaded Judylynn del Rey to take over her science fiction list. Many of its authors were now world famous, having made their reputations through sales of millions of copies of their titles in paperback. Del Rey bet that these devoted followers were now willing to ante-up $16.00 or even $20.00 to buy their favorite writers in hardcover. She was right.

In a way, paperback publishing had come full circle. Fame won in expendable paperback editions was now seeking permanence in hardcover form. This was a bonanza for paperbound publishers who had had to survive on tiny margins of profit, threatened always by rising costs of production and the monster of returns.

Distribution, during the years of these developments, had increasingly moved into the regular bookstores, which had grown in numbers with the growth of the publishing industry overall. National distributors and ID wholesalers had become increasingly costly. Treating paperbacks like monthly magazines, distributors returned only the covers for credit. This procedure, which dated back to the mid-'50s, made returns altogether too easy. By the mid-'80s, publishers were producing two paperbound books for every one that was sold. Returns of 50% continue today to be the industry norm. This was not quite what the wartime administrators had in mind when they declared paperback books to be expendable. Today it can only be called a shameful waste, self-destructive in more senses than one. It is aggravated by a loss of hands-on control in the distribution system caused by shrinkage in the numbers of the all-important ID wholesalers. The more automated distribution becomes, the less likely books are to find their specific markets. The sheer volume of output today is more than all but the largest bookstores can cope with.

On the other hand, the very large bookstores, buying single titles in quantities from 5,000 upwards (naturally at lower purchase prices), have been able to obtain a very commanding position. With the arrival of the superstore, companies such as Barnes & Noble have become chains with huge emporia in diverse locales. Readers have learned to drive to such "destination" stores with the intention of purchasing several books at discounted prices rather than browsing through their traditional neighborhood stores. Thus the small bookstore is the most obvious victim in a distribution system which is once again in a state of turmoil. The superstores, dealing in audio and visual products as well as books – becoming in effect centers of communication – are able to carry a far wider range of titles than any Mom-and-Pop bookstore ever could. Specialization looks like the only salvation for the small bookstore, a long way from the early days when the magazine distributors took paperbacks into every neighborhood. Even so, the superstores are attracting readers who would never have entered regular bookstores. Overall, book sales have burgeoned and the superstores are mainly responsible. In the inner cities, and even in the suburbs, these giant stores have become meeting places for young people, with comfortable areas to sit and coffee or snacks available while they look over prospective purchases, or even do a little studying on the spot. In many ways, the atmosphere in these stores is that of a busy, warm and friendly library, without the imposition of silence. Some superstores have given a new meaning to the expression "dog days", when the local representative of the Society for the Prevention of Cruelty to Animals arrives with a selection of dogs ready for adoption. This is only one example of the kind of events which attract people who would not normally go into a bookstore. Needless to say, dog days are dedicated to the sale of pet care books.

The creation of new readers, a banner now being borne by superstores as interactive participants in their communities, is what the original "paperbound revolution" was all about. What is missing in the '90s, compared with the revolution of the '40s, is the dramatic price appeal. If only someone could reintroduce that, this dedicated reader would sit back, relax and applaud.

One of the founders of Bantam Books, and later of Ballantine Books, Betty Ballantine has in her long publishing career worked with a galaxy of authors, from Westerns to serious non-fiction. At Ballantine Books she brought science fiction and fantasy to a wide audience. Looking back, she says: "Paperback publishing has been a more-or-less continuous gamble: exciting, vital, full of crisis, often cut-throat and always rapidly moving. But withal a load of fun. And it is still developing, and – thank goodness – I am still a part of it!"

10

Book Clubs in America

Al Silverman

Culture came to our home when I was a small child, and its name was the Book-of-the-Month Club.

My mother always believed in culture, but she never could afford it. The Great Depression was on us, and my father, a tailor, brought home almost enough money to cover the necessities of life. But we seldom caught up with the bills.

And then one of my mother's younger sisters came to live with us. Aunt Rose had graduated from "Normal" school, which is what they used to call two-year institutions that prepared you to become a teacher. And now she had a good job teaching at Lynn English High School in my Massachusetts hometown. Aunt Rose brought a breath of fresh air to a constrained household. She was both charming and articulate and, most of all, she cared for culture. She was, after all, a member of the Book-of-the-Month Club. So a house – a rented flat that had never contained a book except those borrowed from the public library – suddenly began to change.

The first book I remember Aunt Rose receiving in the mail – I was eight years old at the time – was *The Forty Days of Musa Dagh* by Franz Werfel, who was a popular novelist of the time in Europe, but little known in the United States. He was one of those novelists who, as Dwight Macdonald would have put it, teetered between mid-cult and mass-cult. But my Aunt loved *The Forty Days of Musa Dagh,* and the books kept coming in until she got married and left our home, taking her books with her along with my heart.

* * * * *

There were 97,000 members of the Book-of-the-Month Club in 1934 when Aunt Rose read Franz Werfel. Imagine the wonder (maybe some trepidation, too) these subscribers must have felt receiving books through the mail. For in that year there were only 500 bookstores in the country and they were mostly in large cities. So at least a third of the population had no direct access to bookstores. It was a barren landscape, this land without books, and Harry Scherman had a vision.

"An institution," Emerson said, "is the lengthened shadow of one man." In the mid-1920s, six men and one woman created institutions in the US that all relied on the power of the written word. In 1922, DeWitt and Lila Acheson Wallace founded *The Reader's Digest.* In 1923, Henry Luce and Brit Hadden started *Time Magazine.* In 1924, Henry Seidel Canby became founding editor of *The Saturday Review of Literature.* In 1925, Harold Ross created *The New Yorker.* And the next year, Harry Scherman invented the book club.

Scherman would have been at home in today's culture, for he was, above all, a marketing genius. And one of the roots of his genius was his conviction that others, the experts, should choose the books, and he would try to sell them.

The notion of book clubs was not entirely new. Germany had its own versions of such clubs right after World War I. But these "societies" or associations mostly distributed books of their own manufacture and publication. Harry Scherman always claimed that the concept of "a Book-of-the-Month program", as he first called it, had been worked out as early as 1916. His idea of a book club was based on three elements:

1. An independent board of knowledgeable and respected judges to pick the "book of the month".
2. This book would be tied to negative option. That is, if members wanted the book, they need do nothing. They would be billed and shipped for each month's Selection, which in those early years was guaranteed to cost no more than $3.00 per book, plus shipping charges. If they

didn't want the book, it would be up to them to return the reply form saying no.

3. Efficient service.

The first ad appeared in the *New York Times* in April 1926 with the headline: You Can Now Subscribe to the Best New Books. With this, a "Book A Month" was launched as the Book-of-the-Month Club.

The first book selected by the Board of Judges was a first novel called *Lolly Willowes,* by an Englishwoman, Sylvia Townsend Warner. Henry Seidel Canby, the same fellow who was running *The Saturday Review of Literature,* was now doubling as chairman of the "members of the Selecting Committee". Canby felt that *Lolly Willowes* was probably too literary and that the "proprietors" of the Club might lose their subscribers "and their collective shirts". (Since there were only 4,700 members signed up at that time, they had few shirts to lose.) The selection of *Lolly Willowes* had an immediate effect: It helped to quickly establish the Club's integrity.

Years later, Sylvia Townsend Warner answered a letter from David Willis McCollough, who was then a Reader at the club (subsequently becoming one of its judges), inquiring about that experience. She wrote, "When I learned that the Book-of-the-Month Club had selected *Lolly Willowes* for its first choice I was astonished, delighted and confident that an organization daring to pick an unknown author would be a valuable asset to contemporary literature."

Harry Scherman didn't lack for competition for very long. Soon England had its first book club, "The Catholic Book-of-the-Month Club". It met a frosty reception. A London trade paper, *Publishers' Circular,* raged: "This sort of thing is likely to do incalculable harm to the book trade and demands immediate action." The Catholic Book-of-the-Month Club went out of business almost immediately.

But the first American competition to Book-of-the-Month Club was here to stay. The powerful Doubleday publishing company started the Literary Guild in 1927. Like the Book-of-the-Month Club, it immediately established its own distinguished board of judges. But the Literary Guild abandoned the system in the early '30s, an executive of the club citing two reasons: "one, the matter of expenses, and the other the matter of efficiency". It also wanted to go after a more commercial novel. Years later, an official of the organization put it more plainly: "We are targeted for the light reader, the in-and-out reader."

By and large, the notion of an independent board of judges, free of management interference, worked well for the Book-of-the-Month Club through the years. A good example of their early perspicacity came in 1931 when the Board selected the second novel by Pearl Buck, *The Good Earth*. Ms Buck's first novel, *East Wind, West Wind*, had received no attention. "Just about broken even," said its publisher. An avid supporter of *The Good Earth* was the only woman judge on the board, Dorothy Canfield. After it was chosen, Ms Canfield wrote to the publisher of the book, saying, "To find such a book among the ones sent to me by the Book-of-the-Month organization gave me a thrill of delight. It's being able to help in the wider distribution of such a book that makes the Book-of-the-Month work seem worthwhile to me." The public certainly found *The Good Earth* worthwhile. It occupied the top of the bestseller lists for two years and helped earn Pearl Buck the Nobel Prize for Literature.

That experience, Henry Seidel Canby wrote in his memoir, taught the judges a lesson. "We began to see," he said, "that there was only one safe procedure, which was to choose what we ourselves liked. If we liked a book well enough, the public, whose taste was perhaps less discriminating but at least as sound and healthy as ours, seemed to like it also."

That suited Harry Scherman. Throughout his life, he always took the long view of things, a philosophy that has become seriously out-moded in our time.

* * * * *

And so, as if preordained, I went to work for the Book-of-the-Month Club. It was Harry Scherman's son-in-law, Axel Rosin, who hired me. Scherman had died in 1969 at the age of eighty-two – remembered by senior judge Clifton Fadiman as "full of goodness and generosity" – and Rosin became President of the company. Axel took a chance on me (I had been a magazine editor and was totally without book publishing experience), largely on the recommendation of his new number two man, Ed Fitzgerald. Way back in another life, Fitzgerald had given me my first job out of college, at *Sport Magazine*. Later, when he became head of the Doubleday Book Clubs, he saw to it that I succeeded him at the magazine. In 1971, he switched to Book-of-the-Month Club, and a year later we found ourselves together again.

Axel Rosin was a shrewd, conservative businessman who steadfastly subscribed to Scherman's values. Rosin loved books, but, like his father-in-law, always left the decision of which books to others. Now in his upper eighties, Axel remains a delightful, courtly, considerate person, a gentle realist who has never treated the past with false sentiments. "You know, the good old days?" he still tells people today, "they weren't so good."

Under Rosin and his successor, Fitzgerald, the Club flourished in the '70s and '80s. By 1988, total membership of Book-of-the-Month Club itself (including Canada) reached an all-time high of 1,600,000. I say "itself" because, by then, the company had begun to follow Doubleday's lead in adding special interest clubs. The Literary Guild today has many more satellite clubs than the Book-of-the-Month Club and, for the most part, they perform more strongly. Its Doubleday Book Club, always considered the second banana to the Literary Guild, is actually the first in membership, 1,200,000 today to the Guild's 800,000, and first in profits. Of course, Doubleday Book Club feeds off the main club, using the Guild's selections and offering them for less money to its members. It is a club securely moored to women's commercial fiction (over 90% women belong to both clubs), particularly romance fiction. Ed Fitzgerald once characterized the Guild (perhaps not when he worked there) as the country's "low neckline book club". The Doubleday Book Club's neckline remains determinedly provocative.

Other successful Doubleday clubs include science fiction, mystery, military history, a health book club and a host of others. A club Doubleday introduced only three years ago, "Crossings", an evangelical Christian book club, already has over 400,000 members. Doubleday Book Club's CEO Markus Wilhelm expects the membership to leap to 600,000 by the end of 1996.

Book-of-the-Month Club, perhaps its answer to Crossings, has successfully begun "One Spirit", a club filled with New Age and Spiritual books. "It will be an asset for the next century," says one Club official.

BOMC also leads the field with its children's book club, now at 250,000 members, well ahead of club officials' own projections. Others include a Money Book Club (named after the magazine), a Homestyle Club, mostly offering cookbooks, and the revitalized History Book Club, which it bought from Harcourt, Brace Jovanovich in 1987.

Book-of-the-Month Club did start a new club in 1973 that has become one of the most significant innovations of the last two decades. The Quality Paperback Book Club (QPB) was the inspiration of Ed Fitzgerald. What he envisioned was a club exclusively offering trade paperbacks aimed at a younger and more sophisticated bookbuying audience. At that time, the Book-of-the-Month Club's average age was creeping up to the mid-forties, and there was a certain restiveness among executives of the Club about the future. Fitzgerald thought that QPB would be a counterweight to the greying of Numero Uno, and that's what it's turned out to be.

But at the time that QPB was still on the drawing board, there were mild dissenters among some of the Club. I was one of them. I was worried about the possibility of QPB cannibalizing the main Club, of members opting for books that sold for 50% less than the Book-of-the-Month Club's hardcovers, thereby reducing the company's profit. But by and large that hasn't happened, and QPB has done nothing but help the company's profit picture.

* * * * *

The book club business revolves around a matrix of considerations – the books themselves; presentation of books; timing of books; pricing of books; sociology of members and knowing about their wants and needs; serving the members; recruiting new members (the major clubs lose about 50% of their active members each year); looking ahead to new ways of reaching members in order to keep them happy in the face of the fierce new competition from the discount superstore chains; and less visible competition from the new and all-pervasive technology – CDs, CD-ROMs, video games, the Internet, all designed to steal more precious leisure time from reading. No longer will you see a cartoon like the one that appeared in a 1959 *New Yorker,* two women sipping espresso, one saying to the other, "He belongs to the Book-of-the-Month Club. I mean how can you reach someone like that?"

One of Harry Scherman's vital rules for succeeding in the book club business, negative option, has been under siege for many years and is an endangered species today. In 1948, Dwight Eisenhower's wartime memoir, *Crusade In Europe,* a Main Selection of the Club, was taken by over 50% of its members. That meant an initial sale of close to 400,000 books. But when the postwar book boom began to ease off, Selection acceptances began to slip for all book clubs. In 1962, at the Book-of-the-Month Club the average gross Selection acceptance rate (members of course have always been allowed to return the Selection,a courtesy they once treated with discretion, but no longer) was 26.8%. In 1972, it had dropped to 17.7%. In 1982, it was 13.5%. Currently, the percentage acceptance has dipped into single-digit figures. Lorraine Shanley, a founding editor of QPB, now a director of the book publishing consulting firm Market Partners International, has always blamed the decline on "a no-strings generation of men and women who didn't want to be pinned down".

Early on, the Book-of-the-Month Club tried to counter the movement away from negative option by increasing the number of new books a member could buy – *positive option.* In 1972, the Club offered, beside the Main Selection, two or three Alternates each cycle. That year, the Club expanded its editorial operations. We added a number of full-time reader/editors to the staff, increased the outside free lance reading group (many of whom were specialists in various fields) and began to buy more books. Soon we were offering a dozen or so new Alternates each cycle. By and large the acceptance rate of these non-Selections, picked by the staff, helped fortify the Club against the diminishing allure of the Main Selection. And the Literary Guild began to do the same.

But the trend away from negative option continues. Members' inertia about returning books they didn't ask for has been replaced by due diligence. Markus Wilhelm says that 20% of Literary Guild members were buying positive option each cycle. "We don't enforce negative option anymore," he said flatly. Wilhelm's counterpart at Book-of-the Month Club, George Artandi, feels differently. Negative option remains an important element in his club and, he says, "it can be improved by segmentation."

Segmentation has become one of these new weapons, like the Stealth bomber. It homes in on a target and delivers a payload in the mail that exactly fits that particular person's wants. But will segmentation, and other exotic new technology on the horizon, be the salvation of book clubs? Some people think so.

Having been out of book clubs for almost seven years, which encompasses at least a generation as time marches on today, I thought I'd better try to find out how the business was doing by talking to the persons who were now guiding the destinies of the two major book clubs in the country. So last summer, I went to see George Artandi and Markus Wilhelm.

Like almost everything else in book publishing, these two organizations had changed hands. In 1987, Nelson Doubleday sold his company to Bertelsmann, a publishing and book club colossus all over the world. Ten years earlier, Axel Rosin, for estate reasons, had sold his company to Time Inc. Time Chairman Andrew Heiskell had long admired the Book-of-the-Month Club. He felt it would be a proper fit for Time to add this cultural icon and cash cow to his Books Group, which then consisted of Little, Brown and Time-Life Books. Indeed, when the principals from both sides met for dinner to get the negotiations going (Time bought Book-of-the-Month Club for $63m), the Books Group CEO Joan Manley threw her arms around Axel Rosin and said, "Will you marry me?" Axel beamed.

Manley, a personable and dynamic person, was the first woman to become a publisher at Time Inc. She had talent, drive and at least one other qualification for the job of supervising the destiny of the club: She loved books. So, like Harry Scherman and Axel Rosin before her, she left the driving to those who understood the business.

But after Heiskell's retirement in 1980, and some sudden and startling financial reversals for Time-Life Books, the new echelon of Time Inc executives began to pay closer attention to the Book-of-the-Month Club. They were a clubby group of individuals, coming from the same kind of background – Ivy or near-Ivy League colleges, prestigious business schools, mainly Wasp, and also very competitive with each other. They were young men perfectly suited to running a huge communications company in the go-go years of the '80s; that is, they were bottom-liners, concerned about return on equity and neutral about almost everything else, including the written word. It is a bit disquieting to note that all of these future contenders for the big banana at Time have long vanished, all with gilded parachutes, to unknown habitats. Gerald Levin, CEO of Time Warner, seems to be the last survivor.

These were reasonable people we were dealing with; they were ambitious, goal-orientated, and wanted all of us to be the same. But in their haste to achieve goals, at Book-of-the-Month Club they neglected to gauge the underlying core of the company's strength, that it was a book club differentiated from all others, that it had a solid nucleus of serious bookbuyers – *preferred* subscribers they might be called today – who really wanted to read the best books and not just the bestsellers. The new tightly structured management, in subtle ways, began to move us off course, off our center, leaving us to drift towards the Literary Guild, the light-reading book club.

These managers also brought with them a bureaucracy of language that was sometimes difficult to decipher. Once at a meeting, talking about the future of the main club, a Time Incer asked, "In five years won't it have obsolesced?" On another occasion, a financial person claimed already to have improved the prospects for the future by identifying "specific quantifiable variables".

So here we were, a mature company full of old hands whose vision indeed may have obsolesced in the '80s, now trying to figure out ways to counter the threats to the future of our business.

* * * * *

By the mid-'80s, a new competitor had emerged: the discount bookstore chain. Before World War II, book clubs represented about 30% of all trade books sold. After the war, with shopping malls and the birth of Waldenbooks, B Dalton, Crown and others, the chain retailers came to represent over 40% of the total market, with clubs declining to less than 10%. Now the mall stores have been superseded by the superstores, where you can sit in comfort and read through 120,000 titles, then amble over to the store's patisserie for espresso. And behind the superstores, casting a deeper shadow over all, are the warehouse clubs, where bestsellers can be bought for 40% below the publisher's price. The competition will not go away.

An even larger aggravation to the Book-of-the-Month Club itself was the increasing difficulty of finding good books for its audience. There are many reasons for this decline in quality, but two stand out. First, the old-line owners of distinguished houses, book people who were willing to take chances on authors, were fading away, selling off their houses to large corporations. Random House was owned by

RCA; Holt Rinehart belonged to CBS; Little, Brown had been bought by Time Inc; Scribner's and Atheneum, two stalwart literary houses, were being swallowed by Macmillan. Other houses would soon be falling. And, by and large, the new owners weren't as willing to take as many chances as their predecessors had. Everyone was cutting their mid-lists, books that could be figured to sell maybe 7,500 copies, except, of course, that you never could tell. And everyone was going after bestsellers; that had become the battle cry of the Republic. As one publisher said to me after watching his old house being nibbled to death by an American industrial giant – "They had such a batch of people looking out for the money that no one was looking out for the author."

Think of how a new-breed owner of a publishing house today might react to an author saying in his face: "I have to deal with people with ideas in my books. Ideas are the only things that will save us." That was Saul Bellow in 1975, talking in the Book-of-the-Month Club News about his novel *Humboldt's Gift,* which had been made a Selection. Today, the question that rings out more than any other is not where you might find good books, but whether books themselves have a future.

All the pundits seem to be chewing on that charged bone. George Steiner, leaning towards the negative (it has become fashionable for intellectuals everywhere to write off the book), blames the book's decline partly on "the consolidating middle class tastes". The trouble is that the middle class, and the upper class, too, are not at all consolidated, but in a muddle trying to sort out the competition for their leisure time. Will riding the information highway, which is apparently everyone's destiny in this post-modern world, still leave a place for books?

Recently, I was caught up short when my five-year-old grand-daughter told me she was going to the library with her mother. "Going to find new books at the library?" I asked Zoe. "Oh, Papa," she said primly, as if I was beyond understanding, "we're not getting books, we're getting movies."

Odd, in the midst of the rubble, the people who run the largest book clubs in our country seem much more assured about the future of books, at least as it will apply to their business in the years ahead.

In 1986, there were 142 book clubs in the US. In 1995, there were

161 clubs. So that tells you something, doesn't it? Well, wait just a second. In 1986, the book clubs' share of the consumer publishing market (adult and juvenile books, mass market, mail order and religious books) was just over 7%. In 1993, it had dipped to a new low of 5.3% (these figures courtesy of the Book Industry Study Group), but in 1994, came back to 6.2%. In unit sales the clubs took their big dip after 1984, when units reached 137 million. In 1994, it came to 119 million, a loss of eighteen million units over those years.

But when I met George Artandi, now in his fourth year as CEO at Book-of-the-Month Club, he was reasonably upbeat. Artandi, a veteran Time Incer, has a face as lean and austere as a monk's but his smile, coming through thick glasses, softens his image. We were having lunch at a Chinese restaurant not far from his Rockefeller Center office, and the first thing he said was that the Club was having a fine year. (Others had told me differently, but this was August and it always comes down to the fourth quarter, which I found out recently was strong for the Club.) But what he seemed most enthused about was the technological advances that would soon be coming to the company.

The Mechanicsburg, Pennsylvania complex – warehouse, fulfillment center and consumer service – "will be state of the art in a year and a half", he said. "Then we'll have variable cycle capability. We'll be able to give the best members the higher number of cycles a year, lower cycles for others. We'll be able to segment beyond Selections, too. We're working towards segmented enclosures."

Segmentation of Main Selections had begun at the Book-of-the-Month Club in the late '80s, with half the membership being offered a book (possibly a thriller) in an area that they had bought before; and the other half being offered a non-fiction work because they had bought non-fiction more steadily than fiction. Robert Riger, also an owner of the savvy Market Partners consulting company, credits Selection segmentation with helping to save negative option. "It brought up acceptance rates some," he says.

What Book-of-the-Month Club seems to have now that the Literary Guild doesn't is unlimited 800 number use. Throughout its magazine the 800 number is visible on almost every page. I couldn't find an 800 number anywhere in the Guild's magazine. "Members now can order by phone," Artandi said, "and also *no-book* the Selection to the operator."

"Doesn't that worry you?" I asked. "Won't you be no-booked to death?" That's what we were afraid of back then when we had begun gingerly to test the 800 number. What would happen to negative option? "I don't worry about that," Artandi said matter of factly. "If members can call in and not be hassled through the mail they'll be satisfied and buy more."

The whole game now for both Book-of-the-Month Club and Doubleday seems to be to get members to buy more, not to try and increase membership. "The trick is to keep good members, replace bad members with good members who'll buy more. The other game," he says, "is to have members buy more from you than from other sources." "How do you do that?" I asked. "The key is effective use of information and creative marketing."

Somehow we didn't talk much about the books. Artandi did say that acquisition of Selections was the editorial function and that "we want them to do more." They have to do more now. The Judges' system, weakened over the years by what was perceived by some to be anachronism in the "modern age", was finally abandoned in 1993. Now a group of in-house editors pick the Main Selection as well as all the other books.

The final question for Artandi was an obvious one. "Do you think you're in a mature business?" He thought for a moment. "I doubt that the business is mature," but a note of doubt hovered in his voice. "Look, if book clubs are going to work in the future, it will be by making secure marriages between books and readers. Everything we're doing now is pointed in that direction."

* * * * *

The first question I asked Markus Wilhelm was what had changed in the business in the five-and-a-half years since he came to run the American book clubs for Bertelsmann. "What has changed? Everything has changed." We were having breakfast at the Millennium Hotel, which was just around the corner from the Doubleday building in Times Square. He apologized for his train from Long Island arriving late. Wilhelm comes into New York only two or three days a week; the rest of the time he spends at the Club's headquarters in Garden City, Long Island. Curly haired and youthful looking, he was carefully dressed in a dark suit, white shirt. He ordered his power cereal and proceeded to tell me what was going on in the book club world.

"As you know," he started off, "in your time" (oof, suddenly I felt ancient), "BOMC was dominating the market. Doubleday had been going downhill since 1983. They'd tried to reposition the Literary Guild by widening the area to include more non-fiction and some literary fiction. I said, forget it. When I came in 1990, you guys had everything on the non-fiction side, two-thirds of fiction. It was scary."

"So what did you do?" "I liked the idea of making long-term commitments, making multi-book deals with all big authors, locking in as many as I could. It worked. We have more than a dozen authors now signed up on three-, four-, five-book deals." He mentioned John Grisham, Danielle Steele, Barbara Taylor Bradford, Judith Krantz, Dean Koontz, Robin Cook, Belva Plain. "This has also helped us establish good relationships with the publishing community. I make a five-book deal, I'm sharing the risk with you."

Then Wilhelm segued into the second prong of his two-prong attack. "Having the books, you then need the marketing strategy to sell these books." He launched into an explanation of that strategy.

"We have to find out what people want to read. We have to present to the members the books they're interested in reading. We're now talking about segmentation – segmentation by interest, by frequency and by monetary value. We started on this six months after locking up the books. We developed segmentation models. We did it by the type of buyer who came in, by zip code." Wilhelm was confident about his segmentation models. "We know the day they join the club whether we've got a preferred member. After three months, it's a very safe bet."

As he went on explaining the various strategies, he sounded very much like George Artandi – giving preferred members a lot more cycles a year than marginal members; offering the preferred member discounts of 50% or more on every book (regular members receive lesser discounts): keeping inventory down; and finding new niches for clubs.

I knew that total membership for all Book-of-the-Month Club active members (actives are generally considered to be those who've bought at least one book in a year) to be about 3.1 million. I guessed out loud to Wilhelm that Doubleday must have about four million actives. He smiled benignly, said I was very close. But I also knew that Book-of-the-Month Club members stay longer than Wilhelm's clubs, two-and-a-half years for BOMC compared to a year-and-a-half for Doubleday. The rivalry between these two institutions continues and is as heated as ever.

Wilhelm mused about that rivalry. He told me what some others had also told me: "BOMC's not focused any more. They've lost their focus. Once they were the upscale club, they had their mandate." He looked at me and, remembering that that's where I came from, he shrugged and said, "We're winning today. Maybe we'll fall flat on our face tomorrow."

*   *   *   *   *

One week in March of 1987, some key executives of the Book-of-the-Month Club and Time Inc journeyed to Santa Fe, New Mexico to talk about the *future* – the future of book clubs and the future of reading. It was as stimulating a site as you could find to discuss books in terms of the '90s and into the 21st century. We had clear, cold early mornings and warm sun and brilliant light during the day – white sunlight, the kind of whiteness Georgia O'Keefe took inspiration from as she created, up in the mountains of New Mexico, her magical paintings.

At this futurist convention we assembled an all-star cast of guest speakers, each an expert in his own area of book publishing – a noted international publisher, a major literary agent, the head of a large advertising agency, the founder of an innovative direct marketing catalog, a prize-winning author, an important financier and Clifton Fadiman.

Fadiman then was in his forty-third year as a judge of the Book-of-the-Month Club; he subsequently passed the fifty-year mark and, today in his ninety-second year, he still advises club editors about books. Opening his talk, Fadiman declared flatly that he could see the future more clearly than anyone else because, in his own words, "I have no future." From the moment he began talking you sensed that he cared more about the future than perhaps any of his juniors.

He suggested issues that would affect reading in the years ahead. Right in lock-step with current book club thinking, he said that we at the Club had to stress and improve the quality of service to our members more strongly than we ever have. He also said that we had to be more "innovative and startling". And he made an impassioned plea for all of us in the book business to make it clearer than ever "what books do offer".

Later that same year, one of the Book-of-the-Month Club's brightest and best young editors, Joe Savago, died of AIDS. Over the years of his life at the Club, Joe's reports on books were almost always impassioned and brilliant, even those he hated. There was one he loved, a novel he read not long before he died, which, he said in his report, "recaptured something I often felt as a child and have rarely felt since". He was referring to the childhood experience with adult books, "about the awesome, the enthralling sense of immersion – of drowning, if you will, and coming back to consciousness in a world so thoroughly peopled and detailed, so fully realized by the author, so morally complete and provocative on its own terms, that I prayed it would not end, that there would always be *more* to read, *more* to return to every night of my life."

That sensation of reading breathlessly is perhaps endangered today. But it is not lost. It can be reclaimed if book clubs, and all of us in any way responsible to readers, will remember.

Currently Editor-at-large and Senior Vice President with Penguin USA, Al Silverman has been editor, author and publisher in his forty-year career. Before joining Viking in 1989, he had been Chairman and CEO of Book-of-the-Month Club, which he had joined in 1972 as Editorial Director. Prior to that, he had edited and written for numerous magazines, specializing in sports, a field in which he also authored many books. A native of Massachusetts, Silverman is a graduate of Boston University, which awarded him a Doctor of Letters in 1986.

11

Very Like a Whale:
The World of Reference Publishing

Joseph J Esposito

> HAMLET: *Do you see yonder cloud that's almost in shape of a camel?*
> LORD POLONIUS: *By the mass, and 'tis like a camel, indeed.*
> HAMLET: *Methinks it is like a weasel.*
> LORD POLONIUS: *It is backed like a weasel.*
> HAMLET: *Or like a whale?*
> LORD POLONIUS: *Very like a whale.*
> —Hamlet Act 3. Scene 2

There is no generally agreed definition of *reference publishing* in the industry today. It is just as well: When publishers agree on anything, watch out. What is peculiar, though, about the lack of unanimity concerning reference publishing is that, at least in my experience, just about every publisher seems to be confident that he or she knows what "reference" is and is equally confident that the world is in happy accord. A reference book, one publisher will say, is distinguishable from a trade book. (But what exactly is a trade book?) Another publisher will point to a huge volume on clinical medicine and state authoritatively that *there* is a reference work. Yet another publisher, reclaiming an editor's eye for a moment, will argue that reference books are the ones with the stops and starts, the ones without narrative.

129

Interesting. But where, we are tempted to inquire, does one place *Encyclopædia Britannica,* whose articles (eg, "China") can reach 200 pages? Blame it on the perversity of the industry's practitioners, but the consensus doesn't hold.

If we are not content to remain up to our noses in this muddle, we can dive deeper. The computer cometh and maketh of all bodies of text a virtual encyclopedia. This is accomplished through the extraordinary facility of Boolean and natural-language searches, database tagging, the Internet, SGML and hordes of unpronounceable and unintelligible acronyms. It is breathtaking. A biography in electronic form need not be read through. It can be sorted and sifted, if not savored. Metaphors can be clustered; all references (!) to the Prime Minister can be viewed at a glance; the mistress in a red dress on one screen of text can be shown to be wearing a blue one on another one. Narrative disappears; the text becomes spatial. When viewed through the various search mechanisms of modern technology, should not the memoirs of Henry Kissinger be renamed *The Encyclopedia of Mr K* ? *Reference publishing* is difficult to define because there is so much of it, because it is growing in size and importance and because increasingly it serves as a cultural metaphor. This last point warrants explanation. A novel such as Julio Cortázar's *Hopscotch* is a reference work of sorts, written as it is in brief fragments, with the reader instructed to read not consecutively, but in a "hopping" order. Even more self-conscious is Milorad Pavić's *Dictionary of the Khazars,* a brilliant confection of a novel constructed as an A to Z lexical work. Or we have the mock-annotated text of Vladimir Nabokov's *Pale Fire.* When novelists begin to use a rhetorical form for their own mischievous ends, it is because the form itself can provide useful insights into the world (or at least into literature). We should not, as reference purists, be surprised to find the chiselled outline of our domain becoming cloudy, but how we long for the days when a dictionary was a dictionary was a dictionary!

Where reference publishers tend to diverge from their brethren in the non-reference world is in their conception of their publications in a larger informational context. Take dictionaries, for example. They are not intended to stand alone (only specialists and madmen read one all the way through). Rather they are intended to supplement other books or activities. A typical desk dictionary in the US today sits in an office, where it assists in such "foreground" activity as writing letters, correcting the boss's spelling and deciphering the charges in the latest lawsuit. The informational context of the modern office determines the role the dictionary is to play. In the drama that is the world of business, the reference work is a supporting character.

Reference publishing, then, is largely the creation, marketing and distribution of "back-grounders". A young boy laboring on a term paper punches up an article in *Microsoft Encarta*. His brighter older sister turns to *Encyclopædia Britannica*. In search of a cobbler, a gentleman turns to the Yellow Pages. Researching a holiday gift for her temperamental boss, a young executive turns to the article on Wagner in *The New Grove Dictionary of Music and Musicians*. Dictionaries, encyclopedias, telephone books: All of these are *referred to* by someone whose investigations were prompted elsewhere. If the high school textbook had completely done its job, there would have been no reason to turn to *Masterpieces of World Literature*. The primary creative task of the reference publisher is to identify the loop and to close it.

In contrast to the reference publisher is the "foreground" publisher of novels, biographies, political essays and scholarly research. It is conceivable, but not likely, that one would look into *War and Peace* for background on the Napoleonic Wars. The memoir of a Hollywood starlet is an improbable place to turn for more information on anything. And although Francis Fukuyama's *The End of History and the Last Man* is much referred to, it is not turned to for information that supplements what is already in hand, but rather to peek at the author's own idiosyncratic argument. Foreground publishers set the stage. They literally provide leadership in entertainment, scholarship and the world of ideas. Followership is the business of the reference publisher.

*   *   *   *   *

The need to close the information loop gives rise to much of the shape and activity of reference publishing today. Take comprehensiveness. The publishers of, say, *J K Lasser's Your Income Tax* begin by identifying a need for more information for consumers on the byzantine US tax law. But *what* information, precisely? The editors must anticipate every possible question someone might ask about taxes. Is the interest on the mortgage for a vacation home deductible? Must I declare as income the value of the rolltop desk given to me by my Aunt Tillie? Not knowing which particular questions a reader will ask, the editors must assume that *Lasser* will be interrogated on every conceivable subject. Thus, comprehensiveness is generally regarded as a virtue among reference publishers. If the importance of this as a distinguishing characteristic for reference works is not clear, think for a moment about what it would mean for a biography to be comprehensive. A horror – page after page on our great man's love affair with a young girl of uncertain origins. *Where are your editors?* we plead to trade publishers. Rather than *comprehensive,* should this biography not be more *selective* ?

Comprehensiveness, reference publishers' *raison d'être,* is also their *bête noire.* This is why reference books tend to be big and fat, why they are often more costly than trade books and part of the reason they are so expensive and take so long to produce. (A more amusing explanation for the urge to comprehensiveness among dictionary publishers was offered by my friend and mentor, the late Jeremiah Kaplan, arguably the most influential reference publisher of his generation. Kaplan blamed it on toilet training: "Lexicographers are all anal-retentives.") If only we knew what questions a reader will ask! Instead we must document everything. I reach randomly for a volume from Mircea Eliade's *The Encyclopedia of Religion* and turn to the article "Celestial Buddhas and Bodhisattvas". Am I the *only* person to look at this article since the editors sent it to press? How much of *The Oxford English Dictionary* is simply, literally, never looked at? There are times, it seems, when we build bridges for no other reason than that there is a river here, a shore on either side: Surely we must connect shore to shore. Thus, we reference publishers document the known, classify the obvious and render the authoritative statement on the back of your hand. As I grow older and wearier, I have come to believe that Kaplan was right.

Connected to comprehensiveness is objectivity (or at least disinterestedness). In their efforts to anticipate their readers' every question, reference editors must also anticipate the perspectives their readers bring to their questions. Rather than side with one group or another, reference editors attempt to stand outside the argument. Does the Emancipation Proclamation mark a heroic episode in the history of liberty or the cunning action of a politician playing to the demands of the press of his time? Well, just the facts, ma'am. There *was* an Emancipation Proclamation and it *was* promulgated in 1863, but the fact is that the motives of President Lincoln are in dispute (though we as reference publishers do not dispute them). Cynics no doubt will find instances of bias in even major reference works, but in my experience reference publishers by and large believe that objectivity is a worthy goal. Occasionally they even fund their editorial departments sufficiently to achieve it.

Comprehensiveness, objectivity and authority: The third member of this triumvirate is the slipperiest. In the continuum that stretches from reference publishing on one side to non-reference on the other, comprehensiveness and objectivity tend more often than not to be found on the reference end. Authority – or, I suppose, authoritativeness – surely can be found on either side. Who better than Margaret Thatcher to speak about Margaret Thatcher? In terms of authoritativeness, where reference and non-reference publishing differ is that for non-reference publishing authoritativeness is an occasional attribute, whereas for reference publishing its achievement (or at least the marketing claim to that achievement) is an unwavering goal. Here again the reason can be found in the reference publisher's aim to close the information loop. When you want more information on a subject, you hardly want something that is less reliable than what is already in hand. It is for this reason that many reference works tend to present a solemn, august image. Authorities all, they preside at the court of information.

What reference publishers will do to establish authoritativeness (or at least its appearance) opens one of the darkest chapters in the entire publishing industry. I know of no aspect of publishing that has more in the way of slippery facts, misrepresentation and outright fraud. (You will excuse me if I stop naming names for a few minutes.) One tactic (valuable when it is genuine) is to create an editorial board of worthies to lend their names to the enterprise. Often their names are virtually their only contribution. Even when such boards do some work, it is often ill-advised. Take the dictionary publisher, for example, that polls its board on matters of usage and then declares "correct" whatever the majority has agreed to. Now, what exactly does it mean when 30% of such a board say *ain't* is an acceptable term and 70% do not? If 55%

argue against the restrictive use of *which,* do we banish the rest to the gulag of illiteracy? What nonsense! It is as though a reference work were being confused with an umbrella, to be carried to work against the chance of rain. Yet unsophisticated customers fall for this stuff, which further encourages unscrupulous and idiotic publishers. Critics, take note!

Citing an editorial board that is poorly used or never used, or whose every member is dead, is akin to the practices of false or misleading attributions of authorship and brand names. Yes, there was a Peter Mark Roget and he indeed wrote a thesaurus, but few of the volumes today identified as Roget's Thesaurus have any legitimate link to Roget's work, including one volume that audaciously declares itself to be "the original". The situation with the Webster name is even worse, but I will recuse myself on this item, as Britannica counts as one of its subsidiaries Merriam-Webster, whose founders purchased the rights to Noah Webster's dictionary from his estate in 1844. Suffice it to say that true authoritativeness is difficult to achieve, is costly and takes a great deal of time. No wonder that many publishers seek short cuts.

*　*　*　*　*

We should dwell for a moment on the use of brand names and trademarks, an area that tends to distinguish reference from non-reference works. The curious fact is that while most (though not all) trade books are known by their authors' names (James Herriot, Danielle Steel, Newt Gingrich, Doris Kearns Goodwin) or occasionally by their titles (*Barbarians at the Gate*), most reference works are known by brand names. This could be a very long list: *Encyclopædia Britannica, The Oxford English Dictionary, Grolier's Electronic Encyclopedia, Fodor's France,* Barron's study aid series, Sybex computer books, *Merriam-Webster's Collegiate Dictionary* and so on. Some of these brands originated with people (Webster, Barron, Roget, Fodor); some are applications of corporate names (*The McGraw-Hill Encyclopedia of Science & Technology*). While branding appears in non-reference publishing (Harlequin Romance, The Baby-Sitters Club), it is only in reference that it dominates. The significance of brand names for reference publishing is enormous, outstripping perhaps even the importance of digital media and the creation of reference content itself.

To begin with, branding speaks to the issue of authoritativeness. We know that these nature guides are good because they bear the Audubon name. It would not occur to a reference publisher to fail to use a brand name; every book must come from *somewhere*. Thus, the straightfor- wardly titled *Directory of Executive Search Firms* becomes the *Prentice-Hall Directory of Executive Search Firms*. Branding sepa- rates products from the undifferentiated pack.

Another advantage of reference brand names is that they allow for line extension. Originally there was only the *American Heritage Dictionary*, but now *AHD* has spawned a family of dictionaries. Each successive member of the American Heritage line costs less marketing money to introduce than the one before, as the various instantiations of the American Heritage brand reinforce one another. The brand becomes the publisher's link to the ultimate consumer, a link that is often difficult to maintain through the thicket of distribution, whether that distribution comes via retail stores, catalogs, classrooms or online services. A reference publisher without a brand name is naked.

Branding is one of the contributive factors to another idiosyncrasy of reference publishing: Reference publishers are less likely than their non-reference brethren to pay royalties. *The World Almanac and Book of Facts* is simply owned outright by its publisher (K-III Communications), as is *Funk & Wagnall's New Encyclopedia* and most products in the Fodor's travel publications series. While the economic benefits of not paying royalties are often exaggerated (someone still must be paid to do the work, and without the special incentives of roy- alties, many reference publishers must deal with the management headaches of industrial production by legions of toilers), the latitude it gives publishers in deriving new works and extending the brand is enormous. No agent need be contacted before Random House decides to create an abridgment of *The Random House Unabridged Dictionary* or to publish the text on CD-ROM. And here we have the core strate- gy of every reference publisher who has the means to pursue it: Extend the brand, derive the content.

The complexity and scope of the products, the often proprietary nature of the brand and the goal of paying small or no royalties natu- rally lead many reference publishers to another practice that is virtual- ly unheard of in non-reference publishing: the creation, maintenance and management of an in-house editorial staff. Whereas trade publish- ing stereotypically involves an author in a garret, an editor at a lunch table and an agent on the phone, reference editors do not lunch; they write. How much they write varies from work to work, but there is little doubt that there is more editorial value added by reference publishers than by their counterparts in the trade. Reference editors tend to view the work submitted by authors (usually called "contributors") as raw material to be pounded into shape by the internal staff. The consistency in voice of some major reference works (eg, the *World Book Encyclopedia*) is entirely a function of a well-trained staff that works and reworks material until they get it right. No Maxwell Perkins of general trade publishing has ever done as much as a lowly editorial assistant at a major reference house.

*   *   *   *   *

To pause for a moment and summarize my argument: While it is hard to define what, exactly, reference publishing is, there are certain attributes we are more likely to associate with reference publishing than with publishing of the non-reference sort. Chief among these attributes are: comprehensiveness, objectivity, authoritativeness, strong reliance on brand names, a disinclination to pay royalties and the common strategy of internal product development. All of these attributes lend themselves to the last that I wish to discuss: the great use of computers in reference publishing, which dwarfs the use of information technology in non-reference categories. The use of computers is of two kinds: in production, which could yield printed works, and in publishing itself, whether on CD-ROM or online.

Virtually all publishers use computers in production. Reference publishers use them more, use them more fundamentally and have been using them longer. I was stunned upon coming to EB in 1991 to discover that the *Britannica* database had been running on an in-house computer system for over twenty years. I doubt any trade publisher could tell a comparable story. Computers in reference production save money, improve cycle times and make the creation of derivative works easier (though never effortless). There will never again be a major reference work created without extensive use of computer technology.

Publishing in electronic media is a different story. While this aspect of reference publishing is immature at best, the inroads electronics are making into the reference world suggest that the printed reference work may someday, perhaps soon, become the exclusive province of the collector. Although it is difficult to assemble reliable figures, it is arguable that more English-language general encyclopedias on CD-ROM have been *given away* – literally given away, a practice called *bundling* – in the past five years than there were English-language print encyclopedias sold since the genre's inception in the 18th century. What is going on here?

Any publisher who has read a newspaper in the past three years knows that we are witnessing a huge battle to create new forms of publishing. Whether those forms are the Information Superhighway, multimedia, local-area networks, CD-ROM, solid-state, or whatever, is beside the point. What is important for publishers is that these are *platform wars,* a competition to control the standard for electronic publishing in the years ahead. To control such a standard platform would be the equivalent of owning a patent on the printing press, enabling the lucky owner to extract a royalty for every book printed. The rivals in this skirmish are some of the world's largest and most voracious companies, ranging from teeny-weenie Microsoft to stout AT&T and IBM. It is always useful to remember how small the book publishing industry is. (The total in the US is less than one-third the size of IBM.) Where elephants dance, small dogs run for cover.

Reference materials on CD-ROM are being "bundled" in order to advance the claims of technology companies (principally Microsoft) to the standard platform for electronic publishing. This has resulted in a dramatic restructuring of many segments of the reference marketplace. There is no turning back.

But why reference works and not, say, *The Bridges of Madison County* on CD-ROM? Unlike the mostly linear text of novels, biographies and other non-reference genres, reference works – with their stops and starts, outright ownership by their publishers, frequent absence of royalty obligations, conspicuous brand names, etc – seem perfectly matched to the branching, interactive nature of computing. (Another factor, ergonomics, is outside the scope of this paper. It is literally a pain in the neck to read a novel from a computer screen.) Indeed, to an encyclopedist the World Wide Web seems to be not so much a new publishing opportunity, but almost the destiny inherent in the very idea of an encyclopedia. The technology companies that have jumped on reference works as a vehicle to promote certain platforms did so because they brilliantly understood what silicon could do and paper could not. From the point of view of value added to customers, in less than one year *Britannica Online* has become the primary form of *Encyclopædia Britannica.*

It is useful to stand back from the millennial spirit that attaches itself to so much talk about electronics and the "information revolution". (Equally, we should resist the Luddite reaction.) Earlier, I argued that reference publishing is a business of backgrounding. I also argued that reference works have been caught up in the creation of new paradigms of digital publishing. What is peculiar, though, is that, at least at this time (I expect this to change by the end of the decade), many electronic reference works are not being used as backgrounders. By my definition, they are not truly reference works at all, but, rather, works of entertainment that superficially appear to be reference works – just as *Pale Fire* and *Dictionary of the Khazars* superficially appear to be reference publications.

Let us picture how some of these electronic reference works are actually used. Johnnie, an eager sixth-grader, sits at his new multimedia computer purchased at a local discount club. With this machine came a half-dozen free CD-ROM titles, mostly reference works. Johnnie loads the *Encyclopedia of Cats and Dogs* (*ECD*). It is a well-produced title, with full-motion videos of dogs at competitions, audio tracks of cats meowing and text covering the various breeds and their evolutionary history. *ECD* looks like a reference work, it smells like a reference work, but it is not a reference work. Why?

There is no foreground activity driving Johnnie to refer to *ECD*. He has no text on the screen from another product or service (say, America Online) for which he wants additional background information. No, Johnnie has turned on *ECD* as a foreground activity, and as a foreground activity it isn't bad. It has sound, it has video, perhaps there are some engaging animations. The text is well-written, too, though why Johnnie would read it isn't clear. The real achievement of *ECD* is that it shows off the technical capabilities of a multimedia PC. *ECD*, in other words, is a showpiece, a form of entertainment. It is more akin to trade publishing than to reference, more like the fictional *Dictionary of the Khazars* than like John Lighter's *Random House Historical Dictionary of American Slang*. *ECD* has accomplished precisely what it has set out to do.

For *ECD* to be a "true" reference work, the hardware must evolve.

It takes too much time to load a CD-ROM onto a computer just to look up a brief article on schnauzers. Nor is it convenient to load reference works of any scope onto a hard disk, unless Johnnie's hard disk is industrial-strength. As a reference work, *ECD* is simply hard to refer to.

This will change and it will change quickly. The world of CD-ROM publishing is already moving swiftly into entertainment publishing, dominated by games companies and Hollywood studios. This is as it should be. Although it is doubtful that any reference publisher will fail to dabble in CD-ROM, reference is going online; and once there, it will stay there. Our company anticipates that by the end of the decade CD-ROM will become the province of entertainment and juvenile titles (that is, another species of entertainment), and virtually all major reference works will be available on the World Wide Web or a successor technology (minor works will come bundled with operating systems). These digital reference works will refer to one another (called *pointing*) in an informal system of hyperlinks. They will provide background to news stories, magazine articles, scholarly research, etc, and they will also supplement one another. From a group of discrete works, all arranged in their separate bindings, reference titles will become integrated with one another, allowing easy passage for the intellectually curious researcher. In a global communications network where it can be difficult to determine where one reference work ends and another begins, we can be sure that publishers will not fail to assert their proprietary trademarks over their library of works.

This does not mean that it is just a matter of time before electronic publishers get reference "right". To do it right will mean to do it differently. With countless databases of information available on the World Wide Web, the challenge for researchers will be to find exactly what they are looking for. Here brand names will serve as navigational tools (because we trust *Le Monde* more than *Weekly World News*). Comparably important will be electronic indexing tools (search-and-retrieval software, classifiers, filters and the like). Reference publishers may have a special role to play in this regard in cyberspace, as their decades, even centuries, of experience in classification and indexing – essential skills for creating major reference publications – may be applied to sophisticated searching beyond their own works to the whole of the global communications network. Our future reference works may be more index than article, more metacontent than content. Stay tuned.

* * * * *

It might be instructive to consider how this essay would differ if it were conceived of as a reference work (instead of as, well, an essay).

For starters, there would be no single author. An editor-in-chief would assemble a staff to begin the difficult task of editorial planning. The scope of the work must be determined; the experts in the various fields must be brought in. The project would be segmented, perhaps into consumer, professional and educational (institutional) reference. An outline for the work would be put together. Then there is the difficult job of establishing the article format and of determining the work's "voice". Contributors would then be approached, but not before article outlines had been prepared to which the contributors' work must conform. Reference is definitely an editor's and not an author's game. At some point in the process, there is a very strong possibility, deriving from the compulsion for comprehensiveness, that the work will begin to become decoupled from users' needs.

It will come as no surprise that this process will yield a much longer work than this essay. Reference editors are constitutionally indisposed to create a short work. Where short reference works appear (the marvelous Lilliput dictionaries from Langenscheidt, for example), it is because a marketing person has – temporarily – risen to power and forced the short work through the organization, or the short work is a long work masquerading as a short work behind tiny type crammed into a barely legible page. In the fullness of time, however, the editorial urge will quietly reassert itself, the small work will become a large volume, one volume will become several, then CD-ROM will be examined, and from there it is but a short trip to the World Wide Web and the vast reaches of cyberspace. It is both a matter of definition and of destiny that all reference works tend to the encyclopedic.

The reference work on reference publishing will be long and well organized; it will have a taxonomy and a board of editors; it will be available in various media; it will get longer and longer; it will be created by an in-house staff; it will get longer and longer; and it will be published with a conspicuous brand name. It is a matter of ecology: The tall trees of Africa give rise to a long-necked antelope, which we know by the brand name "giraffe". The publishing environment gives rise to the reference genre and the genre develops with its own internal rules and conventions.

President and CEO of Encyclopædia Britannica Inc since July 1995, Joseph J Esposito has been with the Britannica organization since 1990, when he joined as President of Merriam-Webster. Since beginning his career at Rutgers University Press in 1978, he has held posts with the New American Library, Simon & Schuster and Random House. A graduate of Rutgers University (summa cum laude with Highest Distinction in English), where he also earned a Phi Beta Kappa key, Esposito attained his master of philosophy degree in English literature in 1978.

12

Medical Publishing in the US: A Competitive Industry Where Readers Need Not Be Buyers

Eric J Newman

Medical publishing in the United States today is a highly competitive business. The entry of major corporations into medical publishing, which began in the '60s, and the opportunity to sell medical publications around the world, whether in English or in translation, led to a great expansion of the business in the '70s and much consolidation in the '80s.

In the '60s, the acquisitions were often by conglomerates, such as Xerox, ITT, IBM or Litton, who acquired medical along with other houses, and subsequently exited. W B Saunders, the largest and most respected medical house in the world, became part of the CBS television network, which also left publishing. Saunders is now a division of Harcourt General. C V Mosby and Year Book became part of the newspaper publisher Times Mirror. Little, Brown Medical followed its trade publishing mother to join Time Life. Waverly, one of the few medical publishers to remain in family hands, itself acquired the oldest medical house, Lea & Febiger, which has recently disappeared as an imprint.

College publishers also moved into the field. McGraw-Hill was the first to make a major expansion of its small medical list with its 1954 acquisition of Blakiston. Addison-Wesley and Houghton Mifflin were among those who tried to enter medical publishing from scratch, but have since given up. Of the late starters, only Prentice Hall, with its purchase of Appleton and then Lange, is still a player in clinical medicine.

The profitability of medical publishing also attracted European companies to enter the US. In the '60s, Bart van Tongeren and Otto ter Haar of Holland's Elsevier and Dr Heinz Goetze of Germany's Springer Verlag guided their companies through an inspired shift into English-language publishing through their branches in New York. The British company Butterworths entered the American market in the '60s, withdrew and then re-entered in 1975. Other major British entrants followed – Churchill-Livingstone in 1974 and Blackwell in 1979. Germany's Thieme Verlag started with a joint venture and then became their own masters. Japan's Igaku Shoin came in 1977. Holland's Wolters Kluwer owns Lippincott, another venerable imprint. All felt the need for an American presence.

During these years, medical publishing was becoming transnational. The Americans also went abroad. Macmillan Inc acquired Balliere-Tindall in Britain. McGraw-Hill expanded in Europe and Asia. Saunders had been active in the UK since the beginning of the century. Mosby and Year Book entered the European market in the '80s with acquisitions in Britain and then in Germany.

Corporate owners who pay high prices naturally expect good financial return. But with so many companies trying to buy their way in or find their way in, delivering the expected returns was frustrating. All struggled as the profits of the '60s proved elusive for late starters in the '70s. Acquisition, particularly early acquisition, proved to be the root of successful market entry. Today, prices stay high and private owners have continually to weigh their current results against the cash offers they regularly receive.

* * * * *

Why is medical publishing so attractive? Although many of the classic works of medical publishing, like *Gray's Anatomy* or *Osler's Textbook of Medicine,* still have popular successor editions today, the estimated shelf life of medical knowledge is five years. *Conn's Current*

Therapy, published annually by W B Saunders since 1949, reflects the rapid change of medical practice. The compounding effects of new drugs, new tests and even changes in disease patterns were tracked in the steady growth and reorganization of this work. Lange's *Current Medical Diagnosis and Treatment,* now in its 35th edition, has had a similar evolution. Not only has the work grown and come to include many new topics, but it has spawned a family of "Currents", now numbering a dozen titles.

As in so many professional and academic fields, the day of the single-authored definitive work has almost entirely vanished. Medical science has become so specialized and the pace of change so rapid that the task of writing must be distributed into the hands of contributors. Medicine is practiced by a team and books are created by committee. Today's authors don't have the time, and the subjects have grown so complex that no single author can do them justice.

With so much to learn, practice has become more specialized as well. This has converted many of the large reference works to series purchased by libraries. Few surgeons would attempt to practice eye, brain and bone surgery as they once did. Works of this type have splintered into sub-sets or died.

The growth of US medical publishing owes much to skilled publishers. Lew Reines, for example, published large comprehensive or multi-volume works at Churchill, Lippincott and now Saunders. His greatest successes were in orthopaedics and anaesthesiology, where British books were displaced by American works, attuned to the American exam structure, authored by the examiners and professors on the local lecture circuit. American doctors loved them. So did doctors in Japan and most of the world. These American books set new world standards.

An early and enduring success was created by Dr Jack D Lange, one of the few MDs in American medical publishing. As a medical student in 1938, Lange and a classmate found that the clarity of their classnotes on neuroanatomy made them popular, even in other medical schools. The model of a carefully edited, concise, authoritative, value-for-money title continues in Appleton & Lange, more than fifty years later. Through Dr Lange's wide travels and generous support of fledgling medical publishers around the world, Lange books, primarily for medical students and non-specialists, are among the most respected and internationally accepted medical titles in the world.

While Reines concentrated on big books in action-oriented surgical specialties, Al Meier at Saunders was developing the cerebral medical specialties, first in rapidly expanding hardcover periodicals called *Clinics*, then in major reference works. These were the specialties where words, ideas and advances in biochemistry played the biggest role. Meier also found the leading authors in emerging specialties who developed cutting-edge ways of looking at problems or organizing data.

There were many others who broke new ground in one way or another. Dr Alan Edelson, who started Raven Press (now part of Lippincott-Raven), concentrated on hot areas with strong pharmaceutical support like cardiology, with new journals, symposia and monographs.

Looseleaf medical publishing was reborn with *Scientific American Medicine* by Gerry Piel. A prolific output of therapy-based books, and lately journals and electronic products, were generated by Brian Decker.

Student textbooks had trouble keeping up. So much has been added to the curriculum in developing fields like cell biology that gross anatomy and other areas have been de-emphasized. Many standard reference works have grown to over 2,000 pages, too much for the student, or even the busy practitioner, to absorb. Some of the most successful publications in recent years have been abridged and scaled-down versions of established works which had grown too large for some readers. "Baby Cecil", a condensed version of the classic Cecil and Loeb, is an example from Saunders in internal medicine. There are spin-off pocket editions of Harrison *Internal Medicine,* Robbins *Physiology,* Sabiston *Surgery* and others.

Students cannot possibly read all that is recommended and do not buy a fraction of the recommended books. They do buy study guides which rehearse test questions for self-examination and review books, however. Medical publishing has long issued brief subject surveys popular with students, such as the Lange books or Little, Brown's *Spiral Notebook Series* based on the *Washington Manual.* Some of the most popular guides were developed by Jim Harris in the *National Medical Review Series,* now owned by Williams & Wilkins. These give very short exam-oriented information bites in bullet form and are heavily illustrated.

One of the strongest trends is the increasing emphasis on the visual. Technology is partly responsible, but so too are educational trends. No doubt television has had an influence, particularly on students and young authors and publishers. Printing advances and the influence of pharmaceutical-sponsored publications have also had an impact. It seems that readers in all countries prefer to receive information through pictures. Several years ago, Al Meier (then at Saunders) worried about the declining sales of *Dorland's Medical Dictionary*. He discovered all dictionary sales were declining. It was one of many signs of a shift away from words to the use of graphics, color photographs, bullet points and summary teaching points.

Medicine never was practiced the same around the world. Even when British and German books were the world standards (as in some areas they were, well into the '70s), there were important national differences in publishing perspectives. Despite their common language, these differences extended to the British and American markets. The British publisher instinctively thinks of a hospital library purchase. The American, just as reflexively, visualizes an individual purchase. These differences produced strains, particularly pronounced when British inflation and a weak dollar shifted the price advantage to America.

The major texts of today generate millions of dollars per edition and usually have several high-quality competitors. Increased competition and high expectations of shareholders are evident in this area. So much is at stake and the top names so important to success that the leading books or their challengers pay royalties approaching 20% of net receipts to attract the best authors. It is now commonplace for these authors to receive advances, artwork grants, loans or grants of computer equipment and secretarial assistance.

These books are such an important investment that enormous efforts are made to protect or exploit the "franchise". McGraw-Hill's Harrison *Internal Medicine* and Lippincott's *DeVita Cancer* are two of many examples. In order to ensure currency, these major works are under almost constant revision, the next edition being planned and organized even as the latest edition is rolling off the presses. Editorial guidelines carefully instruct the listing of references no more than five years old.

Until recently, a new edition every five years was fairly common, but for many of these big books the cycle has been cut to three. Even between editions such works have updates or supplemental volumes periodically published to include the latest developments. These are sometimes supported by pharmaceutical companies or sold on subscription. The primary objective is to extend the shelf life of the book and to keep the attention and loyalty of the buyers for the new edition.

Other materials are produced on the same model. Study guides, slide sets, teaching aids, self-examination books, videos and every manner of information delivery take advantage of the branding of a Harrison. McGraw-Hill has been one of the most successful at exploiting its big names, borrowing heavily from competitive trends in college publishing.

*   *   *   *   *

Medical publishing has become so saturated that despite the consolidation in recent years, few publishers see significant growth in traditional lines of business. By contrast, nursing and allied health, the myriad of health care professions that are neither doctors nor nurses, have grown rapidly in number and importance. Nursing is primarily a student market and is one of the few areas of medical publishing with which college publishing seems to have a strong affinity. Nursing is a smaller market than college, highly contested by a few big players, usually with a medical heritage, such as: Saunders, Lippincott or Mosby-Year Book, but college publishers like Addison-Wesley have established themselves as well.

Springhouse, founded by two veterans of advertising-based magazine publishing in 1970, has one of the few book programs which concentrates on practicing nurses. Gene Jackson and Dan Cheney started a hugely successful magazine *Nursing 1996*, plus heavily illustrated books and continuity series and other services directed at the magazine's nearly 500,000 readers. Following magazine practice, the books were authored in-house.

The allied health fields of optometry, physical therapy, nutrition, speech pathology, laboratory medicine, x-ray technology and podiatry are some of the fastest growing professions in most employment forecasts. This growth is built on the health needs of an ageing population and efforts to control cost of health care by transferring work to specialized, less expensive health providers. One example is the shift of much prescription work from ophthalmologists (medical doctors) to optometrists (not licensed to do surgery or to handle certain complicated conditions).

Very often it was the smaller publishers who seized these opportunities first. Butterworth-Heinemann in Boston moved to take a major share of the optometry market, and College Hill Press in San Diego staked out an early claim in the speech pathology market. Aspen came to dominate the non-clinical but rapidly growing market of hospital administration and related legal and insurance issues.

Books are only one of the ways health care professionals receive information. Depending on their specialty and prescribing habits, some American doctors receive more than thirty free publications a month. Most are clinical review publications, some carrying pharmaceutical ads, some more subtly seeding the market by their selective coverage of meetings. Others are lifestyle publications carrying medical advertising.

Medical research also has its share of high-priced, narrowly-focused journals which circulate to a few thousand or even a few hundred hospitals or university libraries. These publications from Elsevier, from Marcel Dekker and others reflect the levels of government funding of fundamental research and the trend of science to twig into narrower and narrower disciplines.

* * * * *

But it is the advertising, largely from the drug companies, that sets medical publishing apart. In most countries, doctors have great influence over pharmaceutical subscriptions. Hundreds of millions of dollars are spent on advertising drugs in the pages of the top 200 American medical journals alone. This is unique in journals that carry high-level scientific content and has permitted most doctors to buy individual subscriptions to a number of journals. But it is also a fickle market. Ad revenues are down sharply from 1992, when a burst of drug approvals from the Food & Drug Administration swelled ad sales.

Many of the world's leading medical journals are published by and for major national or regional medical associations, eg, the *Journal of the American Medical Association* (JAMA) or *The New England Journal of Medicine* (NEJM). Many specialist journals are the official journals of specialty societies, eg, the *Journal of the American College of Cardiology* (Elsevier) or the *Journal of Bone and Joint Surgery*. Because the societies see publishing primarily as a member service, they are tax-sheltered. Reaching sufficient readers to generate enormous pharmaceutical advertising income, these journals can be offered at unusually low prices.

The journal may be owned by a society and published under contract with a commercial publisher for a commission, profit-share or similar arrangement. Many of the Lippincott-Raven, Academic Press, Williams & Wilkins and Mosby-Year Book journals fall into this model. Editorial control usually rests with the society, while subscription sales and the important advertising sales are handled by the commercial publisher.

In recent years, the number of medical journals has continued to grow. Physicians came to specialize more and more and demanded publications which fitted their clinical needs. New societies grew and created publications as badges of legitimacy and as their financial underpinning. Societies also grew more sophisticated or more demanding financially.

Leading journals have also become franchises, with foreign editions translated into local languages around the globe. Depending on the market, the journals are subscription-based, advertising-based or a mix.

Not surprisingly, the most successful journals are in subjects flush with advertising. Advertising also allowed many of the better supported of the new sub-specialties, ie, better drug areas, to have their own journals at prices within reach of individual doctors. Journals in cardiology, internal medicine and infectious diseases benefited most by the increase in advertising, with the launch of many new drugs backed by unprecedented ad campaigns, and by the advent of the supplement in the '70s and its blossoming in the '80s as a major marketing tool and publishing phenomenon.

As pharmaceutical advertising grew, it became apparent that many medical titles could be supported by advertising alone. These controlled-circulation titles are sent free to highly sophisticated mailing lists and tailored to deliver readers whom the advertiser wants to reach. If one of the most desirable reader groups were heavy prescribers of anti-hypertensives, a list was available for rental and a journal could be launched reaching every doctor who fitted that profile. An editor could be chosen among the leading figures and paid handsomely. The editorial was usually clinical, but it could be anything that grabbed the attention of the reader: lifestyle features, financial or travel advice. In general, these advertising vehicles were created by communications companies or advertising agencies, not the traditional publishers. Superior artwork and graphics were part of the package.

The logical extension of this approach was not long in coming. A publication could offer a solus position for the sponsor's ads or, more subtly, the editorial slant could emphasize meetings or studies favorable to a single drug's mode of action. The circulation list could be targeted with the drug's marketing objectives in mind.

* * * * *

One of the fastest growing areas of medical publishing in recent years has been neither book nor journal publishing, but that catch-all of new technology and new media. This includes online services, CD-ROM, software, video, slides and other non-print formats. While the growth has been technology-based, usage by practicing doctors has been quite different from that by professionals in law, science or engineering. They are accustomed to getting it free or at pharmaceutical industry-supported prices. However, slide sets and videos have established a major presence in the medical schools, particularly in visual subjects like embryology and pathology and in gross anatomy, where there has long been a shortage of cadavers.

The path to commercial success for these electronic initiatives is far from proven. *The Online Journal of Current Clinical Trials*™, started in a blaze of publicity by the American Association for the Advancement of Science, was sold to Chapman & Hall. BRS/Colleague™ was a disappointment in its efforts to reach the practitioner, as was MEDIS™. Today, IVI has cost its investors millions of dollars. ADAM has established a following in medical schools and, in the best tradition of print publishers, has found ways to use a common core to create multiple products. Geomedica was taken over by Reuters. It has been slow to grow.

One online service has established its niche in research, rather than with practicing doctors. MEDLARS™ (Medical Literature Analysis and Retrieval System), a computerized bibliographic system of the

National Library of Medicine, is an indispensable part of the medical research network.

Though doctors have been reluctant to pay for new media, they have been exposed to plenty of it. Increasing competition between pharmaceutical companies and larger budgets have led to an explosion of new ways to deliver medical information. The ad dollars are flowing into these new vehicles. Desktop media, seminars, symposia, investigator meetings and audiovisuals are taking an ever greater share of the total spend – and of the total share of information reaching the doctor.

The book and the ad-based journal are both under fire. Professional books are over-published, and students ignore all but a fraction of the recommended books. The new media are unproven, but promising. But somehow, a core of healthcare professionals still read and some even write. Both are necessary for publishing, even if this market has long since proven that the reader need not be the buyer. Somehow medical publishing continues to attract new entries and high multiples.

Current President of the American Medical Publishers Association, Eric Newman was raised and educated in Califonia. He began his publishing career in 1973 with Butterworths in Australia. He spent nearly twenty years with Butterworths, moving from Sydney to Singapore to London to Boston, where he assumed executive responsibility for STM operations in the US and Europe. In 1993, he was appointed President of Appleton & Lange.

13

Journals Face the Electronic Future

Pieter S H Bolman

The issues to be discussed in this article concern *scientific* journals, a breed considered well nigh indestructible for a great many years. In an era in which the *book* publishing industry (scientific, professional, trade and mass-market) went through great turmoil, and when the fortunes of periodicals publishing for professional, business-to-business and mass markets rose and fell with the tides of the advertising business, scientific journals seemed to be totally unaffected by all this. Publicly quoted companies such as Elsevier, Maxwell (before the sale of Pergamon), Wiley, Plenum, etc, were reporting steady, if not explosive, growth, which the financial press to a large extent ascribed to the strength of their scientific journals programs and the rich cash flows associated with them.

At the same time, but less in the public eye, learned societies all over the world who were engaged in journal publishing, either directly as publishers or indirectly through third party commercial outlets, were able to expand missions and enhance services for their members as a result of the surpluses generated by their journal publishing programs.

All of a sudden (or has it been visible all along for those who wanted to see it?), the scientific journal publishing enterprise is rocking on its foundations[1]. The Internet seems to offer boundless opportunities at minimal cost. Growth in funding for (academic) research libraries (who are the buyers for all these journals) has come to a grinding halt.

153

Scientists and librarians have combined in revolt against journal publishers, be they for- or not-for-profit. A new paradigm has started a new era in which the individual scientist takes his fate in his own hands, retains his copyright and does away with the centuries-old shackles of thralldom and dependence on print-on-paper.

What I write below is a personal view on some of the most pressing aspects of these new waves, keeping in mind the condition imposed by the editor of this special issue to highlight the US publishing scene (even though the phenomena are worldwide). Because of the limited space allowed, it is only possible to present a very selective treatment of issues that are exceedingly complex. Even so, having not yet been able to sort through all the relevant phenomena and, as a result, having not yet arrived at simple representations of what is actually happening, I am writing a long story because I haven't yet the insight to write a short one.

* * * * *

It is estimated that the international research journal publishing business is worth about $2.5bn. As such, it represents about 2% of worldwide research expenditures. In the late '60s, this ratio was about 3%.

In 1991, US authors published over 142,000 articles in the natural sciences and engineering in some 3,500 journals. Over 70% of these publications came from academia. The total number of US articles accounted for 35% of the world's output in these fields[2].

In the US, learned societies dominate scientific journal publishing, especially in areas such as mathematics, physics and chemistry. In Europe, commercial publishers play the larger role. This stems from the fact that after World War II, when the real expansion and internationalization of science started, European learned societies were still very much organized on a national basis, publishing mostly in local languages, and they were slow to respond to their scientists' needs for international outlets for their research results. Commercial publishers in the Netherlands and the UK responded by creating English-language journals with international editorial boards and, within a relatively short time, grew to major forces in the scientific publishing world.

Commercial publishers in the US had less incentive to do so, if for no other reasons than the attractiveness of the emerging large US textbook market and the fact that US learned societies already had strong journal programs in the by then lingua franca of science, English. It is not coincidental that those commercial publishers in the US that did become successful in scientific journal publishing, such as Academic Press, Interscience (now merged with Wiley), Dekker, etc, mostly have very direct European roots: They were started by German and Dutch émigrés who fled Europe in the '30s and '40s [3].

* * * * *

Science is a truly international endeavor and the scientific community forms one of the few true international markets currently in existence. It comes as no surprise, therefore, that science publishers, whether in the US, Europe or elsewhere (and to a large extent also the publishers of journals in technology and medicine), all face similar challenges in connection with the rapid changes that are occurring both in information technology and in the funding of information dissemination and delivery. In order to get a better idea of the significance of these challenges, we must briefly review the role of the journal in the scientific enterprise as a collection of certified scientific documents.

The purpose of a scientific article, and hence of the journal as a collection of articles, is not merely to disseminate scientific information. Without claiming to be exhaustive or complete, it is clear that at least the following functions are served: [4]

1. The preparation of a research report represents completion of a piece of research. The document is the ultimate evidence for the new discoveries that are being presented, usually building explicitly on what was known before through the citing of appropriate references, among other things. Even if the document is not published, eg, in the case of proprietary research, writing is an essential final act in any serious research project.
2. The document becomes an article if the author wishes to have it published and succeeds in doing so. It then becomes the unique official and formal means of distributing the scientific information in space and time.
3. The published peer-reviewed article is the basic means of establishing the priority of the researcher for this piece of work and for assigning credit. Hence it becomes an important stimulus for the

researcher's self-expression and a confirmation of his/her position in the scientific community.

4. The total number of published peer-reviewed scientific articles is a generally accepted measure of the creative work of researchers.

5. By becoming a component part of the public archive of science, an article acquires a quality of authenticity. It is transformed into a small part of the grand human design of science.

Even a listing as cursory and non-exhaustive as the above makes it clear that any proposed changes to the scientific information system that have to do only with the dissemination function are either doomed to failure or will result in fundamentally changing, or even damaging, some of the other functions of journals.

As a result of the tremendous growth of research activities after World War II, the quantity of scientific output increased correspondingly, and so did the journals that "keep the minutes of science". They grew not only in number but also in size. As a result, costs of journals have risen at least proportionately. As the bulk of these costs has to be borne by scientific research libraries, library budgets should also have grown correspondingly. They have not, however, and this in turn has led to the tremendous squeeze that has essentially been in effect since the early '70s, resulting in the elimination of duplicate subscriptions, monographs and other non-essential information products (at least in the short term), the replacement of non-core subscriptions by Current Awareness Services and Individual Article Supply, etc. In order for this to happen, libraries have had to engage and invest in laborious and time consuming photocopying and interlibrary loan activities, resulting in an even further reduction of funds available for journals and exacerbating the financial squeeze further.

Publishers, who wanted to maintain their margins, responded each year with price increases, caused not only by inflation in production and overhead costs, but also by the growth of the literature and by the erosion of their subscription holdings. Certain learned societies, in order to compete effectively with commercial publishers for the best authors, abandoned or drastically reduced their page charges to authors and compensated for this by extra increases in subscription prices. These page charges had provided a significant contribution to prepress costs. Eliminating them further added to the overall financial problem.

In the US and Canada, libraries also suffered from the weak dollar effect, which made it increasingly difficult for them to buy material from some of the very large European publishers.

All this contributed to a deterioration in the relationship between librarians and publishers; the former often accusing the latter of price gouging and the latter telling the former that they were barking up the wrong tree and that they should ensure that their funding kept pace with the growth of the scientific enterprise as a whole, pointing out to frustrated librarians that publishers are merely trying to satisfy market demand (the market in this case arising from the needs of scientists as authors, and not from the librarians who have to foot the bill).

Meanwhile, information technology grew exponentially in terms of memory, band width, resolution, speed, etc. Most scientists now have access to work stations and expect the information they need to be presented to them on their screens. The Internet (and especially the World Wide Web) has made tremendous inroads during the last two years. The concept of a "wired campus", which seemed so remote only ten years ago, has now become a reality. The costs associated with this remain fairly invisible to most players (scientists and librarians) and, in any event, costs per unit of performance continue to drop.

Librarians fully expect that cost savings on the part of publishers will be passed on to them so that expectations of improved service for less money are rife and, ultimately, not totally unjustified. In the meantime, scientists have become increasingly involved in debates about the plight of the libraries and have started to come up with experimental solutions of their own.

*   *   *   *   *

In June 1994, Steve Harnad, then at Princeton University, published his "subversive proposal" [5] to have all ESOTERIC (ie, non-trade, no-market) scientific and scholarly publications published for free via PUBLIC File Transfer Protocol (FTP): "If every esoteric author in the world ... established a globally accessible local ftp archive for every piece of esoteric writing ..., the long-heralded transition from paper publication to purely electronic would follow suit ..." He states: "For centuries, it was only out of reluctant necessity that authors of esoteric publications entered into the FAUSTIAN bargain of allowing a price-tag to be erected as a barrier between their work and its (tiny) intended readership, for that was the only way they could make their work public at all during the age when paper publication (and its substantial expenses) was their only option."

I will not dwell on the historical accuracy of this description, except to say that it is good to remind ourselves that the scientific journal as we know it now grew and evolved from the *Journal des Scanvans* and the *Philosophical Transactions of the Royal Society of London*, started in 1665 [3], and that both journals were set up by scientists themselves and had as their stated goals to "make known experiments in physics and chemistry that might serve to explain natural phenomena ..." and "to give some account of the present undertakings, studies and labours of the ingenious in many considerable parts of the world". The journals originally started as archives and systematic catalogs, on the basis of which the scientists could be "invited and encouraged to search, try, and find out new things, impart their knowledge to one another, and contribute what they can to the Grand design of improving Natural knowledge".

It was only in the 19th century that the pursuit of priority became an important factor in journal publishing (up to that point definitive research on a subject was still written up as a monograph) and that the journal started to play the more complex roles described earlier. Presumably the "Faustian bargain" set in then, if one equates the author's pursuit of priority with Dr Faust's desire for "youth, knowledge and power".[6] Later, Harnad claims he meant PAPER to be the Devil (not the paper publishers). The seemingly catchy metaphor then reduces to a pedestrian observation to the effect that new technology can offer many "liberating" options and possibilities, something we have all known for some time.

Dr Harnad's other claim, viz that esoteric information (intended for a tiny readership) has no market value and should therefore be free, does not seem to bear scrutiny. It negates the variety of functions of scientific journals listed earlier and assumes that the only purpose of scientific publishing is to inform (a few) other scientists. The scientific archive that has been built over the centuries at tremendous cost and that exists in distributed form in libraries throughout the world, clearly has immense value and as clearly deserves to be preserved and further built upon. The infinitesimal parts of this archive, each individual scientist's contributions, may only have infinitesimal market value at the time of their origination (this is true by definition: Scientific knowledge is knowledge for knowledge's sake, it gains in market [or other] value when it can be applied), but to say that infinitesimal equals zero is going a bit far, it seems.

Dr Harnad has yet another claim: He figures that the per-page costs in an electronic medium should be about 75% lower than for the paper medium. No further comment on this seems necessary: Excellent rebuttals were given from non-commercial sources such as the American Chemical Society and, unwittingly, from his "comrade in arms" Paul Ginsparg (a High Energy physicist at Los Alamos). For $1m one can produce a lot of pages, be they paper or electronic!

In mid-1991, Ginsparg set up an "e-print Archive" system for the distribution, archiving and searching of scientific preprints [5]. So far, the e-Print Archives have been set up for at least twelve sub-disciplines, and it is expected that more disciplines will follow in time. Early in 1994, Ginsparg and co-workers requested, and subsequently obtained, National Science Foundation (NSF) support to the tune of $350,000 per year for three years for a software development effort that "will expand the use and increase the effectiveness of the current systems, and furthermore, focus on the design, implementation, and incorporation of new, innovative tools for electronic communication of research results".

It is claimed that for some fields of physics the e-print archives have become the primary means of communicating research information, entirely supplanting conventional journals in this role. In a recent survey conducted by the American Physical Society [7], 30% of the (9,000) respondees were stated to have used preprint servers, 13% on a regular basis. This finding neither proves nor disproves the claim. What is known is the following:

High Energy physicists have for a long time been dependent on the exchange of preprints as their primary means of communicating ongoing research information. In the early '70s, just before I entered publishing, there already was talk about giving all physicists access to the information thus distributed (then very unevenly) through the start-up of a "preprint grinder", an effort that eventually led to the start of a review section in the journal *Physics Letters* under the name "Physics Reports". In 1987, North-Holland (the physics imprint of Elsevier) conducted formal market research into the possibility of electronically collecting and distributing these preprints under the project name HEP-base. There was considerable enthusiasm for the plan, both from physicists, who were eager for complete information, as they could never be sure that they had seen *all* relevant paper preprints, and from the librarians, for whom the preprints were a nightmare, as they were largely unindexed when they arrived, took up a lot of space in the library and were constantly missing. However, the plan was abandoned for two main reasons: 1) the technology, although there, was not ubiquitously available and was too primitive to gain acceptance; and 2) although the librarians could save a considerable amount of money by not having to deal with paper printings (about 6,000 were produced then on an annual basis), these savings were largely in the overhead sphere and could not easily be freed up for other purposes.

So far, the existence of the electronic preprint database seems not to have led to a decrease in submissions to the conventional journals. This is not surprising, as the preprint database is just that: It does not provide authentication and quality control (there is no peer review), nor does it guarantee permanence in an archival sense. As the refereeing process quite frequently leads to modifications in the original submission, the version that is eventually published can differ significantly from the one circulated as preprint. Whereas in the "paper days" the official publication was a sign that the paper version (the preprint) could finally be thrown away, thus significantly uncluttering library shelves and personal files, the continuing existence of the e-preprint (which served as an "early communication version") now can lead to a by now classic "version control" problem. The problem is exacerbated by the fact that authors increasingly tend to refer to preprints in their articles, rather than wait until the "official" citation is known, or bother to look it up when it is available. . The result is that these preprint citations disappear: The Citation Index does not pick them up (thus also influencing the Impact Factor of the journal), nor do other Abstracting and Indexing Services, and gradually this "virus" eats into the "collective memory" of High Energy Physics (HEP).

As it turns out, this is a much more "subversive" proposition than Harnad's. And what is more, it is government-subsidized. If not checked, it will lead to a considerable contamination of the body of HEP literature, for which future generations may not be grateful. One of the things that could be done now is to make the NSF support contingent on implementing a requirement to remove preprints from the database after official publication (and in any case after a certain period of time, eg, a year). Also, there should be more stringent guidelines on citation behavior in official journals, a job that should be spearheaded by the learned societies, in this case the American Physical Society in the US (and even the IUPAP [the International Union of Pure and Applied Physics], as this is a worldwide phenomenon). In HEP there actually exists an "Anti Preprint Database" service that essentially allows authors to check on the "fate" of a preprint in terms of its official publication. The importance for other disciplines is clear: HEP is in the vanguard of these developments because of its publishing traditions.

* * * * *

The new technology is very seductive for solving such immediate, short-term problems. In some cases, the resulting "paradigm shift" can be very beneficial even though not very pleasant and convenient for the people who earn their living under the old paradigm. In science publishing, however, we are continuing to build on foundations constructed in the past and are dependent on them: A clean break, without taking care of building bridges from the old to the new, could lead to discontinuities and mismatches in the fabric of scientific literature that could be very difficult to remedy, if allowed to fester.

In the US, the learned societies displayed a variety of responses to the electronic challenges. The ACM (Association for Computing Machinery), a relatively small publisher in terms of number of articles published, was one of the first to come out with a well reasoned "strategy" and position paper on electronic publishing, notably on copyright, submission policies, etc [8]. It declared its intention to have the entire ACM literature in an online digital library, to be stored in original and SGML files, and possibly Postscript, PDF and Lectern format. It will also allow authors to post collections of their works and obtain public comment on early versions of them. The author retains the right to post a personal copy on non-ACM servers for limited non-commercial distribution, provided that the ACM Copyright Notice is attached.

The Institute for Electrical and Electronics Engineers (IEEE[9]) requires the author to clearly mention on the paper or electronic preprint version that the paper has been submitted to the IEEE for publication and that copyright may be transferred without notice and that, in the case of an electronic preprint, "this version may no longer be accessible". When the IEEE publishes the work, the author must replace the previous version of the accepted paper either with 1) the full citation to the IEEE work or 2) the IEEE published version, including the IEEE copyright notice and the full citation.

The American Physical Society (APS) [10] is also developing online distribution systems for its journals. It chose OCLC's Electronic Journals Online System for its flagship journal *Physical Review Letters* as did the American Institute of Physics (AIP) for its *Applied Physics Letters* . Other journals from these two related stables are to follow suit (in terms of number of articles published annually, the AIP and APS combined are not only the world's largest physics publisher but also the second largest overall journal publisher in the world, after Elsevier Science).

Of the commercial journals publishers in the US, Academic Press [11] has recently announced the International Digital Electronic Access Library (IDEAL), in which all its 180 or so journals (published in the US and UK) are published on the World Wide Web as of January 1996, using servers on both sides of the ocean. Academic Press has adopted a deliberate policy to use standard World Wide Web browsers and the ubiquitously available (and mostly free) Adobe Acrobat Reader, to give its subscribers access to journal articles, including full text and graphics, in a form practically identical to the printed pages.

In order to give the maximum number of users access to its material, the Academic Press Print and Electronic Access License (APPEAL) was developed. Under this scheme, consortia of libraries can join up and enjoy limited access to all or a substantial part of the AP program, depending on the initial breadth of coverage of the aggregate members of the consortium in the aggregate. For the initial three years of the license, individual library members are entitled to additional paper subscriptions of journals to which they get electronic access at greatly reduced prices, based on the (not insignificant) marginal costs of supplying these subscriptions. Provided it takes place *within* the consortium, there are no limitations on the use of the material, ie, interlibrary loan (if still needed), course pack use, etc, are allowed.

The philosophy behind this approach is to create a relatively "quiet" period of three years, in which both the consortium and the publisher can experiment freely with value-added services, customized for (groups of) individual end-users. At the same time, demand for such different services can be measured and new charging mechanisms explored. It seems clear that the current paradigm (library pays all and "up front") may have to be replaced by a program of enhanced services designed to meet the needs of the individual end-users, while retaining a basic service paid for by the library.

The first such "consortium license" agreement has been signed with HEFCE (the Higher Education Funding Council for England) and its counterparts in Scotland and Northern Ireland. Other publishers signing a similar deal with HEFCE et al are Blackwell Scientific and the Institute of Physics (UK).

From the publisher's and library's point of view, such an arrangement has the advantage of falling under contract law, not copyright law. Parties enter into it on a voluntary basis and the agreement allows considerably more freedom on the part of the customer. If such an arrangement gains wide acceptance, expensive infrastructural arrangements for interlibrary loan, copying services, etc, can be curtailed to a considerable extent. At the same time, libraries with very limited, but finite demand for high-level scientific information (eg, public libraries) can become members of an appropriate consortium for very limited extra cost. The end result can (and should) be greatly enhanced access for the research worker and a secure (financial) basis for the continuation of the building of the scientific archive.

Born in Groningen, The Netherlands, Pieter Bolman entered publishing in 1972 as physics editor for North Holland Publishing Company (Elsevier Science), of which he became Deputy Managing Director in 1976. After three years in New York, as Vice President of Elsevier/North Holland, he moved back to Amsterdam to become Managing Director of one of the Elsevier Science Divisions. Bolman was Managing Director and Chief Executive Officer of Pergamon Press (Oxford and New York) from 1988 to 1991. He became President of Academic Press (San Diego, Boston and London) in 1992. He holds a PhD in chemical physics from the University of Southampton, UK.

Notes

1. See eg, "The Internet's First Victim?", Forbes , December 18, 1995 issue
2. Science & Engineering Indicators 1993, National Science Board, Washington, DC (Netsite: http:// x.nsf.gov:80/sbe/srs/seind93/main/seitoc93.htm)
3. See description in eg, "Development of Science Publishing in Europe", Ed. A J Meadows, 1980, Elsevier, Amsterdam
4. See eg, "Scientific Communications and Informatics", A I Mikhailov, A I Chernyi and R S Giliarevskii (trans R H Burger), 1984, Information Resources Press, Arlington VA
5. See eg, "Scholarly Journals at the Crossroads: A subversive Proposal for Electronic Publishing" (An Internet Discussion about Scientific and Scholarly Journals and their Future), Eds. A Shumelda Okerson and J J O'Donnell, 1995, Office of Scientific & Academic Publishing, Association of Research Libraries
6. "Faust", J W von Goethe, various editions: Netsite: gopher://gopher.vt.edu: 10010/02/89/1
7. APS News, January 1996 edition
8. The ACM Publishing Plan, P J Denning and B Rous, available from ACM, New York and at Netsite: http://www.acm.org
9. The Institute for Electrical and Electronics Engineers, Inc, Netsite: http://www.ieee.org
10. APS Netsite: http://www.aps.org
11. Academic Press Netsites: http://www.apnet.com, http://www.hbuk.co.uk/ap/, http://www.idealibrary.com/

14

The US College Textbook:
A Learning Tool without Rival
If Values Are Maintained

Robert R Worth

The 1990s have not been the best of times for college textbook publishers in the United States. Why that is so, and what might be done about it, are questions I would like to discuss in the course of describing some of the privileges, peculiarities and peccadilloes of our particular brand of publishing. My perspective is that of someone who is grateful for, and takes pride in, having been a publisher of introductory textbooks for undergraduates.

The conventional image of textbooks as boring, leaden, opaque, etc, has a long history, during most of which time it has probably been deserved. If we consider only the mission of the introductory textbook, however – not how successfully it's been fulfilled – it is, without question, an extraordinarily ambitious one: to present the basics of an entire academic discipline in an order, scope and depth that satisfies experts in the field and in a manner that has the potential to spark the intellectual curiosity of someone who may not have any special aptitude for, or preconceived interest in, the subject matter. What's more, in the absence of a nationally accepted syllabus, introductory textbooks define to a great extent what sociology or economics or botany *is* – that is to say, they set, for a time, the paradigm. It's clearly an important pursuit and a challenging responsibility to publish such books.

How successfully have we met this challenge? I believe that many recent college graduates will admit, if bullied, to having encountered as undergraduates one or two textbooks that succeeded in firing their imaginations and enriching their minds. The unheralded truth, in fact, is that the period from about 1950 to 1990 was one of vast improvements in American college textbooks. There are now quite a few that are truly masterful expositions – engagingly written, logically organized, encompassing an extraordinary range of information and knowledge, building incrementally from *tabula rasa* to considerable sophistication, imaginatively illustrated and beautifully designed. The fine textbooks that existed before this were much rarer, pitched to a fairly sophisticated audience, and invariably owed their distinction to exceptional authors, such as William James.

College textbook publishers deserve some of the credit for this flowering, of course, but conditions were so propitious that we might not have been able to prevent it had we tried. (This praise is grudging because so many copy-cat, pedestrian textbooks were also published during these bountiful years.) Over most of this time, college enrollments were expanding rapidly, not only due to the post-World War II baby boom, but also the growing percentage of the population seeking higher education at junior colleges, colleges and universities – soaring from 1.4 to 14 million students in less than fifty years. (In 1950, less than 10% of Americans went to college; now, almost 60% do.) Technological leaps were being made in printing, binding and in paper manufacture, enabling much better reproduction of type and photographs, color as well as black and white, on far thinner paper. Graphic designers of distinction, like Malcolm Grear, were repealing the conventional image of textbooks as bland and dreary, and creating pages with enormous appeal. There was no competition from foreign publishers for the large US and Canadian markets. And, in the '50s and '60s, pioneers like Gordon Graham were opening up to American textbooks English-language markets in India and other countries previously dominated by British publishers. With colleges and universities flourishing in this large, youth-oriented and increasingly affluent country, and with college professors industriously expanding the horizons of their disciplines and inventing new and better ways to teach them, what more could we have asked for?

The last five years have been much more difficult. Consider some current market dynamics:

- College enrollments in the US have leveled off. There are now about 15 million students in US colleges, 12.6 million undergraduates. Although enrollment growth is predicted to pick up by the turn of the century, the total is not forecast to reach 16 million until about 2005.
- The number of college textbooks sold by publishers (not counting, that is to say, the sale of used books) has diminished (or risen only slightly) each year; and price increases well in excess of inflation have been essential (and sometimes insufficient) to cover rising costs in a flat market. Total US college textbook sales are roughly $2.5 bn – about 93.5% to the domestic market, 6.5% foreign. A recent study reports that the annual growth rate of spending on college textbooks from 1989 to 1994 was 3.4%. As inflation for those years averaged about 3.9%, the "growth" cited is really contraction. And these figures are in dollars, where annual price increases mask the decline in numbers of copies sold. (Between 1980 and 1992, the American Association of Higher Education reports, textbook prices increased 250% compared to a 70% increase in the Consumer Price Index.) The same study predicts that the annual growth rate of spending on college textbooks from 1994 to 1999 will be 3.5%, far less than the yearly growth projected for adult trade publishing (10%) or for book publishing at large (6.9%).
- Used book sales continue to grow at a faster rate than the sale of new books and now exceed in dollars a fourth of the sales by publishers. As James Lichtenberg of the Association of American Publishers pointed out in a 1992 article: The used-book marketplace, with its active on-campus promotion of used books and of textbook buy-backs from students, reinforces the attitude that textbooks are simply utilitarian commodities to be purchased only when absolutely essential to passing the course, as cheaply as possible, and sold back as soon as the course is completed. College bookstores now buy used books first and turn to the publisher only as supplier of last resort.
- "Price resistance" – by which publishers refer to all the ways students manage to get through a course without buying the textbook (by relying exclusively on used books, by sharing one copy among several students, by using library copies, by photocopying, etc) – is on the rise. Introductory textbooks range in price from $40.00 to

$75.00. While publishers point out that students get an awful lot of book for that price (typically 800 to 1,400 large-format pages full of attractive color graphics and photographs), young people acculturated to instant gratification and lacking the mind set for serious reading may fail to see the value of tomes 9 1/4 by 11 by 1 3/8 inches in size weighing four to five pounds. It is not until their freshman year in college that they have ever had to buy a textbook, as high school texts are provided to students without charge in the US.

- Returns inch ever higher as a percentage of sales. They are now about 22% of dollar volume. College bookstores are ordering fewer books than previously in comparison to enrollment size and then finding themselves obliged to return more of them to the publisher.

As if all this weren't enough, larger publishers have been gobbling up smaller ones, until now the seven largest college textbook publishers account for roughly two-thirds of the industry's sales. It is hard to understand the rationale for some of these acquisitions. Presumably acquirers believe they can downsize staffs and facilities without diminishing revenues. Except for the rare instance when there is no overlap in lists, however – a science publisher acquiring a humanities publisher, for example – there is bound to be some sales fallout. How many directly competing textbooks can a unified sales staff effectively promote? Although there may be some advantages of scale with regard to finance and distribution, and even in sales, no such advantages are evident for the editorial aspects of publishing. Book publishing companies are a lot like restaurants, in my view: The cuisine is likely to suffer if they get too big.

Perhaps most troublesome of all, there have been almost no new college textbook publishing companies founded since the late '60s. Is there another sector of the economy in which, during a twenty-five year period of growth, there have been so few successful start-ups? Is there a message here?

The US has always been a country that places enormous value on education. To send a child to a four-year private college now costs parents about $100,000. In recent years, however, there has been much wringing of hands about the wretched state of primary and secondary education. By some measures, only a third of current US high school graduates have achieved a twelfth grade reading level. Some of this dissatisfaction and insistence upon "accountability" is now turning to colleges, with their continually rising tuitions and tales of graduates lacking basic skills. The response of state and federal governments has been punitive: massive annual cuts in school and college budgets and in student loans. Much of the support for privatizing schools and relying more on technology to do the teaching is driven by such cost-cutting considerations. Whether this is the beginning of a sea change in our society's love affair with education is still in doubt, but it's worrisome.

Finally, there are the anxieties posed by the electronic wonders so widely touted to be changing our world forever – multimedia, the Internet, the virtual university. A college president speaks glowingly about providing a "technology-mediated model of customized learning experiences". Academics enamored with the new technologies rail against "the tyranny of the textbook". In *Science* last October, Professor Eli M Noam of Columbia University persuasively questions, in "Electronics and the Dim Future of the University", whether the economic foundation of the present system of higher education can be maintained. (He points out that tuition fees at private universities are nearly $50.00 per lecture hour per student.) It's not hard to imagine a 2-pound, 7-by-10-by-1-inch slate with a comfortable handle for portability and a durable fold-out screen, into which libraries of reference works, maps, movies, paintings and recordings have been loaded, with more continually available on disks or on the Internet, from which high-fidelity sound issues, on the screen of which are displayed high-resolution text and full-color graphics and, via modem, rapid feedback from tutors, and with which one can interact via a keyboard and by voice. The world at one's fingertips, but textbooks, as we know them, in the dustbin of history!

Beleaguered and confused by all of this, we publishers seem to have (with some justification!) lost our bearings – to have forgotten, in our apprehension about what comes next, the importance of what we are doing. It is said that the curse of journalists is to be dazzled by ephemera while verities go unseen. We may have contracted the same disease. Perhaps, by taking a tour through contemporary college publishing, we might be better able to discern what is valuable and important about what we do. For, to be really pessimistic about the future of textbooks (whatever their mode of delivery), one has, it seems to me, to be pessimistic about our society's continued adherence to classic liberal values, or even about the future of literacy.

* * * * *

The greatest pleasure of college textbook publishing, for me, has been that quality is almost always rewarded – the sometimes subtle factors that distinguished a very good textbook from an ordinary one are discerned by a sufficient number of conscientious and discriminating professors that it has always paid to publish better books. (By "better" I don't mean more inclusive or rigorous, but simply more appropriate and effective for the audience intended.) In my darker moods, I worry that this is becoming less true, but in fact the proportion of good books to bad, if it has shifted at all in recent years, probably has done so for the better. What *is* remarkable is how often the leading textbooks in a discipline are the 5th, or the 12th, edition of a book that was first published in the '60s or '70s. Although this underscores what a rare thing a book that works well for students and teachers is, so much conservatism has also riveted authors' and publishers' attention on competing against the successful models, with the result that we bring out look-alike books, which, in turn, increases professors' temptation to take textbooks for granted.

From an outsider's point of view, the most suspect feature of US college textbook publishing is the frantic revision cycle of successful texts. "Is it really true," I've been asked, "that publishers bring out a new edition every three or four years simply in order to circumvent the used book market in textbooks? Isn't that extremely artificial and wasteful? Surely the basics of a subject such as calculus, say, don't change enough to warrant continuous new editions." Such criticisms don't take sufficient account of the modern compulsion for being up-to-date. How many times have I heard the lament: "Your introductory sociology text by Ian Robertson is far and away the best book available, but if a new edition doesn't come out soon, I'll just have to stop using it." A professor using a 1989 textbook in 1996 is thought hopelessly out-of-it. Even if the used book market didn't exist, the innovative publisher who significantly revised successful textbooks every few years would soon capture the lion's share of the business. Although the calculus may not change, ways of teaching it do. New technologies like the hand-held graphing calculator provide exciting new opportunities for learning, and textbooks must be quick to adapt to them. It is the pressure to come up with significant improvements in each edition that has catalyzed many of the advances in textbooks.

This great churning of editions certainly has its sick side: It is driven primarily by the need to kill off used books, and it can burn out authors and breed ennui in editors and sales people, but it is also a reflection of one of the healthiest aspects of our business: its fierce competitiveness, which drives us to provide professors and their students with ever better teaching packages. This very competitiveness, however, is also the source of one of our peskiest current problems: the escalation of money spent on giveaways.

Textbooks are purchased from publishers by college bookstores and sold by the bookstores to students, who usually send the bill to their parents. The publishers' marketing effort is directed, however, not to the eventual purchaser but to the college professor who decides which textbook to adopt. This system usually works well when limited to the choice of a textbook. But when the selection process is confused by the consideration of additional inducements that teachers may find of interest but that may not enhance the student's experience, it becomes more problematic.

We supply teachers, for instance, with fat, three-ring notebooks filled with all sorts of resources for teaching each topic, with overhead transparencies for lecture illustrations (which can cost the publisher as much as $100,000 per edition for a successful textbook), with test banks (primarily multiple-choice questions, dozens per text chapter) available in print and on computer disks (separate sets for IBM and Macintosh computers – another costly item), with solution manuals that contain step-by-step solutions for all the end-of-chapter problems in the textbook, with sets of computer disks for class demonstrations or labs (again, necessarily available for both IBM and Mac), sometimes with videos (a recent example contains forty-two segments lasting over seven hours) and/or a videodisk for class presentations, with software for student projects ... the list is endless and growing longer, as publishers attempt to outdo each other. Most of the value of this vast investment in giveaways – intended primarily to persuade faculty to choose one text over another – is invisible to the end purchaser, the student. Publishers are left with inflated faculty expectations on the one hand and price resistance among students on the other. Perhaps the only escape from this bind will come when the current crunch on publishers' profits renders us unable to make available the latest teaching timesaver or resource, but I fear that market forces will first tempt us into cutting back on the quality of our offerings rather than their quantity. At some point, we are going to have to draw a line based on what is best for the student.

Could it be that our priorities need to be re-examined? Why, despite all this competition, *are* there so many indifferent textbooks? With the investment (the plant cost) required to publish a basic text and its ancillaries ("the package") mounting to the million dollar mark – not including the cost of the paper, printing and binding needed to manufacture an inventory of the book – you would think that a manuscript would have to be awfully good to earn the publisher's OK, that no decision would be more worthy of the publisher's time and attention. Instead, the sieve seems fairly coarse. Why? I believe there is something in the culture of US college textbook publishing that prompts us to take our eye off the ball.

*   *   *   *   *

Let's first consider the people, starting with those employed in the business: editors, managers, sales people, and then go on to authors and, finally, manuscripts.

We have to do a better job of attracting first-rate people to college publishing, of training them to know what is expected of them rather than letting them sink or swim, of holding them to a high standard, and of honoring and rewarding them adequately once they've proven themselves. (Not having given enough attention to these things is one of the mea culpas that have hounded me in retirement.) At a time of cost and staff cutting and depleted morale, that may seem a crazy recommendation, but jobs in the overall economy are scarce and we have a persuasive and powerful story to tell. At its best, a college textbook is the most effective tool available for imparting knowledge, broadening minds and instilling culture. The rare human beings who can write an outstanding college textbook are (*almost* always!) a delight to work with, as are a great many of the faculty one meets in selling textbooks to them. Publishers of college textbooks can play a far more significant role in creating and "perfecting" the final product, and can thus take more pride in its success than can, for example, successful trade book publishers. The excitement among young people about new media should help us to bring some of the brightest into the business. As someone who happened into college publishing purely by good fortune, and has thanked his lucky stars ever since, I feel sure we could do a much better job of recruiting good people.

Do we use our employees appropriately once we have them? I'm not sure we do. Take developmental editors, for example. College textbook publishers provide their authors with a lot of editorial help, but primarily in the form of reviews. Developmental editors (as we call the editors assigned to assist authors with the manuscript) are rarely asked to do the extensive editorial work that most introductory college textbook authors must have if they are to elevate their manuscript out of the "also-ran"category. It is, for one thing, expensive in time and money, and it's hard to tell whether you are throwing good money after bad, vainly trying to make a silk purse out of a sow's ear. Editors with a talent for this kind of work are rare, and the more such help an author needs, the less likely it is that he or she will have the objectivity and self-confidence to acknowledge that need and be willing to share in the expense of it. More and more, managers are trying to make ends meet by turning for such services to free lance editors. Because most managers are not aware on a firsthand basis of the manuscript's shortcomings, they are unlikely to take kindly to editors who tell them that a schedule cannot be met or blow the whistle on incompetent or uncooperative authors. The upshot is that, comes the crunch, developmental editors – whether on staff or free lance – are likely to be considered expendable. Development is shortchanged and the books come out half-baked.

There is an additional wrinkle to this story. An odd culture has long been in place among the managers of college publishing houses: that of not reading manuscripts and not taking a lively interest in the subjects about which they are written. Thus the work done by developmental editors is undervalued and the need for that work to be done is underappreciated. Most managers have had sales and editorial experience by the time they reach the top. Do they therefore appreciate and take advantage of their great good luck in being able to discuss with their editors and with the best expositors of the day the latest findings and controversies in sociology, psychology, physics, economics, etc? Sad to say, many do not. What a letdown for authors truly committed

to their subject! No wonder such managers fail to themselves appreciate or to inspire their employees with the potential and the importance
of our calling.

The morale of a company depends to a great extent on its sales representatives – college travelers. Wheras the soul of the firm may be in
its editorial staff, its spirit is in the sales staff. If the sales people don't
take pride in the unique attributes and quality of the books they are
selling, their voices will simply add to the pressure for books that conform to the bestsellers, for more giveaways, for more of anything that
garners sales. If these eyes and ears of the company aren't vigilant
about what's happening on campus – not just scouting for manuscripts,
but reporting, for example, how faculties are making use of the World
Wide Web and the other multimedia technologies – the publisher could
quickly fall behind the times. Nothing is more important to success in
college publishing than a highly motivated, literate and experienced
staff of sales reps. And yet this is an area where publishers are going
to have to find less expensive ways of reaching and influencing professors. It has simply become too costly to keep a large field staff traveling to college campuses throughout the US and Canada. Smaller,
more experienced staffs of the ablest travelers – with their reach
enhanced, perhaps, by multimedia – would seem the best of the available options.

Next, the authors. The greatest challenge in our business is finding
those rare teacher/writers who have the enormous strength of ego, per-
severance, empathy, scholarship and intelligence it takes to write a successful college textbook. The exponential growth of many branches of
scholarship, particularly in science (doubling every ten to fifteen
years), has obliged college professors to become ever more narrowly
specialized. The demands on their time also seem to grow exponentially. Writing a textbook is not – in most colleges (there are some
happy exceptions) – considered serious academic work for purposes of
promotion and tenure, and there is jealousy toward successful textbook
authors. Because the paragons who can surmount such obstacles are so
rare, publishers are continually tempted to lower our standards, to hope
against hope that someone who isn't keenly interested in the potential
of young people, or doesn't really have anything fresh or original to
say, or isn't highly respected by colleagues, or whose sample chapters
were only so-so, etc, will rise to the occasion. Every publisher has to

take a few such gambles; the risks, after all, are part of the fun – and some of them pay off handsomely.

As someone who has too often given in to such pressures, however, I can only advise others to be more obdurate. While the pleasures of working with rational, competent authors are great, on the reverse side of the coin are the expensive and emotionally wrenching disappointments with authors under contract who haven't got what it takes. If we're lucky, we discover this quickly. If not, there is hell to pay, more of it the longer we put off facing up to the awful truth. And more often than you would think (for reasons I'll get into later), we do our company and the author the injustice of publishing the book, only to see it fail. No matter how author-oriented a publishing company prides itself in being, it is the manuscript that counts. We do authors no favor by acceding to their pleas and imprecations and publishing a mediocre book.

There is, on the other hand, nothing more rewarding than the author-publisher partnership when you have a basic textbook author who is up to the job. Listen to a successful author explaining what motivates him: "To present our discipline to the next generation, to convey the power of its ideas, to help students think more critically, to gain insight into the phenomena of their everyday lives, to sense the extraordinary wonders beneath seemingly ordinary processes – such aims make our work intrinsically worth doing." To have a hand in that noble undertaking is our enviable lot as textbook publishers.

Creating a basic textbook is truly a partnership from start to finish. Such a book isn't its author's personal achievement in the same way a novel or a poem is. Although it is the author's vision that must guide the effort and the author's words that make the book lucid or pedestrian, what is being built is an educational tool. Making sure there are no important concepts missing, no errors, no unclear statements; that every point which can be better made or enhanced with a photo or graphic is; that every end-of-chapter problem is unambiguous and the solution provided correct; that the design of the page, of the book, of the cover has just the right mix of aesthetic appeal and authoritativeness – these are the publisher's responsibilities as well as the author's. In recent years, the publisher's share of the load has had to increase as the demands on faculty time – particularly getting funded, but also supervising graduate students, running labs, teaching, doing committee work, etc – have burgeoned. Add to this the fact that if the text isn't accompanied on publication by a cornucopia of supplements at least as good as the competition's, it will not be widely used; and this is primarily the publisher's responsibility.

Next, there's the raw material: the manuscript (one hopes not so raw). Textbook manuscripts should be held to a higher standard than they are, and this means they should be judged guilty until proven innocent, not just by favorable reviews, but by the reading of at least a few chapters by *all* of the company's responsible decision makers. Most publishers, however, allow the crucial acceptance of the manuscript for publication to be based primarily on reviews, together with the advice of the acquisition, editorial and sales managers, some of whom are also unlikely to have read the manuscript. (Some consider it nothing short of arrogance to rely upon one's own judgment in such a matter, particularly when that judgment runs counter to the consensus of reviews.) The reviews are written by college professors who teach the course or are experts in some aspect of the subject matter of the manuscript. First rate reviewers are almost as rare as superb authors, but most college professors are conscientious about constructively criticizing any manuscript they agree to review. This process of the author's peers extensively reviewing all aspects of the manuscript is at the heart of editorial development. But to take the next step and base the publishing decision almost exclusively on the appraisals of these third parties seems to me a great mistake. It is, however, the way things are usually done. Intelligent and successful people who wouldn't purchase a $15,000 automobile without test driving it will commit their companies to a $1m investment based primarily on the recommendation of people who have no stake in the outcome! I believe that no manager should consider letting a basic book into production without reading at least a few chapters of it. The people who have made it to the top in our industry don't lack the ability to do this; they just lack the self-confidence and the belief that it would make a difference. I am certain that it would.

Not paying enough attention to recruiting the ablest people into our business, not always honoring their importance or making the best use of them once they've proven their worth, not holding our authors and their manuscripts to the highest standards, not trusting our own judgment in evaluating manuscripts, not always treating our calling or our products with the respect they are due – these are the ways in which I and my confreres have too often let down our side; and these practices are partly responsible for the existence of too many also-ran textbooks. But the main culprit, in my estimation, is the gigantic moment of inertia that often builds around a project. There are so few authors willing and able to undertake the life's work – for that's what it is – of writing a successful introductory textbook and revising it every three or four years. Once you have, with high hopes, signed someone who you pray can do the job; once you have spent years and tens of thousands of dollars developing the manuscript; once the long-expected book is a significant factor in the year-after-next's sales budget; etc; it becomes exceedingly difficult for any one manager to face up to the fact that the manuscript, even with all the work that has gone into it, still isn't good enough. That is why the reading of a few chapters of the manuscript plus the reviews, and looking through a few competing texts, and only then coming to a publishing decision, should be carried out by a *group* of editors and decision makers for a project of any size – with a budget of over half a million dollars, say.

Textbooks are educational tools, and no tool can incite intellectual curiosity or inculcate critical thinking skills or instill a love for learning the way a gifted teacher can. Personal contacts with mentors, role models, teachers and other students are essential catalysts to an inquiring mind. But most of what students actually learn from most undergraduate survey courses is obtained – not from videos, not from innovative computer software, not from CD-ROMs (which, as textbook replacements, have thus far been a lead balloon), not even from the lecturer or the class instructor, but from the textbook. In a 1992 survey, college students said that as much as 55% of the "knowledge" they received in college courses came from textbooks. A 1994 survey of 5,000 randomly selected professors found that 81% agreed that textbooks are "critical to students' success". Rather than being expensive, textbooks are, if judged by the value provided, or by comparison to the costs of tuition, a great bargain. Undoubtedly forty years in the business have brainwashed me, but I believe that college textbooks are woefully underrated – by students, by professors and, most tellingly and ironically, by textbook publishers. It is we who have allowed college professors to take our books for granted.

How many college professors start off their courses by telling the class: "There were many textbooks available to choose from in giving this course, and I spent a few days last spring evaluating them in order to provide you with the best choice. I hope you will be pleased, but I welcome your feedback. It is you, after all, who can best judge whether this is a book that excites your interest in the subject and is relatively easy to learn from. I know that the author would be glad to have your and my appraisals of the book and suggestions for its improvement, at the end of the course. Now let me tell you something about the author and about the book's special features, and suggest how I would go about using this book and its study guide if I were taking the course." Some teachers do take this approach, knowing that if their students begin to read the textbook with interest and respect they are much more likely to derive full value from it and do well in the course. But others choose to enhance their own charisma by regarding the textbook with indifference, or even with disdain, thus treating what could be their greatest ally – in bringing the intellectual excitement of their discipline to their students – as either a rival or a necessary evil. We publishers could do a much better job of helping college teachers to see how self-defeating this is. To its great credit, the Higher Education Division of the AAP is now addressing this problem.

To make our case effectively, however, we have to realize ourselves how important textbooks are and how enduring they will be. We have allowed all the excitement about multimedia and the Web to weaken our confidence in the efficacy of the textbook as a device for learning. These challenges should prompt us to raise our standards, not to model our offerings on the current market leader but to go beyond it. Market research will always tell us, if we let it, to "do likewise" and copy the leader. We've got to go deeper, to find out the whys of its success and devise better ways to satisfy those requirements.

"Content is king," according to current jargon. What publishers do best, electronic apostles claim, is to add value to that content in meaningful, "contextual" and appealing ways. These are scarcely new perceptions for college publishers – rather an opportunity and an invitation to do better what we have always done. So far, *as a tool for learning the sciences and social sciences, the textbook has no rival.* Someday, something electronic may well challenge the textbook, but for now the new baubles in the bathwater should not divert our attention from the baby. Even if the hard copy textbook does give way in the 21st century to an electronic successor, that learning device will still be a textbook, in essence. It will still have to be read, it will still have to be written and reviewed and edited and illustrated and designed. Authors and publishers will still have a role to play.

Just as textbooks are not rivals or necessary evils to teachers, multi-media may well be publishers' greatest ally in removing the curse of familiarity from our products and in bringing the excitement of learning to tomorrow's students. At least that's how it will be if we hold our textbooks to a higher standard and do a much better job of conveying their true value to professors and students.

A Cautionary Tale

The story of how college publishers meandered into the sorry practice of bribing college professors to adopt their books shows how fine a line separates legitimate from illegitimate sales tactics – so fine, in fact, that a few publishers profess not to see it.

As I've mentioned, it has long been the custom to provide professors not only with a complimentary copy of the textbook but also with free ancillaries that complement the text and facilitate its use. These supplements are prepared by the publisher specifically for the textbook.

In the late '60s, a short-lived California publisher by the name CRM arrived on the scene with the creative idea of producing films to go along with its new introductory psychology textbook. The book took the market by storm, selling 160,000 copies in its first year, primarily due to the offer of complementary films (but also because there were good psychologists connected with the project and it was the first introductory psychology textbook to be printed in full color). Other publishers were caught flatfooted, having no films to offer. In a panic, some of them made arrangements with film libraries, like the one at Indiana University, to rent films for use in courses where their book was adopted.

Note that unwittingly an ethical boundary had been crossed: Instead of preparing and providing a product intended to enhance the experience of those using its textbook, the publisher was buying in the open market a product not originally designed for use with its, or anyone else's, textbook. Almost immediately, the inevitable happened.

Psychology departments with plenty of films available, or with no interest in films, asked to be provided with the same amount of money the publisher was willing to spend on film rentals for some other educational purpose, say a new IBM typewriter for the department secretary. So money began to be exchanged for adoptions. It wasn't long before an enterprising publisher began to offer a $1.00 "rebate" for every textbook sold (only the money went to the department, not back to the student who purchased the book). An even more enterprising publisher raised the ante to $1.50. While only a half dozen or so publishers stooped to these practices, it didn't take an ethicist to see big trouble looming. Under the aegis of the Higher Education Division of the Association of American Publishers, college publishers took the pledge to sin no more. As far as "rebates" go, that pledge seems to have held , but bribes still occur in the form of pieces of equipment (currently videodisk players) or other incentives, such as "America Online" or *Wall Street Journal* subscriptions. And the Higher Education Division has decided not to try again to play policeman. (Film supplements *were* a great idea from a marketing point of view, but a disastrous one financially, which is why CRM is no longer with us and no other publisher has started up film production.)

So it seems that a minority of publishers will continue to clutch for immediate gain despite the doleful long-term effects on the integrity of our business and the quality of our books. (Why spend money on the development of the manuscript when with far less money you can buy the adoption?)

This tawdry saga is indicative of the ways in which publishers sometimes demean their products and their calling, and a few professors shortchange their students by looking for "deals" rather than for the best textbook.

Starting his career as a college traveler with the McGraw-Hill Book Company in 1956, Bob Worth has spent forty years in college textbook publishing. After a period of editorship at McGraw-Hill, he joined Bill Benjamin in 1960 just as W A Benjamin Inc was being launched. In 1966, together with Walter Meagher and Neil Patterson, he founded Worth Publishers, Inc, from which he retired in September 1995.

15

The American University Library:
Embattled by Economics and Technology

Hendrik Edelman

Are the book collections in American university libraries becoming white elephants in the virtual information environment? Many in the profession like to predict so. On some campuses it appears to be becoming a self-fulfilling prophecy, as the need for further expansion of library space is being questioned. If the last years of the 20th century were indeed to see the beginning of a shift away from the book as the central resource of America's university libraries, they would have had a shortish history, for it was only in the latter part of the 19th century that libraries began to play an important role in their institutions. Prior to that time, library collections consisted largely of uncoordinated gifts – albeit sometimes very valuable – which were accessible only to faculty and students on a very limited basis.

The basic service patterns that are still the tools of the university library trade were developed under the leadership of Justin Winsor and Melvil Dewey: systematic current and retrospective collection development; standardized cataloging and classification; the dictionary catalog; reference service; and building design conducive to study and research. Remarkably in a nation of great distances and competitive higher education systems, a national interlibrary loan was established early on.

The collection development concepts were initially patterned after

German models. The great corpus of knowledge, documented since the 17th century and embedded in the annals, proceedings and other publications of national and regional scientific academies of the Western world, had to be made available to local scholars. In addition, extensive scholarly book collections were acquired, often by private purchase. Extensive bibliographical apparatus, substituting, in many cases, for real holdings, complemented book, series and periodical collections.

A unique feature of these early days was Winsor's call to Harvard alumni to donate American imprints to their university library. Such locally produced books and pamphlets had hitherto been collected only by historical societies. Library collection development was made a high priority both by the newly established universities and the older ones which had established new graduate programs. There was much competition for collections. As early as 1910, worries about extensive duplicate holdings began to be heard among academic administrators.

Needless to say, most of the materials had to be procured from Europe. A well-organized export book trade developed and flourished in the UK, Holland, Germany, France and Italy. Dealers such as Martinus Nijhoff in Holland and Otto Harrassowitz and Gustav Fock in Germany, who had previously concentrated on the antiquarian book trade, established agencies for new books and periodical subscriptions. The need to monitor the current book and periodical production became more and more apparent and resulted in the establishment of specialized acquisitions and serials departments in university libraries. Annual budgets became standard – as did the debate on how to allocate funds to different departments.

By the time of World War I, American scholarship and science were firmly established. Virtually all academic disciplines were represented as university departments, as scholarly associations and by major periodicals. American universities began to compete internationally, and their library collections were by now good enough to attract scholars from around the world.

After the first World War, financial support for higher education lagged. The continuing rapid growth of the production of scholarly and scientific publications, notably in Germany, strained acquisitions budgets in US universities. That was the time when American university libraries first began to protest against the proliferation and high cost of

European periodicals. While some of the better endowed institutions were able to keep up with the new production, and to continue to develop their retrospective collections, most began to suffer. The acquisition of foreign-language material declined sharply, especially after the stockmarket crash of 1929. Calls for more national coordination in the acquisition process went unheeded.

It was only in 1941, when the effort to mobilize resources for World War II began, that it was recognized that American libraries had failed to acquire the necessary European materials, particularly in the sciences. The academic library community rallied, and soon a large number of major German standard works and periodicals were being reprinted by subscription. An ambitious plan to overcome the collection gaps after the war through a coordinated foreign acquisitions plan, called the Farmington Plan, was initiated.

*   *   *   *   *

The end of World War II saw not only a massive infusion of undergraduate students under the GI Bill of Rights, but also the enrichment of the library profession by the entrance of many highly qualified and motivated veterans. Established universities added many new programs and capacities. Existing institutions such as Southern Illinois and Michigan State were upgraded, and brand new universities in several states, such as California, New York and Florida, were established.

The deficiencies of the '30s and early '40s, combined with the needs of newly started libraries, led to a demand for older materials that could not be supplied by the antiquarian book and periodical trade, either in the US or in Europe. The market's response was quick and efficient. Using the experience gained during World War II in reprinting German books and periodicals in relatively small numbers, entrepreneurs began to reprint standard books and journals from the US, the UK and Europe. Initially issued on paper, many of these titles also were produced in a variety of microforms. Ultimately, whole collections were reproduced in microform to satisfy the bibliographical needs of new and expanding college and university libraries.

This catch-up on the past coincided with the remarkable rise in scientific research and the explosion of new research literature in the post-war Western world. New books, book series and conference proceedings were published in all major disciplines. New disciplines emerged with their own publications. Sub-specializations engendered new journals. The traditional society-based publishing structure was augmented by enterprising commercial publishers, who transposed the old German publishing model of systematic subject coverage into an international English-language model. Library acquisition budgets kept pace with these developments. Book and serial vendors, especially in Europe, happily rode the waves of a fast-growing US market.

University library collections also benefited from the establishment of so-called area programs in research universities. With funds from the US government (obviously much of it from the Department of Defense) and private foundations, new academic programs directed at cultures of Asia, Africa, Latin America and Eastern Europe came into being. New acquisition techniques had to be developed. New linguistic capabilities had to be attracted for processing and cataloging. Even fumigators had to be installed to cope with the masses of materials imported from all parts of the world.

Following the model established by the Farmington Plan and with leadership from the Library of Congress, arrangements were made with foreign booksellers for blanket orders to provide systematic coverage of new publications from each country or region. Often books were bound and cataloged in foreign countries before shipment.

The acquisitions process in the US also became more systematized. Oregon bookseller Richard Abel translated the European service model into an American one, establishing subject-based approval programs for academic libraries. His programs were ultimately adopted by most of the US book trade. The use of computers greatly enhanced the service capabilities of book and periodical dealers.

To cope with the dramatic rise in worldwide acquisitions, subject bibliographers were now appointed. The coordination of the development of collections (a term introduced in the early '60s) became the responsibility of especially assigned assistant or associated university librarians. Faculty input, in most cases, had now become advisory.

In addition, departments of special collections were strengthened or established. The acquisition of special subject collections and older material required different housing, different cataloging and different service modes. These departments increasingly also took charge of growing archival and manuscript collections.

*   *   *   *   *

This unprecedented period of collection growth came to an end in 1969. The last of the nation's new universities and colleges had been built. Enrolments were no longer growing. The number of PhD degrees declined. Amidst the social and political turmoil of the late '60s in most university campuses, library acquisition budgets ceased to be "untouchable". The publishing industry was slow to notice this and kept up its growing pace. But when President Richard Nixon devalued the US dollar in 1971, the gap between collection development ambitions and actual purchasing power became real and painfully visible. Book and periodical acquisitions became internal competitors, and the first of what were to be many rounds of systematic periodical subscription cancellations took place.

Not surprisingly, the academic library profession reacted. A group of collection development librarians of large research libraries convened in 1971 to discuss their common agenda. As a result, the much-heralded, but never really functioning, Farmington Plan received its coup de grace. An attempt to inventory and compare the nation's major research library holdings through common shelf-list measurements was initiated. Ultimately, this led to the now well-established National Collections Inventory Project, which uses a sophisticated common reporting and evaluating scheme known as the Conspectus method.

Another result of those early meetings was the development of a series of guidelines for the articulation and implementation of collection development and evaluation policies and procedures. Published under the aegis of the American Library Association, these standardized tools have had a considerable impact on the rapidly increasing professionalization of collection development.

While 1969 marked the end of a powerful collection development era, it also marked the start of a new era: collection management. In that same year, the Library of Congress launched its MARC (Machine-Readable Cataloging) Project. As bibliographical data began to be supplied in electronic formats, university libraries were quick to accelerate their fledgling automation programs. At first mainly local, then

regional, and ultimately national and international, bibliographical networks facilitated the sharing of holdings data in a standardized language. One of the basic requirements of resource sharing began to be
fulfilled: access by libraries to each other's bibliographic information.

Inevitably, this increased standardization in procedures led to
renewed expectations of budget relief as a result of coordinated development among research libraries. With much public fanfare, the university libraries of Harvard, Yale and Columbia, together with the New
York Public Library, announced the formation of their Research
Library Group (RLG) in 1974. While the reality was far from the
rhetoric, the publishing industry, already jittery about the proliferation
of copying machines in libraries, saw this cooperation as the beginning
of an organized attempt to erode their markets.

This marked the beginning of a long and protracted battle between
publishers and academic librarians. While largely based on miscon-
ceptions and lack of information, acrimonious relationships surfaced
during copyright discussions and contributed to the demise of a
planned cooperative venture, the National Periodical Center.
Librarians, with their back against the budget wall and facing continued increased journal production and ever rising prices, tried to depict
publishers as the source of their woes. Even today, some twenty-five
years later, some academic librarians continue to call for the "libera-
tion" of scholarly and scientific information from commercial influ-
ences.

*   *   *   *   *

The erosion of the buying power of university libraries has continued, however. Not only have budgets not kept pace with increased
book production and inflation, internal pressures such as automation
costs have begun to compete with acquisition dollars. Initially, the cost
of subscriptions forced a decline in book purchases. One cancellation
round succeeded another – of duplicates, of foreign-language materials and of expensive sub-specialty journals – but were never enough to
regain balanced budgets. In most recent years, the advent of very costly, but high profile, reference tools in digital formats has forced further
reallocations.

With a few notable exceptions, most university libraries have de
facto abdicated their long-standing goal of supplying their clientele

with the books and periodicals they need through local collection development programs. Under the slogan "access versus ownership", resource-sharing and document delivery services are the supposedly attractive alternatives. However, the long-term retrenchment programs and lack of active involvement in collection development matters have alienated faculty members of many campuses, leading to a visible decline in the status and standing of the library and its professionals in the academic community.

Collection management concerns also include the growing awareness of the decline in the physical condition of the stock of America's research libraries. Survey after survey has demonstrated the seriousness of the deterioration caused by high acidity, often poor environmental conditions, heavy use and years of physical neglect. Successful lobbying efforts in Washington and state capitals and private foundations have led to availability of large sums of money to address this issue. Technological and economic problems of mass-deacidification and digitalization have caused serious delays. The lack of a national preservation plan, paralleling the absence of a national collection development plan, often has led to conflicting goals and objectives.

Today, the US academic library community faces more questions than answers, more dilemmas than solutions. The continuing production of books worldwide; the continuing need of faculty and students to consult them; and the professional responsibility to select and preserve for the future – all of these are challenges begging to be resolved. With the rapidly evolving information technologies, a new (or renewed) vision of the future role of the academic library needs to be articulated. The library leadership, especially in the nation's most prominent libraries with their rich historical collections, needs to rise to the occasion.

The current political climate may not be conducive to new initiatives. Nevertheless, to address the proper role of university libraries is a matter of national concern. In the fierce competition for funding, there is need for a united front. It would seem that a new alliance between publishers and academic librarians is essential for the survival and future of our collections.

Professor of Library and Information Studies at Rutgers University, Hendrik Edelman has served as a senior library administrator at

Vanderbilt, Cornell and Rutgers. In the early part of his career, he worked in the Netherlands for Dutch publishers Martinus Nijhoff and D Reidel Publishing Company. Edelman is a frequent consultant to international publishers, booksellers and academic libraries.

16

The Mixed Blessings of Society Publishing

Judy C Holoviak

Learned societies, of which there are more than 3,600 in the United States, have as their primary mission the advancement of the fields of science, literature or the arts, from which their members are drawn. Publishing is part of this mission and will remain so even in this period of rapid change. However, society publications are also shaped by the unique way in which societies are managed, by their not-for-profit status and by various government regulations.

Most US societies own journals associated with their names. A few endorse the journal of a commercial publisher in exchange for a significant voice in the journal's editorial direction. Most of those that publish journals undertake all of the functions of a publishing house – editorial, production and distribution. A few societies buy production and distribution services from university presses or commercial entities, while retaining ownership and editorial control.

The size of society publication operations varies greatly. At the modest end of the scale, there any many one-person, fully volunteer operations. These are at the greatest risk of failure as they try to contend with the increasing pressures on research funding and the challenges of electronic distribution. At the other end of the scale, there are societies publishing more than 100,000 pages annually, employing large professional staffs and operating their own composition and printing equipment. Between these extremes lies every possible variation of size and function.

Although some societies publish books, the majority concentrate on or deal exclusively with journal literature. This focus on the journal is a direct outgrowth of each society's mission; it also complements other society functions. Initially, individual scholars banded together to share the results of their research. From such initial ad hoc assemblages, societies were born. Oral presentations at society meetings soon spawned the need to develop more lasting ways of sharing information. The desire to assure quality and assist colleagues in preserving the best of their work underscored the premium given by society publishers to a solid peer-review system. The membership list easily and naturally became the journal subscription list.

Most society journals started their lives as member benefits. Today, societies employ a wide variety of journal distribution models. Those publishing only one journal, or with a very highly focused membership, are likely to bundle journal subscriptions with dues. On the other hand, societies publishing very large journals, or with memberships characterized by many sub-specialties, sell their journals separately from their dues. These societies are typically more sensitive to the market because each journal subscription is the result of a specific purchasing decision on the part of a member. By the same token, membership in such societies is also subject to market pressures. The decision to become or remain a member of a society is not driven by the desire to obtain a journal, nor is it influenced by the requirement to purchase a journal as part of the dues.

Members of societies in which journal subscriptions are optional receive special member rates. Non-members can be asked to pay from twice to ten times as much as members. Very large scientific journals usually have the largest subscription price spread. The vast bulk of non-member subscriptions are taken out by libraries in which multiple users have access to the information. (For an explanation of the pricing of society journals, see A F Spilhaus, Jr's "The right price: One not-for-profit publisher's perspective" in *Scholarly Communication Around the World: Proceedings of the Fifth Annual Meeting of the Society of Scholarly Publishing* , Washington DC, pp 107-108, 1983.)

In some societies, journal publication is the major source of revenue. In such cases, journal revenue not only recovers the direct and indirect cost of publication, but also provides income for other activities, such as education programs or public outreach. The American Geophysical Union is one such example. Other societies expect their journals to cover only direct costs and all or a portion of attributable overheads. Others subsidize journal publishing with revenues generated by other activities, such as meetings and conferences. A few find themselves in the happy situation of mounting journal programs from endowments, most of which come from well-respected and financially successful members. These various financial models bear no necessary relationship to the size of a society or the field it serves.

The variations in financial models make it extraordinarily difficult to compare publishing operations between societies; and almost impossible to compare society publishing with commercial publishing. Societies receive publication-related income from one or more of the following sources: proration of membership dues, member subscriptions, institutional subscriptions, paid advertisements, page charges, direct grants, gifts or endowments. Few society journals benefit from all these sources. Setting subscription prices thus becomes a delicate balancing act in the context of the net return expected. This can range from a deliberate subsidy (when other society revenues support the journal) to zero (when the journal is expected to support only itself) to a positive number (when the journal helps support other activities).

Societies differ fundamentally from their for-profit counterparts in what they must or may do with income received from publishing. Because they have as their primary mission the cultivation of intellectual goals in the public interest, most seek tax-exempt status and as a consequence receive a number of government benefits. Learned societies in the US have their own special tax classification within the structure of tax-exempt organizations. This classification recognizes the fact that societies complement the government's support for educational, scientific and charitable endeavors. As a quid pro quo, the societies are required to use all of their financial resources for the furtherance of the scholarly fields they serve. Additionally, societies may not use any of their funds to the inurement of any of their members. Commercial publishers by contrast are obliged to serve their shareholders and are expected to generate profits, so there are no legal restrictions on the amount of revenue that they generate and few on the uses they can make of their profits.

The nature of learned societies, however, provides many advantages for their journals. Foremost among these is the immediate call a society has on the loyalty and intellectual talent of the most out-standing individuals in the field it serves. Because the members *are* the society, they are more or less deeply involved in the success of its journals. They tend to develop and even exercise a quasi-ownership posture towards their society's publications. Many members feel an obligation to serve as editors and reviewers. More importantly, they provide advice on ways of improving the journals, never hesitating to make their views known, even when they are not asked. The only dis-advantage of this is that vocal minorities can become too influential in decision-making.

The pricing of society journals is also influenced by their desire to disseminate research as widely as possible. Pricing at rates affordable by individuals (as distinct from institutions) maximizes distribution. Researchers who possess personal copies can refer to them at their convenience. The lowest rates offered by many societies are to stu-dents enrolled in a college or university and actively pursuing their degrees.

Maximum dissemination brings further advantages. Researchers with ready access to society journals turn first to them. In the sciences, citation statistics reveal that society journals are read more than com-mercial journals. Authors seek to publish their best work where their colleagues are most likely to see it. Thus many society journals enjoy a vigorous competition among authors seeking to be published. This competition, together with the high standards expected by member-ships, brings much prestige to society journals. Developing and main-taining reputations for superior quality are primary goals for societies.

Many US scientific societies finance their journals in part through the collection of page charges. These fees usually are not mandatory. Acceptance of an article is never guaranteed by the author's willing-ness to help support publication through the payment of page charges. Some commercial publishers who are associated with societies also enjoy access to this revenue source. Until two years ago, the policies of the National Science Foundation prohibited the use of grant funds to pay charges to journals "operated for profit". That prohibition was lifted over the protests of many scientific societies and some library associations.

Most learned societies also enjoy special postage rates. These rates used to be the subject of congressional whim as part of the annual federal budget process, so that nobody knew what the rate was going to be from year to year. While this political vagary has now been removed, the replacement system is still under development. Societies are still uncertain about the postal rates that they will pay, but they know that over some yet-to-be-specified timescale, the benefit of special rates will be eroded.

Revenue from advertising in society journals is not treated so kindly. Government regulations work against the not-for-profit, tax-exempt publisher, since US law views advertising per se as an unrelated business activity. Not only is income generated from advertising space subject to taxation, but attendant expenses cannot be charged against the income. Thus, a not-for-profit organization is likely to incur a higher rate of tax from this revenue source than does a commercial operation. There have been cases where the tax levied has exceeded the gross income that the advertising sales generated.

*   *   *   *   *

While membership support is a great source of strength in societies, it has some disadvantages. The decision-making process tends to take more time than it would in a commercial environment. Committees review each proposition to make certain that members' opinions are reflected. While such reviews improve the likelihood of acceptance by the ultimate readers, they take time. Furthermore, decisions that are vested in the staffs of commercial enterprises must pass the boards of directors of learned societies. These boards meet infrequently, and this can delay the development of new projects. Furthermore, the membership of society boards turns over frequently. Each change in the volunteer leadership is likely to introduce significant changes in the agenda of a society. Whereas the basic objectives of societies do not change from term to term, the means of realizing these objectives may change quite drastically over a short timeframe. Publishing staffs are accustomed to maintaining continuing education programs for those newly introduced into the leadership structure. This process has its rewards, but can also be frustrating.

Society governance also makes it difficult to keep proprietary information confidential. Scholars often have difficulty in recognizing potential or even actual conflicts of interest. Members of a society's board of directors often serve as editors or advisers for competing publications and see no reason to keep information they gain from their directorships of a society from benefiting other organizations they serve. So the generosity of members who give freely of their wisdom and energy can be a mixed blessing.

The relationship with the volunteer structure provides unique challenges for the publication staff of a society. While the benefits of access to this pool of talent can hardly be underestimated, members can be difficult. Memberships of societies include authors, who are thus shareholders in the publishing enterprise. Some (not all) do not hesitate to use this special relationship when they disagree with a staff action. Even when a staff member is clearly implementing a policy of the society, the occasional society member can take exception and become very insistent about having his or her own way. Some authors become members of boards of directors and may temporarily overlook, or wish to ignore, society policies. Dealing with such situations requires a special combination of tact and persistence on the part of the staff. To understand the special inter-personal skills required, those working in commercial publishing houses would have to imagine that all the articles in their journals were authored by stockholders, many of whom are personal friends of the chairman of the board.

Member volunteers play a great variety of roles in the publishing activities of a society. While most of these involve their scholarly expertise, they are also called upon to make or influence economic decisions. The setting of subscription rates is commonly subject to the democratic process. Societies offering journals as separate membership options thus find themselves in the curious position of being purchasers who decide the rate they will be charged. The possibilities of conflict of interest clearly loom large. Furthermore, the directors or committees that must vote on the subscription rates may also have influence over the library purchasing decisions at their home institutions. This puts a great burden on them, since they must balance the economic needs of the societies against their desire to make limited library resources serve as many researchers, faculty members and students as possible.

In times of tight library budgets, the mandates of societies to achieve the widest possible dissemination can put society journals at special risks. The fact that many individuals have access to a society journal by virtue of their membership leads to fewer calls for it in library surveys. Faculty members making recommendations about which journals should be maintained and which should be cut are faced with the choice between journals they can afford for their own personal libraries and those priced with only an institutional market in mind. In a few institutions, members may even be encouraged to subscribe at member rates and donate their journals to the library so that institutional subscriptions can be cancelled in favor of other publications for which this option is not available.

Some of the very large society journals in the sciences are faced with yet another problem. Although they are typically less expensive on a per-page basis than many of their counterpart commercial journals, their absolute prices are often higher because they contain many more pages. These high absolute prices make them likely candidates for cancellation. While some librarians and faculty members have become very astute in comparing prices with the amount of material provided, others look only at the price per title. Most surveys of journals prices do not yet take into account the amount of material provided, so large society science journals look expensive.

Similarly, the differences between the numbers of possible customers in different fields are not considered in library pricing surveys. For scientific journals, fixed costs and many variable costs (those depending on the number of pages, not on the number of copies produced) account for 80% of the total costs. These costs must obviously be recovered from subscribers. The incremental savings to the publisher resulting from dropping a subscription has a virtually meaningless impact on the costs of publication. Thus, in fields with limited circulation, the price of a journal will necessarily be higher since the expenses must be recovered from the subscription income.

The relationship between fixed and variable costs had much to do with the introduction of page charges for US scientific journals in the '30s. It was recognized by various funding agencies that a key element of "doing science" was to make the results easily available to other researchers. Building on past research would become more efficient, it was reasoned, if results could be assessed readily by others. In theory, if another source of revenue to cover "first copy" costs of scientific journals was available, subscribers would need only to pay the incremental copy costs in order to receive the journal, and the journal would be assured of recovery of full costs. First copy costs include all expenses related to the review process, copy-editing, composition and setting up the presses and the bindery and mailing equipment. Many of the journals that adopted page charges as part of their financial models contained significant amounts of mathematics which, in the days of hot metal composition, was much more costly to produce than straight text. (For further discussion of the origins of page charges for US physics journals, see H A Baritone "The publication charge plan in physics journals" in *Physics Today*, 16, 1963; and R H Marks, "Publication charge plan: Wider circulation at lower subscription rates", in *IEEE Transactions on Professional Communication*, PC 20, 1977.) Today, page charges cover only a fraction of first copy costs. They are not part of the international culture of funding science. So journals with a large international clientele find that a growing percentage of the articles they publish do not receive page charge support. Likewise, tight funding in the US is causing a decline in page charge support. The subscription prices, therefore, must cover an even larger fraction of the expenses than the simple model described above.

Page charge support is in great jeopardy in today's financial and political climate. As institutions look for ways to stretch their budgets, directing page charge funds to cover other activities is an increasingly tempting option. Additionally, this source of revenue could be removed instantly by political directive. As societies move into the age of electronic publishing, page charge financing grows in importance. Yet it is at greater peril than at any time since it was introduced six decades ago.

*   *   *   *   *

Why is page charge financing particularly important in the electronic environment? The first and obvious answer is that, if income is derived on a per-use basis, the whole financial model is turned upside down. Journals receive their funding up-front and must manage that source of income each year as the publishers produce and deliver each issue. If "per-use" becomes the dominant income source, the cash will follow, instead of precede, the expenditure, and few societies are equipped to deal with such a wrenching change. Amassing large financial reserves is looked upon with some suspicion by the US federal government. Further, society directors, while fully committed to meeting their fiduciary responsibilities, find it difficult to justify to themselves and their colleagues budgets that provide regular surpluses which in turn could be used to build financial reserves of the size that electronic journal publishing will require.

All of this must change if the scholarly community is to have a stable electronic publishing enterprise. The technology of electronic publishing is becoming easier to handle. Even the changes in the financial model can be addressed if given time to adjust. But societies will have to develop reserves if they are to meet their obligations to the scholars they serve, both today and into the future. Societies must develop systems for maintaining their electronic publication files for tomorrow. These files must be regularly refreshed, must be moved to new storage media as today's standards become obsolete, and must be ported to new computer platforms. These new responsibilities bring with them additional expenses that have not previously been a concern for publishers, whether not-for-profit or for-profit. Learned societies cannot shirk their responsibilities to the disciplines they serve, nor can they be satisfied by simply serving the present community of scholars. One might think of this new challenge as the need to create a fund for the perpetual care of electronic journals. Monies must be earned, earmarked and invested to provide a source of cash to cover the expenses of the future.

Electronic publishing challenges are not specific to societies. All publishers face the same uncertainties. What will be the most likely delivery mechanisms? To what extent will present financial models be disrupted? How do we learn and adopt new technologies? However, learned societies are set apart by one overriding consideration: Their charter is to service the individual scholar. For societies, there is never any question about who is the market – it is the end user. Likewise, there is little question about the need to reach out to non-member scholars in all parts of the world. Societies pride themselves on the openness of their activities. They seek ways of assuring that any individual scholar with intellectual interest and a sufficient command of the subject can participate in their publication programs as authors, reviewers and subscribers. As societies take greater advantage of the new technologies, subject matter expertise may not be enough to entitle individuals to participate. For the first time, there is evidence that a technological élite is being created. Some scholars will not be able to participate because they do not have the technological wherewithal.

This is a very troubling prospect for societies, and reducing it will be a driver in some actions that they will take.

To lessen the possibility of such disenfranchisement, learned societies are forecasting the need to provide their journals in both print and electronic format. Probably societies will persist longer in providing dual formats than the commercial and university presses, and to do this they will incur correspondingly higher costs. So long as societies manage to serve their memberships worldwide, their governing bodies are likely to press that they find the means to do so. Meeting this goal will undoubtedly add further strains on society resources – both financial and intellectual.

Learned societies will face other challenges as they try to replicate in the new media the most highly valued aspects of their current publication activities. Access to publications by individual scholars – any society's most important role – is likely to be expanded by the development of the World Wide Web. Until the last few years, it had seemed that electronic publishing would in the near term require specialized hardware and software and that electronic formats would be beyond the reach of many individuals.

On another front, the value of the peer review system has again come under significant question, particularly by those who see it as a deterrent to the dissemination of novel ideas. Many proponents of electronic publication through the Web argue that the speed of Internet, coupled with the absence of cost to most users, will bring about the demise of journal publishing. The time lapse between submission and publication, largely a product of a well-established review system, is under closer scrutiny today than ever before. This occurs because instantaneous publication, in the absence of any other criteria or value, is practical on the World Wide Web. Will the need to provide a vetting system to ensure a superior intellectual product by the author and to serve better the legitimate expectations of quality by the reader survive this pressure? So long as authors seek the help of their colleagues to make their arguments clearer and reduce the likelihood of publishing foolish errors, the review system will survive in society publishing. So long as readers prize their time, they will appreciate a system that sorts out much of the chaff from the kernels of wisdom. Open peer review systems on the Web, being touted by some, will not serve either of these ends. Those whose opinions and judgment are likely to be of greatest value to both author and reader will probably not take the time nor have the inclination to surf the Web in order to provide unsolicited reviews. Self-selected reviews, which some propose, could well be worse than no reviews, because the remarks of the unknowledgable and the disgruntled cannot be deleted.

Some authors will undoubtedly bypass the review system and self-publish on the Web. After all, it does not take any particular talent to master hypertext mark-up language or to set up a simple home page. Self-publishing has suddenly become easy and free. For most users, its costs are buried in institutional overheads and so are evident neither to authors nor to readers. Why should societies object to self-publication, if it means broader distribution to individuals? Because, while self-publishing may serve today's scholars, future scholars will not have access to the work that has preceded their own. Archiving functions are utterly lost in a world of self-publication. Since the advancement of a field of study relies on the availability of the entire body of knowledge which gives the field intellectual cohesion, learned societies must and will take a stand to ensure that self-publication does not become the norm.

Learned societies recognize the problem of archiving their publications for the future. In addition to assuring future generations of scholars access to the full body of work preceding their own, society-managed archives will provide sources of the authentic versions of the articles they publish. It is very easy, in the electronic medium, to alter content, either inadvertently or deliberately. Users will require the means to ascertain that the version they are using is unadulterated. Only society policies can help to ensure that future publishing practices serve the best interests of each field as a whole. It would be tempting for authors who have self-published to correct little errors that slipped into their first versions mounted on the Web, without considering that others have seen these first versions and referred to them in other papers. Chaos could replace the orderly approach to published literature unless the interests of all parties in the information chain are considered in the development of policies and practices to govern the future. Societies are uniquely positioned to bring the views of all these parties into play and to develop and propagate policies that do not favor one segment over another.

The membership of many societies is imbued with a strong spirit of adventure. Such members will press their societies to try new approaches to serve the needs of individuals. Because, in the course of their research, many use the newest technologies in their fields, they will encourage their societies to exploit the medium to enhance the value of the information that the societies publish. For example, three scientific societies – the American Geophysical Union, the American Meteorological Society and the American Association of Geographers – are working together on a fully electronic journal that will do just that. Although joint ventures are not unique to societies, it is perhaps easier for societies than for commercial publishers to come together to develop new products. By pooling their intellectual and financial resources, societies can do together things they could not do independently. Furthermore, societies, individually or jointly, can seek grant funds to support projects that will benefit the broad mass of scholarship.

Society publishing in the US is generally healthy and robust although, in addition to sharing the difficulties facing all kinds of publishers, it has unique challenges of its own. Whether society publishing will flourish in the future depends simply on the extent to which it meets the mission of all learned societies. My prediction is that, in those fields where publishing is critical to the advancement of a field of study, ways will be found.

Director of Publications for the American Geophysical Union, a scientific society with a worldwide membership of more than 30,000 researchers, educators and students, Judy C Holoviak has been engaged in society publishing for thirty years. She was a founder of the Society for Scholarly Publishing and served as its President from 1990 to 1992. In recognition of her publishing service, an iceberg in Antarctica was named in her honor.

17

Between Academe and the Marketplace: University Presses Face the 21st Century

Naomi B Pascal

The lore of American university presses includes three frequently quoted statements that reflect evolving perceptions of scholarly publishing. The first was pronounced by President Daniel Coit Gilman more than 100 years ago when he established the Johns Hopkins University Press. "It is one of the noblest duties of a university," he said, "to advance knowledge, and to diffuse it not merely among those who can attend the daily lectures – but far and wide." The second statement was made by Thomas J Wilson, Director of Harvard University Press, in 1947: "A university press exists to publish as many good scholarly books as possible short of bankruptcy." The third statement, made in the '50s by Chester Kerr, Director of Yale University Press, was even more graphic: "We publish the smallest editions at the greatest cost, and on these we place the highest prices, and then we try to market them to people who can least afford them. This is madness."

The second and third of these statements reveal economic pressures which the university presidents who founded the presses had not envisaged. They took it for granted that, like other university activities, scholarly publishing would require financial support. Direct financial subsidies from a parent university now range from adequate to nonexistent, averaging approximately 10% of the press's total operating budget. Over the years, universities under increasing budgetary pressure have asked the university presses to be self-supporting, or nearly so. On the one hand, they are expected to fulfill their mission of making significant scholarly research available to the academic community, regardless of the limited market such publications may find, and to bear in mind also that young scholars are still required to publish in order to attain academic recognition and professional advancement. On the other hand, since publishers produce a tangible "product" that is sold in commercial establishments, the presses are viewed as business operations that may actually be expected to return a profit to their universities.

This paradox at the heart of scholarly publishing has been both a challenge and an opportunity for American university presses, which, from their first appearance in the late 19th century, have reflected the common concerns, the diversity, the achievements and the problems of their parent institutions. Five of them are more than 100 years old: Cornell (first established in 1869, discontinued in 1884 and re-established in 1930); Johns Hopkins (the oldest in continuous operation); Chicago, California and Columbia. (Not counted here is Cambridge, founded in 1534, which lists 1949 as the year of the establishment of its American branch, or Oxford, established in the US in 1895.) They were never supposed to provide college textbooks, as do university presses in some parts of the world, but to publish scholarly research – "contributions to knowledge", in the words of Nicholas Murray Butler of Columbia University, "usually destitute of commercial value".

Eight more university presses in the US (and one – the University of Toronto Press – in Canada) were founded in the first decade of this century and seventeen more by 1947, when the Association of American University Presses (AAUP) was established. By 1995, the Association had eighty-four regular members, twelve affiliate members (presses too small to justify full membership), thirteen associate members (presses attached to non-degree-granting institutions and associations who qualify otherwise), and five international members.

Although differing in size, internal organization and editorial programs, the university presses as a whole retain today many of the characteristics of their earliest years. The AAUP bylaws define a university press as "the scholarly publishing arm of a university or college, or of a group of such institutions, with an estate or geographic region located within the Americas". In order to be admitted to membership, the press must be "devoted to scholarly and educational ends", and there must be a "committee or board of the faculty of the parent institution or institutions .... charged with certifying the scholarly quality of the books and journals that bear the institutional imprint". On this basis, an American university press is considered part of a non-profit, tax-exempt educational institution. Some presses are separately incorporated; some represent more than one institution within a state system or in several states; but all report in some way to the administration of the parent institution or institutions.

* * * * *

When I joined the University of Washington Press in 1953, the Director – a professor in the Classics Department – held the belief that the Press had the obligation to publish any manuscript, in any field, whose worth was validated by scholars in that field. He also believed that any book for which a sale of fewer than 1,500 copies could be anticipated should be published as cheaply as possible, even printed by photo offset from typewritten copy. At that time, academic libraries were still the primary market for university press books, although some presses were beginning to send sales representatives to call on bookstores in the hope that they might be persuaded to stock at least some of their titles despite the "stigma" of a university press imprint.

In my forty-some years of involvement with scholarly publishing, I have seen the number of copies of a scholarly monograph that one could count on selling to academic libraries shrink from 700 or 800 to 200 or even fewer. This situation has led to spirited discussion among the presses, most recently in the Association's Internet mailing list, as to whether manuscripts with such a limited potential market can, or should, continue to be published, at least in conventional book form.

Among reasons for the dramatic decline in library sales have been:

- Increasing costs of labor and raw materials, causing book prices to rise at the same time that library budgets, especially at state institutions, suffered drastic cuts.
- The so-called "serials crisis" – the proliferation of scholarly jour-

nals, especially in the sciences, some of them sold at inflated prices by commercial publishers, compelling libraries to devote a larger proportion of their budgets to periodicals.

•   Ubiquitous and inexpensive photocopying machines, reducing the number of copies of titles needed by libraries – although questions of what constitutes "fair use" in photocopying are still being hotly debated twenty years after the passage of the revised US copyright law that attempted to define this.

•   The use of library funds for the acquisition and implementation of computer hardware and software, in which academic libraries have played a leading role.

The net result is that the large number of libraries that once automatically ordered all university press publications, usually through a wholesaler, are now vastly more selective in their purchases.

University presses have responded in various ways to the challenge of their ambivalent position between the academy and the marketplace. Recognizing that it is more economical to promote a list of related books than a single title, most university presses now tend to emphasize certain areas in their publishing programs, rather than attempting to serve the whole range of scholarly activity. Thus it is not uncommon for an editor to refer the author of a promising manuscript to another press with a stronger list in that particular subject. In the absence of adequate funding from the parent university, some presses have relied on related enterprises such as a bookstore or a printing plant to help support the publishing operation. Several derive income by providing warehousing and order-fulfillment services for other publishers. Others have undertaken the marketing of publications produced by museums or other institutions lacking adequate access to distribution channels. Many have joined together in marketing consortia, sharing the cost of hiring sales representatives for the export as well as the domestic market, or in opening a sales office in London or elsewhere.

University presses seek title subsidies from public or private foundations to support the publication of books that cannot be expected to break even – an endeavor that was dealt a grievous blow in September 1995, when the National Endowment for the Humanities announced that the severe budget cut voted by the US Congress was forcing it to suspend its program of subventions for scholarly publications. Some presses have begun to engage in aggressive fund-raising in their own communities in order to establish endowments that will provide a measure of stability and flexibility for their future operations.

* * * * *

The most significant response to the challenge has been a conscious effort to broaden the audience for university press books. This change in editorial focus has been evolving for some time, but has accelerated in the past several years. Scholarly research, whenever possible, is to be published not exclusively for scholars, but for the use and enlightenment of a more general public. Indeed, non-academic authors are sometimes enlisted to interpret the writings of scholars who are incapable of expressing themselves in terms comprehensible to non-professional audiences.

As long ago as 1980, the *New York Times Book Review* reported: "Anyone who thinks that academic publishers in this country limit their lists to donnish studies or arcane matters has not been paying attention. Perhaps there was a day when our university presses catered exclusively to a specialized professional readership, but in recent times they have aimed shrewdly at a wider audience of intelligent general readers .... Serious non-fiction for serious laymen has lately been finding shelter in the groves of academe." A glance at current catalogs of American university presses will reveal the continuation and extension of this trend.

Titles dealing with the history, politics, flora and fauna, folklore, art, architecture, cuisine and other cultural aspects of the region in which the press is located were the first kinds of books designed for this wider audience. This kind of publishing was pioneered in the '30s by William Couch of North Carolina and later championed by Savoie Lottinville of Oklahoma and Frank Wardlaw of Texas, among others, especially at presses in southern, midwestern and far western states. Far from the centers of publishing in New York, Boston, Philadelphia and Chicago, these presses were often the only – or at least the leading – book publishers in their areas. They had the pick of manuscripts that might otherwise have gone to commercial publishers.

When I began my career in scholarly publishing at the University of North Carolina Press in 1948, they had just broadened their program of publishing significant studies dealing with contemporary problems of the South by issuing a *Southern Cookbook* . This title was, to the best of my knowledge, the first cookbook to be published by a university press. Despite the inadvertent omission of a crucial cup of flour from one of the recipes in the first printing, the book was enormously successful and remains in print in a revised edition. Today, cookbooks – either regional or historical – can be found in the lists of many university presses.

To scholars who were critical of the idea of regional publishing, Frank Wardlaw made an eloquent rejoinder: "There is no necessity for making the sharp distinction between traditional 'contributions to knowledge' and 'regional' books which some scholars make. It is a narrow view of scholarship indeed which holds that the Medici banks of Florence are legitimate subjects for scholarly inquiry but that the operation of a big cattle ranch in the Texas Panhandle is not."

The broadening of the curricula of American universities has also provided publishing opportunities related to courses in subjects such as environmental studies; the history of sports, of jazz and of films; women's studies; black, Native American, Hispanic and Asian American studies; and gay and lesbian studies. Even science fiction became a university press subject, as Paul H Rohmann, then Director of Kent State University Press, observed in 1983: "Science fiction and fantasy are playing ever larger roles in the curricular and scholarly interests of college and university faculties and students. University presses are established to serve the interests and meet the needs of denizens of the scholarly community. If they want to orbit around a new constellation, we'll don our space suits and go with them."

Self-help and inspirational books, medical books for lay audiences, and "how-to" or craft books, once frowned on by university press editorial committees, are now published routinely. A book on paper sculpture by a professor of art education at the University of Washington came close to being rejected by our committee in the '50s, although a preliminary version was already being used in courses taught at the university. Grudgingly approved, it became one of our all-time best-sellers. A volume on weaving had an easier passage through the committee because it dealt with an historical reconstruction of the techniques of ancient Peruvian textiles and was a translation from French. This University of Washington Press publication from the '60s is still in print.

The 1995 "University Presses" issue of the *New York Times Book Review* (October 29) published reviews of university press publications in traditional fields of scholarship – studies of James Madison (Cornell), Barry Goldwater (Yale), Vladimir Nabokov (Princeton), US foreign trade policy (North Carolina) and forest ecology (Washington). Also included were reviews of books about the great jazz singer Billie Holiday (Northeastern), vampires (Chicago), the notorious photographer Robert Mapplethorpe (California), the lyricists Oscar Hammerstein 2nd and Alan Jay Lerner (Oxford) and Molly Spotted Elk, a Penobscot Indian woman who became a celebrated Parisian dancer (Oklahoma). None of the latter would have survived the scrutiny of an academic editorial board in earlier times.

The publishing of fiction has proved to be even more controversial. With the exception of edited and annotated editions or translations of works of fiction that might be required for use in college courses, university presses have not traditionally viewed the publishing of original fiction as appropriate for a scholarly publisher. Many university presses still adhere to this belief. Some have concluded, however, that just as university presses had earlier begun publishing poetry, largely because it was neglected by commercial publishers, they had a similar obligation to writers of fiction, since independent publishers who once had been willing to take a gamble on previously unpublished writers of short stories or novels were increasingly being swallowed up by large corporations interested only in their bottom lines.

Sometimes such ventures hit the jackpot. Norman Maclean's *A River Runs Through It* (University of Chicago Press 1976) came very close to winning the Pulitzer Prize, is still in print in several editions and was the basis of a successful motion picture in 1992. In 1980, *A Confederacy of Dunces* by John K Toole, published by Louisiana State University Press, did win the Pulitzer. Today, more than two dozen university presses list fiction as one of their areas of editorial interest.

*   *   *   *   *

No aspect of university press operations has been free from change under the pressure of financial imperatives. For years, the primary concern of university presses was editorial content and presentation. Many of the editors trained in the strong editorial departments of university presses made significant impact upon publishing standards throughout the publishing industry. These departments were often headed by women who became legends in their profession, although not until recent decades did a significant number of women become press directors. The *Chronicle of Higher Education* (August 4, 1995) noted that eleven university presses are now headed by women.

Design and production quality were first formally recognized in 1965 by the establishment of the AAUP Book Show, now an annual juried competition. The increased attention given to bookstore sales has helped to make university presses aware of the importance of attractive packaging for their publications.

Marketing was the last of the primary components of the publishing process to be recognized as critical by the university presses and so to become thoroughly professionalized. Today, marketing – direct mail, advertising, publicity, book exhibits and sales organization – is recognized as a major function. Marketing considerations have come to play a significant role in editorial decisions and have a strong influence on design, especially of dust jackets and paperback covers.

Notable, too, has been a change in relationships among presses. The AAUP has a long tradition of mutual assistance and exchange of information among its members. This spirit of cooperation survives in informal conversations among individuals and in workshops sponsored by the AAUP, but now coexists with vigorous competition among editors vying for the same high-profile academic authors. Many presses now offer contracts, including advances, for manuscripts still to be written. Such contracts, however, are likely to include a proviso that publication is contingent on the approval of a faculty editorial board, such approval being typically based on favorable reviews from outside readers. Editors have also become accustomed to dealing with literary agents, whose demands in terms of royalties and control of subsidiary rights typically go well beyond the traditional arrangements with academic authors, whose interest was more in professional advancement than in financial return.

* * * * *

Like the rest of the publishing world, university presses are struggling to understand and adapt to the electronic revolution. The use of the computer as a tool – in typesetting, for example, or for the business operations of the press – is by now taken for granted. Almost all manuscripts submitted for publication have been prepared on computers, and more and more press staff members edit and design on screen. Computers are used to prepare catalogs and ads and to maintain mailing lists of various kinds. The AAUP has developed an online catalog that will eventually, it is hoped, include all the publications of all its members, and many individual presses are putting their own "home pages" on the World Wide Web. Electronic publication as an end product, however, either complementing or substituting for a book, remains a controversial issue, evoking responses that range from enthusiasm to outright rejection. Some presses have created a new staff position of "electronic publisher" or "electronic project manager". Others remain skeptical of the extravagant predictions made by champions of the new technology.

The impetus for the development of electronic projects comes sometimes from authors and sometimes from academic libraries, many of which are far more advanced technologically than the university presses. Some librarians have entered into lively debates with scholarly publishers. Some challenge the very idea of publication in codex form as the ideal medium for the preservation and dissemination of scholarly research. One of the consequences of this debate has been the generation of a number of projects in which academic libraries, university computer centers and university presses are working together to explore the potential of electronic media for scholarly communication.

Several of these pioneering projects involve applications of the newest technology to the most ancient materials – an affinity of opposites. The Perseus Project, for example, established in 1987 at Tufts University and marketed by Yale University Press, is an "interactive multimedia digital library of Archaic and Classical Greece". It is funded by a combination of public and private foundations.

There are more than thirty electronic publications either completed or under way, according to an AAUP survey of August 1995. Three of the presses that publish scholarly journals (Johns Hopkins, Chicago and Colorado) are making them available on the Internet, often – but not always – concurrently with the print format. Colorado states flatly that "at first the journals will be offered concurrently in print and in electronic formats, but our plan calls for the eventual discontinuance of the print format." Chicago describes one of its journals as "a peer-reviewed electronic journal" in which every article will have "a file of associated comments which will be unrefereed, unmoderated and easily accessible from the article".

Reference works have also been converted into vehicles electronically transmitted. The *Columbia Electronic Encyclopedia,* the *Columbia Dictionary of Quotations* and the *Columbia Granger's World of Poetry* are all available on the Internet, the last of these also on a CD-ROM. Indiana is putting Stith Thompson's *Motif-Index of Folk-Literature* , originally compiled in the early '30s, on a CD-ROM, and Nebraska is creating an online "Library of the Frontier", including 400 public-domain publications relating to the history of the American West.

MIT Press's *The City of Bits* – "a comprehensive introduction to a new type of city, a largely invisible but increasingly important system of virtual spaces interconnected by the emerging information superhighway" – was published in an online version on the World Wide Web before it appeared in conventional form in bookstores. The author, Dean William J Mitchell of MIT's School of Architecture and Planning, introduces himself on the computer screen: "My name is wjm@mit.edu (though I have many aliases) and I am an electronic *flâneur*. I hang out on the network."

Also available in both book and hypertext versions is Chicago's *The Electronic Word: Democracy, Technology and the Arts* by Richard A Lanham, a professor emeritus of English whose message is that "electronic expression has not come to destroy the Western arts but to fulfill them." At Washington we are working on a CD-ROM version of Glenn White's *The Audio Dictionary* which will add animation and sound to the diagrams that lie fixed and silent on the book pages. Whether such electronic extensions will encourage or compete with sales of their sibling books remains so far an unanswered question.

*   *   *   *   *

In the last years of the 20th century, American university presses face a variety of dilemmas and paradoxes, some of which are their own and others shared with the rest of the publishing industry. As computers become more affordable, more prevalent and more sophisticated, the boundaries between the roles in the process of book publishing are shifting and blurring. Authors are being asked to assume greater responsibility for the preparation of their manuscripts; editors are acquiring some of the functions of the production department; design and production people find themselves setting type, scanning illustrations into their layouts and performing other tasks traditionally entrusted to outside suppliers.

The conundrum of the scholarly monograph with a limited audience continues to be unsolved. Academic committees, especially in the humanities, still require the publication of one or more scholarly books for tenure and promotion. Yet the universities do not support such publications, either by direct subsidies or by purchasing enough copies to make them economically viable. A solution may be some form of peer-reviewed electronic publication that will provide access to the materials and will simultaneously provide the opportunity for criticism and further development of the theses so presented. Academic tenure and promotion committees, however, have not yet indicated a willingness to accept such innovations. Ironically, if electronic publication of specialized monographs does attain formal recognition, university presses may find themselves marginalized. Academic libraries, one school of thought claims, are in a better position than presses to distribute scholarly materials electronically. In such a scenario, acquisition, evaluation, editing and design of manuscripts will be "folded into" the library structure. Libraries providing photocopies are, of course, already de facto on-demand publishers.

As communication via the "information highway" becomes easier and more universal, the principle of copyright and the very nature of intellectual property are being called into question. "Fair use" and limitations on what should be considered to be in the public domain are seen by some librarians as restrictions on a fundamental public right to knowledge. In this construction, copyright becomes a symbol of greed on the part of the author, the author's heirs and the author's publisher. It is further contended that since much scholarly research and writing are carried out on university time and with university facilities, the copyright, if there is any, should be held by the university.

It may be true, as some believe, that the last years of the 20th century mark the beginning of the end of the post-Gutenberg age. Electronically conducted university seminars already draw participants from anywhere on the globe. They still rely, to some extent, on printed materials, but it is not difficult to imagine a time when they may be completely paperless. Students brought up on hypertexts may not be concerned about the longevity of electronic archives or the integrity of original texts – problems that concern those of us who are still struggling to adapt to the new technology. It has been suggested that linear thinking, which is linked to a fixed text, may itself be obsolete, although it is the basis of our present logical and legal systems.

American university presses, which tend to be liberal in their thinking but conservative in their actions, will undoubtedly continue to modify their publishing programs in response to changes both within their parent universities and in society at large. There are at least two possible directions they may take, becoming either more independent of the university or more closely integrated with the libraries as part of the university's system of scholarly communication. In any case it seems likely – given its attractiveness, portability, cheapness and accessibility – that the printed book will be with us for some time to come; that university presses will continue to occupy their small but significant niche in the US publishing community; and that they will be agile enough to avoid collapsing into a black hole in cyberspace.

Associate Director and Editor-in-Chief at the University of Washington Press in Seattle, Naomi Pascal worked previously as an editor at Vanguard Press in New York City and the University of North Carolina Press at Chapel Hill. She has served on the Board of Directors and numerous committees of the Association of American University Presses, and in 1991 was given the Association's first Constituency Award "for her outstanding contribution to scholarly publishing". She frequently writes and lectures on various aspects of publishing and has presented or participated in seminars on publishing in China and Latvia. She is a co-author of Glossary of Typesetting Terms , published by the University of Chicago Press in 1994.

18

Electronic Publishing and the Indispensability of Publishers

Sandra M Whisler

I define electronic publishing as publishing activities that have as their end the distribution of knowledge by electronic means, not the use of electronic technologies to speed up or reduce the cost of print publication. Nor do I include in my definition the rapidly spreading use of World Wide Web home pages for innovative online marketing.

Discussions of electronic publishing often pose two extremes: either extravagant and sometimes fantastic predictions of a revolution that will transform the entire publishing industry in eighteen months or a deep sense of anxiety and foreboding on the part of those whose professional lives center round print media. Neither conclusion is justified. In fact, the next ten years will be a time of transition, during which publishers and librarians will live in a dual paper-electronic world, in which "reader" and "user" will be increasingly used as synonyms.

Since a tour through all of electronic publishing – from computer games to the huge NEXIS (newspaper) and LEXIS (law references) databases and CD-ROM encyclopedias – is beyond the scope of a single article, I shall concentrate the argument on professional and scholarly publishing (PSP). What is happening and what is about to happen in this sector will offer some illumination of trends in the whole spectrum of publishing. Electronic capabilities are uniquely suited to some scholarly enterprises, and PSP audiences are already widely familiar with the Internet. What scholarly associations, university presses and commercial academic publishers are doing, should do and should not do, has implications for other publishing sectors.

Twenty years will probably pass before PSP switches over to entirely electronic delivery of information, in spite of the fact that there are some disciplines, notably the physics community, who believe that this transition will occur much more rapidly. But even if the transition is slow and uneven, it will happen. Publishers who ignore electronic publishing do so at their peril.

What PSP publishers are facing is an increasingly complex and multi-layered publishing environment. Publishers will provide knowledge in a variety of print and electronic formats, depending on the nature of the materials, the audience, the needs of libraries, the unique contributions that electronic publishing can offer – and the economics of it all. Traditional publishing duties will be restructured as publishers produce single works in multiple formats. Work flow processes will change and the implementation of electronic production technologies and approaches will eliminate old jobs and create new ones. Electronic publishing also offers exciting opportunities to expand the audience for scholarly materials as well as to enhance the presentation of knowledge and to publish entirely new kinds of scholarship.

Our anxiety, our ignorance and our alienation from the often daunting technical jargon sometimes prevent publishers from seriously exploring the electronic future. This is a mistake for publishing professionals and a disservice to scholarship. To date, much of the material that has been published electronically falls at two extremes: good content presented without sufficient thought to format and delivery (sometimes characteristic of works mounted on the Internet by their authors); and sumptuous multimedia presentations and interfaces without sufficient depth of content (this applies to the vast majority of non-bibliographic CD-ROMs).

Traditional publishers are professionals who understand both presentation and the need for genuine content. They have important contributions to make to electronic publishing:

- First and foremost, *the ability to identify superior scholarship* and the resulting reputation for publishing quality. The peer review and validation provided by a quality imprint will be even more important in the electronic world than in the print world to help readers to be better able to sort out what's good from the huge mass of sometimes mediocre electronic materials now available.

- *Skill in matching presentation to content* in ways that increase accessibility. Copy-editing, design, choice of format and fit of content and format to market – all functions that publishers perform every day in the print world – are also needed in the electronic modes. The answers are different, but the questions are the same: What format and approach will present authors' messages most accessibly to the audience, at a price that the audience can afford? If a system of scholarly information bypassing publishers and publishing functions were to come into being, the world would be poorer.
- *Familiarity with scholars,* both as authors and readers. What publishers already know about their customers can help to avoid the who-did-they-think-would-use-this? mistakes that plague so many multimedia publications.
- *Marketing expertise.* The suggestion that marketing will disappear on the Internet, as Web crawlers and intelligent agents present their personalized lists of discoveries each morning, is naive. In the exceptionally noisy, overwhelmingly large world of the Internet, marketing will be different, but its function – to notify the appropriate audience of the existence of new work of high quality – will be more important than ever. The same is true of CD-ROM. In 1994, space on computer store shelves accommodated only one-fourth of the CD-ROM products on the market. Marketing and distribution savvy were survival issues for many companies. Whether online or on-shelf, marketing will continue to be a sine qua non in the publishing business.

Despite a lot of talk among multimedia enthusiasts that content will drive the process, so far glitz and technology have been consistently in control. PSP publishers, and indeed all publishers, have the opportunity – and the challenge – to do electronic publishing right. Only when they do this will online and stand-alone projects fully demonstrate the potential of electronic publishing.

* * * * *

The very rapid pace of technological development – seen, for example, in the growth of the Internet or the installation of CD-ROM drives in homes – leads many to predict that the rate of change within publishing will be equally fast. I believe, however, that the transformation will happen very unevenly. Some academic disciplines (physics, for example), some sectors of society and some applications will develop much more quickly than others. Each enterprise will have to decide for itself its own pace and direction.

In planning the electronic future at the University of California Press, I work on the assumption that scholarly publishing will take twenty years to switch to a wholly digital mode. Nevertheless, the electronic revolution has to be seen as inevitable. The publishers' task is to prepare their staffs and their organizations to live in constant change during these transitional years. In an environment of harsh economic pressures and continually evolving technology, publishers must develop strategies that allow them to respond flexibly, creatively and rapidly. Format and publishing will vary not only from company to company, but from one project to the next in each company, according to the demands of content, audience and economics.

Titles published by the University of California Press ten years from now are likely to fall into four groups: electronic, print-only, multiple-format, and hybrid.

Exclusively Electronic Titles

About 15% to 20% of all publishing will be books and journals that will exist only in electronic formats, either published over the Internet or as stand-alone projects sold in units, probably as CD-ROMs. Both stand-alone and networked products will be characterized by a great need for speed of publication; by multimedia facets and interactivity; or by enhancement as parts of larger databases. Electronic-only products will include everything from multimedia CD-ROMs (which will take full advantage of visual and aural possibilities and target audiences beyond the academy) to electronic books and journals (including multimedia materials as large bandwidth capacities become more widely available) that will be available only over the Internet. Such online projects will earn revenue through a combination of institutional domain licensing (ie, licenses to universities, associations and other organizations for unlimited use by their members) and on-the-spot sale of chapters and articles to individuals.

Print-Only Titles

About 10% to 20% of all titles will be books that will exist only in print. Most of them will be trade titles and perhaps textbooks – although how the textbook adoption market will develop is one of the great open questions of electronic publishing. Even some print-only titles, however, may have electronic supplements.

Multiple-Format Titles

The majority of our titles will be published full-text in both electronic and print formats, the print version being increasingly on demand (ie, without inventory in the warehouse). Offering the same material in multiple formats to different audiences will ease the transition into wholly electronic modes, allowing the publishers to acquire expertise before abandoning print. However, the use of multiple formats will also require the re-engineering and management of our entire production process to eliminate inefficiencies and maximize flexibility. If this is not done, the overheads associated with each step or format will make the projects unprofitable.

How will such multiple formats work? UC Press's plans for publication of special interest or small-market books provide one example. As any publisher of such books (traditionally called monographs) knows, sales are collapsing as a result of the ongoing library budget crisis. The Press is developing a plan to publish such works as a combination of ultra-short-run printing for pre-release orders from libraries with subsequent on-demand printing, done either by the Press or by printing facilities in libraries and bookstores. These monographs will also be available online over the Internet, through domain licensing to libraries and through sale of chapters to individuals. The goal is to maximize both income and availability, while reducing the unit and inventory costs of the print editions.

Making such a combination successful will require rigid economy of handling, in peer review, copy-reading and copy-editing, as well as absolutely standard design. To control overhead costs, such a multiple-format model demands strictly limiting the work that must be done to the digital file each time the material moves from one format to the next. To accomplish this, the Press is developing a work plan for implementing Standard Generalized Mark-up Language (SGML) coding as part of the electronic manuscript editing process. This will ensure that files are portable from one format to another with the least possible additional staff time.

The online "editions" of such multi-format titles will be available over the Internet as parts of discipline-focused databases. Such databases will comprise both frontlist and backlist titles and current and back volumes of journals. It is also likely that the Press, in collaboration with the university library or scholarly organization, will add related materials to these databases, such as primary source documents (including art and photographs) or out of print works.

Hybrid Titles

These will be print publications with electronic supplements. For example, CD-ROMs or computer disks can either be bound into the backs of volumes or offered as materials from the Press Internet site. The Press has already begun work on a project that will offer a wealth of original source materials to scholars, online and without charge, to supplement the much more trade-oriented printed main text. MIT Press, among others, has already published books with CD-ROMs of images bound in the backs. These split formation formats will become more common as publishers become accustomed to dealing with electronic media and as the requirements of authors change in response to such opportunity.

Thus, in ten years' time, the Press will be publishing electronic versions of the vast majority of its publications in one of these four categories. The implications for staff development and the re-engineering of work flow, scheduling and procedures are enormous. It will not be possible to live in such a dual world with a small autonomous electronic publishing division, while the rest of the house remains unchanged. If 80% of the Press's titles are to appear electronically, it follows that most staff must be not only familiar with, but fully competent in the use of, electronic technologies. Investment therefore must cover not only equipment and software, but staff training. This presents a particular challenge to non-profit organizations. Few university presses or scholarly societies are spending even the 4% of revenues recommended for non-profit investments in new technology, let alone the 8% average annual expenditure by commercial firms. How to maintain the current print business while diverting increasing staff time and equipment resources to electronic publishing, without new sources of capital, is a major conundrum.

* * * * *

What is happening NOW? Is this all still just a dream? Faced with the need for more investment and lulled by the thought that the transition is just beginning, publishers can be tempted to say to themselves, "Oh, but there'll always be books," and postpone all things electronic. Instead, a cursory survey of PSP publishers reveals a wide assortment of not simply pilot projects, but fully developed products, often produced in partnership with outside organizations, in both stand-alone and online configurations.

The following networked projects are a sampling of what is currently going on (see the end note for a listing of URLs for these sites.) It is important to keep in mind that these are publisher-sponsored, fully peer-reviewed and edited undertakings developed within the confines of full-cost recovery models, unlike ostensibly free publications being mounted on the Internet by individual scholars.

- The SCAN project (Scholarship from CAlifornia on the Net). This is the major online enterprise of the University of California Press. It currently consists of a 19th century studies database, of which domain-licensing to libraries will begin in 1996. Unit sales to individuals (of chapters or individual articles) will be offered by late 1997. The database will include current and back issues of *Nineteenth Century Literature* and a number of monographs and mid-list books in the field, together with a variety of original source materials. In the following years, the database will be expanded and new databases in history, musicology and other humanities and the social sciences will be added. A full-scale operation, with a viable cost recovery mechanism, is foreseen by the turn of the century. SCAN is partially funded by the Andrew W Mellon Foundation and is created in collaboration with the UC Berkeley Library, the UCLA Library and the UC Irvine Library.

- Johns Hopkins University Press is sponsoring Project Muse [see LOGOS 6/2]. At least forty journals will be online within the next two years. Like SCAN, Project Muse will go first for domain licensing and then for sales to individuals. Again, like SCAN, partial funding has been provided by the Andrew W Mellon Foundation, together with the National Endowment for the Humanities and in collaboration with the Johns Hopkins Library.

- MIT Press, working in collaboration with the MIT Library, is publishing two new journals in electronic form only: *Chicago Journal of Theoretical Computer Science* and *Journal of Functional and Logic Programming* These will be sold on subscription to institutions and individuals for online access. MIT is also planning to develop electronic services related to and expanding on print journals, such as the *Leonardo Electronic Almanac*.

- Scholarly societies are also moving quickly into online publishing. The On-line Computer Library Center, Inc in Ohio (OCLC) is currently publishing thirty-six journals online, including *Physical Review Letters On-line,* published in cooperation with the American Physical Society; *Applied Physics Letters On-line,* published in cooperation with the American Institute of Physics; and *Electronic Letters On-line,* published in cooperation with the Institute of Electrical Engineers.

- Among other initiatives: The American Astronomical Society and the University of Chicago Press are mounting the *Astrophysical Journal Letters* online. And five societies – the American Geophysical Union, the American Meteorological Society, the Association of American Geographers, the Ecological Society of America and the Oceanography Society – are cooperating to publish a new, exclusively electronic journal called *Earth Interactions,* which will include computer animation and other visualization techniques. Leading commercial journal publishers such as Elsevier and Springer are rapidly moving beyond their pilot projects. Elsevier, for example, is offering electronic access to its full journal list from 1996 through OCLC.

* * * * *

Online PSP publishing to date remains largely focused on journals, although there are a few experiments at commercial sites like the Online Bookstore, as well as the sometimes substantial text samples appearing on Web sites. In contrast, a wide array of stand-alone projects are appearing, some of them quite profitably. For example:

1. The American Society for Microbiology and the American Psychiatric Association have produced journals and standard reference works on CD-ROM. The majority of the sales have been not to libraries, but to individual professionals, who need the capacity for quick searching of databases and are prepared to pay for it.
2. The University of California Press is offering *Introduction to Attic Greek: An Electronic Workbook,* for which it expects sales for classroom adoptions, from individuals and for site licensing to schools.
3. Columbia University Press has had excellent success with the *Grangers World of Poetry '95,* selling for $600.
4. Yale University Press is hard at work on the second edition of the *Perseus Project,* a multimedia database in classics, and also reports substantial success with its multimedia interactive French language program, *A la rencontre de Philippe/Meeting with Philippe.*
5. Princeton University Press is developing a number of CD- ROMs,the most notable being a hypermedia version of *The I Ching,* with the full Wilhelm/Baynes text and some supplements. It will contain an elaborately cross-referenced textbase for both study and divination; engines for yarrow-stalk or coin generation (or direct entry) of hexagrams; indexing and filtering of commentary levels; help tools; study resources; a diary for reader note storage; text-printing facilities; and browse functions for searching, viewing and reading the texts or commentaries. This digital publication should make the Bollingen *I Ching* far more accessible than its print counterpart.

* * * * *

Developments in trade publishing are better capitalized than those in PSP. There are several elaborate Web sites, with free access at the moment, but sufficiently well developed to show how they will work as income generators (see the end note for a list of URLs). An example is Macmillan USA's Information Super Library, not currently full-text, but demonstrating how full-text would function.

One of my favorite publisher sites is the Moon Books home page, with a complete hypermedia edition of *The Big Island Handbook.* Traditional trade book publishers such as Simon & Schuster, HarperCollins and Times Warner are all creating stand-alone electronic lists. What is happening in PSP is not a parochial development, but part of a larger endeavor.

Additional places to find projects on the World Wide Web are listed below:

- SCAN project (Scholarship from CAlifornia on the Net): http://sunsite.Berkeley.EDU:8080/scan/
- Project Muse: http://muse.mse.jhu.edu/
- MIT Press projects: http://www-mitpress.mit.edu/
- OCLC (Online Computer Library Center, Inc.) Electronic Journals Online: http://www.ref.oclc.org:2000/
- *Physical Review Letters Online*: http://aps.org/Journals/PRL-online/
- *Applied Physics Letters Online*: http://www.aip.org/epub/aplointro.html
- *Electronics Letters Online*: http://www.iee.org.uk/publish/journals/profjrnl/eleclett.html#ele
- *Astrophysical Journal Letters*: http://www.aas.org/ApJ/
- *Earth Interactions*: http://earth.agu.org/kosmos/homepage.html
- *Introduction to Attic Greek: An Electronic Handbook* : gopher://gopherlink.berkeley.edu:3112/11/Classics%20Department/
- Macmillan USA's Information SuperLibrary: http://www.mcp.com/
- Moon Books: http://www.moon.com
- Times/Warner: http://www.pathfinder.com/
- Copyright Clearance Center: http://www.openmarket.com/copyright/

All of these developments do not signal the demise of the codex, any more than television signalled the end of radio. Early experience in this transition period seems to indicate that online access, even to full-text, often boosts sales of the print product – provided both are reasonably priced. Academic libraries often report that electronic products bring new users (especially undergraduates) to the publications (ie, the electronic version, not the print version), actually expanding the user base. In the long run, provided publishers take advantage of the transition to gain skills and reorganize work flows, it won't really matter to them whether scholars prefer online, stand-alone or paper versions. Publishers will be offering them all. And for some kinds of materials, PSP publishers may be able to expand their market beyond their traditional scholarly constituency to undergraduates, public libraries and the educated general public.

There is also a possibility that PSP publishers will be able to continue the publication of specialized monographs, which has been their traditional mission – provided their production processes can be sufficiently streamlined and there is additional revenue from access to portions of the online full-text. It would ʻamount to a kind of publisher-controlled electronic "document delivery". These are, of course, big "ifs".

A major concern for both authors and publishers during the transition period will be the protection of intellectual property. A vigorous program of user education, combined with mechanisms to make compliance easy, will be indispensable to effective monetary copyright protection. Widespread, low-level copying by individuals, like the widespread photocopying of print and the duplication of audio tapes, is to be expected. But I believe that systematic abuse can largely be stemmed. To do so, however, publishers must first clearly assert copyright ownership. (In the SCAN project, for example, a discussion of what is and is not permissible appears as the first screen of any down-loaded document.) Secondly, it is of paramount importance to make it easy and cheap to do the right thing. Most people will comply relatively happily, if it is not too difficult to do so. By the end of '97, commercial transactions on the Internet will be secure. This should make it easy for publishers to charge a reasonable fee for downloading an article or chapter, and safe for the buyers to do so without risking the confidentiality of their charge card numbers. In most cases, readers will choose to pay the fee in order to obtain the fully authenticated copy, rather than run the intellectual risk of obtaining a corrupted version from a friend. The Copyright Clearance Center has a pilot project in electronic delivery of rights-cleared material. Copyright concerns won't go away, but the problem of protecting intellectual rights will not be so overwhelming as to freeze development of online publishing.

The strategic partnerships that publishers are undertaking with libraries, scholarly societies and with one another will, I believe, greatly enrich the whole art of publishing, beyond the success or failure of specific projects. Collaborating closely with individuals representing key markets can only enhance publishers' overall understanding of and responsiveness to those markets.

Publishers who regard themselves as electronic neophytes should subscribe to *Internet World* and *Wired*. They should also talk to colleagues who are knowledgeable about electronic publishing. The exposure to a unique approach to strategic thinking, included in the intensive "Mapping the Future of Information Commerce" seminar offered by Northwest Consulting (617 654 0600, Boston, MA, USA) can be very useful – and eye-opening. Talking with librarians about their visions of the future can also be instructive. Upgrading hardware and software and encouraging staff to spend time on the World Wide Web are investments that will surely pay off later. In every publishing house there are electronically adept employees who should be invited to work on some electronic project, provided they can be given relief from their other duties.

Even organizations that decide not to enter electronic publishing in the near future need to encourage management and staff to acquire expertise. The learning curve for the technologies is steep. It will be too late to acquire familiarity and expertise in the year in which the first electronic title is to be published. Publishers have vast experience in fitting content to format and to market. Developing expertise in electronic media will complement that experience and make publishers' potential contributions to the world of electronic communication a reality.

Prior to her appointment as Assistant Director for Electronic Publishing and Serials at the University of California Press in April 1994, Sandra Whisler spent more than twenty years in journals publishing at the University of Chicago Press, Springer Verlag New York and the University of California Press. She has been active in the Association of American University Presses (AAUP) and the Society for Scholarly Publishing (SSP) and is currently serving on the Board of Directors for the SSP. She can be reached at smw@garnet.berkeley.edu.

19

The Positive Role of Large Corporations
in US Book Publishing

Martin P Levin

There is a widely held view that in the second half of the 20th century the ethos of American book publishing has been damaged by concentration in the hands of a small group of large corporations. I was first invited to debate this proposition in public twenty years ago on the McNeil Lehrer Report, the prestigious Public Television news program. My opponent was Roger Straus, the founder of the independent Farrar Straus and Giroux publishing house. I was then President of the Book Publishing Group of the Times Mirror Company which, beginning in 1962, had built a major publishing entity by acquiring six independent publishers, including such icons as the New American Library, a leading paperback publisher, and Harry N Abrams, the world-famous art book publisher.

Roger Straus mourned the acquisition of distinguished publishing houses by conglomerates (ie, companies with diverse interests beyond publishing) and also by mega-publishers such as Times Mirror. He predicted that concentration in the hands of "big business" would be the "end of the golden age" of publishing in the US. Corporate management, he argued, would diminish the vigor of the industry and stifle growth by limiting publishing to titles deemed profitable.

The principal offenders, according to Roger, were corporations such as IBM, Xerox, GE, Litton, Raytheon, CBS and NBC, all of which had acquired independent publishers in the 1960s in the belief that there would be a holy marriage between the printed word and their electronic resources, cemented by the new owners' management skills. Independents, Roger argued, would continue to be ravaged by these giants and other corporations until, as in television, only the big and bad would survive.

I did not agree then and I do not agree now. To support my views, I would like first to review briefly the history of corporate participation in publishing over the past fifty years.

* * * * *

The situation in the '60s, when Roger and I had our debate, was already the sequel to earlier developments; and the situation in the '90s is quite different from that of the '60s. The history can be conveniently reviewed in three phases – the forty years from 1940 to 1980; the '80s; and the '90s.

The period from 1940 to 1980 is described by historian John Tebbel as "The Great Change" in Volume IV of his landmark work *A History of Book Publishing in the United States*. In this period, there were three intermingled, but distinct, developments:

1. the rise and decline of the "conglomerate" (the concept that publishing can be combined with other businesses);
2. the invasion of, and withdrawal from, publishing by the major communications companies; and
3. the rise of the big publishing investor.

Each of these phases can be neatly illustrated by case histories of three famous imprints – Macmillan, Random House and Simon & Schuster.

1. *Macmillan*, once described by Edith Stern as the "Mayo Clinic of book publishing", offered shares to the public in 1951 – one of the earliest issues by a publishing house. It made the move in order to free itself of its eponymous parent in the UK, which until then was a major shareholder. Ten years later, Crowell Collier, whose primary business was magazine and encyclopedia publishing, bought control of Macmillan. With additional financing obtained from Wall Street, Crowell Collier Macmillan (CCM), as it was then called, embarked on

an acquisition spree. Raymond Hagel, a chief executive recruited from outside publishing, assembled scores of companies under the CCM ownership, including such uneasy bedfellows as the high-quality non-fiction imprint The Free Press (acquired from the young Jeremiah Kaplan); the Schirmer Music Company; the C E Ward Company, a manufacturer of band instruments; Berlitz Language Schools; and Gump's department store in San Francisco. By 1980, the "Mayo Clinic of book publishing" had become a Turkish bazaar. However, Wall Street loved the profits, which also attracted suitors. A takeover bid by Mattel Inc, a toy manufacturer, was resisted. Then a bid by the American Broadcasting Company, which CCM regarded favorably, was withdrawn. Shortly thereafter, in an executive suite confrontation, Raymond Hagel, the architect of combining books with non-books, was dismissed by large shareholders (the Evans family, father and son). However, traces of the conglomerate model lingered into the 1990s, when this great American publishing house was purchased by Maxwell Communications, on whose dissolution it was dispersed.

2. *Random House* was a prime candidate for takeover at the beginning of the 1960s, when the communications giants – from ABC to Xerox and many other letters of the alphabet in between – all believed they should invest in book publishing. Random House, so named because Bennett Cerf and his close friend Donald Klopfer claimed that they founded the house "at random", had long attracted an all-star roster of editors and marketers. Bennett Cerf, author, television personality and friend of the rich and famous, was a highly visible publisher. Random House became a leading trade and juvenile publisher, with a reputation for being independent of mind. It was therefore a shock to the publishing industry in 1960 when Random House offered 30% of its shares to the public. Many of its publishing friends believed that its action was opportunistic and cynical. Public esteem for Random House sent the shares from the initial offering price of $11.25 to $45. Later, they fell back to a more realistic $17. With its newly found source of capital, Random House acquired the venerable publisher Alfred A Knopf, and then a series of smaller and talented publishers. It was not long before the communications industry took notice of Random House. CBS, the television network, turned away because it felt Random House's revenue was too small. Time Inc, the magazine

and book publisher, was frightened off by the Department of Justice, which threatened to block the acquisition. In 1965, RCA, the third suitor, acquired Random House for $40m in cash. Bennett Cerf and his associates, conscious of the dangers of being owned by a rich and powerful corporation, obtained a pledge that RCA would not interfere in any way with what was published. This pledge survived until 1980, when, after fifteen years of constructive association that enabled Random House to diversify and grow, RCA sold its shares to the privately held Newhouse organization, whose primary interests were newspaper and magazine publishing. This sale symbolized the fading interest of the communications industry in publishing. Today, ABC, who owns the modest Chilton Publishing Company, is the only broadcasting corporation in the US involved in book publishing.

3. *Simon & Schuster* illustrates the third phase in "the years of change" – the rise of the big investor. Max Schuster and Richard Simon had founded their business in the ebullient '20s. Astute merchandisers of popular books, they surrounded themselves with talent. They were innovators. With Robert de Graff they created the paperback line Pocket Books and, with Albert Leventhal, Little Golden Books, a pioneering inexpensive line of picture books for children. At their side was Leon Shimkin, a financial genius who, through a series of alliances, provided capital that enabled Simon & Schuster to grow dramatically. During the feeding frenzy for publishing stocks which began in 1960, Shimkin sold Pocket Book shares to the public. When Dick Simon died, Shimkin acquired control of Simon & Schuster, again using Pocket Book shares. This was followed by acquisition of numerous smaller houses, by now a familiar pattern. In 1975, Simon & Schuster itself was sold by Leon Shimkin. The purchasers were Gulf & Western, a conglomerate with holdings that ranged from Paramount Pictures to the United Fruit Company. Although Shimkin remained the nominal chairman until he died, the command of the company was handed to Richard Snyder, who began, with Gulf & Western cash, the most extensive acquisition program ever conducted in publishing history. Noting that there were many excellent publishing businesses for sale, Gulf & Western proceeded to buy them with gusto. The results showed that it paid to invest in publishing and that size brought with it an opportunity for enhanced profits. Other US companies with signif-

icant resources have followed in Simon & Schuster's wake, but even today have not been able to catch up.

During "the change", there were many takeover attempts which failed. Three major examples at the end of the period were assaults on Harcourt Brace Jovanovich, McGraw-Hill and Houghton Mifflin. William Jovanovich fought off a bid by Robert Maxwell to buy the company he cherished and to which he had added his name. He won, but in the end, because of decreased profits and an extraordinarily generous distribution of cash to shareholders, he ran out of resources and was forced to sell to a corporation which owned movie theaters and retail establishments.

Harold McGraw defeated a bid from American Express for McGraw-Hill in a prolonged and bitter battle. Harold Miller, President of Houghton Mifflin, successfully fought off the entreaties of a conglomerate called Western Pacific Industries. McGraw-Hill and Houghton Mifflin are still publicly held, still unaffiliated and still in the forefront of US publishing. These episodes put corporate raiders on notice that unfriendly takeovers of publishing houses were difficult to execute, and led to the development during the '80s of consensual mergers. The lessons learned from 1940 to 1980 laid the foundation and set the pattern for the extraordinary consolidation which took place from 1980 to 1995. The takeover and merger techniques used in the above examples were a testing ground for the growth to come.

* * * * *

In the Fall 1989 issue of *Book Research Quarterly* , Professor Albert Greco reported that US publishers had invested over $23.1bn in corporate takeovers. This figure, he emphasized, was based on incomplete information. He ventured an estimate that the actual amount spent for publishing acquisitions up to 1989 was in the region of $40bn. Whatever the figure, big publishers grew bigger in the '80s. Huge sums were invested to improve portfolios. New players appeared.

One corporation alone (Gulf & Western, the rich parent of Simon & Schuster) spent $1.3bn acquiring publishing companies in the years 1984 to 1986. Prentice Hall, the leading college publisher, went for $710m. Two school publishers (Ginn and Silver Burdett) became part of Simon & Schuster for $500m and $125m respectively.

With investment dollars available and publishers willing to sell, the '80s saw a virtual blizzard of acquisitions. For example:

- In 1984, CBS sold its Education and Professional Division to Harcourt Brace for $500m.
- In 1988, McGraw-Hill acquired Random House's School and College Division, enabling the latter to augment its presence in trade publishing and subsequently become the largest trade book publisher in the country, with revenues in excess of $1bn.
- Between 1984 and 1987, Macmillan, in the course of divesting some of its non-book companies under its new management, purchased thirteen publishing companies, including the family-owned Scribner Book Company, publisher of Ernest Hemingway and other notable authors.
- In 1983, Times Mirror elected to leave the trade book business and concentrate more on professional and scientific publishing. This caused it to sell the New American Library to Odyssey Partners, an investor group, who did not keep it for long. After adding the family-held E P Dutton, Odyssey sold both imprints to Pearson, owner of Penguin and Longman.

This last example draws attention to another major development of the '80s: the arrival of the Europeans. Leading publishers from Germany, Holland, France, Canada, the UK and Australia made significant investments in the US market, of which the following are examples:

- In 1986, Bertelsmann, the internationally-minded German group, combined three US purchases into Bantam Doubleday Dell, creating thereby a major presence in the hardcover, paperback and book club markets. This represented an investment of more than $500m.
- Elsevier, the Dutch specialist in journal publishing, acquired during the period 1985 to 1988 twelve modestly important professional and scientific publishers.
- Germany's Verlagsgruppe Georg von Holtzbrinck in 1986 made the first of its many US acquisitions when it bought the magazine Scientific American and its college imprint W H Freeman, with a winning bid of $52.6m in a spirited bidding contest.
- In 1988, Hachette, the French publishing giant, acquired Grolier, the encyclopedia and children's book publisher, for $462m.
- International Thomson, the Canadian newspaper and travel conglomerate, acquired no fewer than fifteen professional and reference publishing houses during the '80s, primarily from the entrepreneurs who had founded the businesses.

- In 1988, Maxwell Communications, the publishing empire of the late Robert Maxwell, set some kind of record for investment in the US by spending $3.5bn to acquire Science Research Associates (a counselling and testing publisher); the Official Airlines Guide (a directory publisher); and, adding a new chapter to its chequered career, Macmillan.
- In 1987, the shareholders of the venerable and distinguished Harper & Row were persuaded to part with their company to Rupert Murdoch's Australia-based News Corporation for a consideration of $330m. Murdoch followed this up with the biggest single deal of all (up to that time): the acquisition of TV Guide from Walter Annenberg for $3bn. With other acquisitions, Murdoch invested a total of $4.5bn in book and magazine properties in the US during this period, in the process marrying the great British imprint Collins with Harper.
- The UK's Reed International acquired fifteen media companies in the US between 1983 and 1987, the most notable being the R R Bowker company, publishers of Publishers Weekly and The Library Journal .

In brief, the '80s saw the emergence of the mega-publisher. By the end of the decade, publishing was concentrated in the hands of about a dozen corporations, none of which was a conglomerate. They were all devoted to forms of what they variously called communications, information, entertainment and education.

* * * * *

US book publishing in the '90s is even more heavily concentrated than it was in 1980 and at the end of the '80s. By 1994, twenty publishers accounted for approximately 84% of all sales of books in the US (see table on p. 232). In 1980, the thirteen largest companies accounted for 54.6% of sales. These figures rose to fifteen companies and 62% of sales in 1985. By 1994, the top thirteen accounted for 74%, the top fifteen for 79%, and the top ten for 62%.

Heavy though this concentration is, it is less than that of television, which had been dominated by only three networks for decades until Rupert Murdoch invested millions to create a fourth. Recently, one of the top twenty book publishers (Times Warner) has merged with Turner Broadcasting to create an entity generating a revenue of $18.7bn – comparable to the revenue of the entire US book publishing industry in 1994.

Simon & Schuster, on whose earlier adventures we have touched

TABLE 1
The Largest American Book Publishers

1994			1985			1980		
Rank	Publisher	Est. Sales (Millions)	Rank	Publisher	Est. sales (Millions)	Rank	Publisher	Est. Sales (Millions)
1	Simon & Schuster	1,786	1	Simon & Schuster	921	1	Time Inc.	498
2	Reader's Digest Books	1,449	2	Reader's Digest	550	2	McGraw–Hill	355
3	The Thomson Corp.	1,361	3	McGraw–Hill	460	3	Reader's Digest	340
4	Random House	1,315	4	Time Life	420	4	CBS	320
5	McGraw-Hill	1,162	5	Macmillan	405	5	Doubleday	316
6	Time Warner	1,140	6	Harcourt Brace Jovanovich	401	6	Grolier	312
7	HarperCollins	1,096	7	Random House	385	7	Harcourt Brace	294
8	Addison Wesley, Penguin	962	8	Doubleday	380	8	Encyclopaedia Britannica	280
9	Bertelsmann Book Group	950	9	Scott Foresman	379	9	World Book	273
10	Harcourt General	920	10	Encyclopaedia Britannica	345	10	Scott Foresman	225
11	Times Mirror	880	11	International Thomson	310	11	Times Mirror	214
12	Scholastic	613	12	Grolier	296	12	Macmillan	208
13	Houghton Mifflin	483	13	CBS Educational	286	13	Prentice Hall	189
14	Harlequin	474	14	World Book	282		Total Top 13	$3,824
15	Encyclopaedia Britannica	454	15	Times Mirror	270			
16	Grolier	410		Total Top 15	$6,090			
17	John Wiley & Sons	331						
18	Putnam	278						
19	Rodale Press	231						
20	Western Publishing	175						
	Total Top 20	$16,344*						
	All of US	$19,414**		All of US	$9,800		All of US	$7,000
	% Top 20 of US	84%		% Top 15 of US	62%		% Top 13 of US	54.6%

Source: Simba Information, with permission of © holder

* Estimates provided by Simba Information with permission of © holder.
** US Dept of Commerce, Bureau of Census and International Trade Administration.

and who has been number one on the list since 1985, now dominates the industry with nearly $1.86bn of revenue – 12% of the industry's total sales. When the industry sales are tabulated for 1995, Simon & Schuster will report revenues of $2.17bn, the first publisher to reach this lofty level. However, its leadership may not last long.

The Thomson Company, in February 1996, announced a merger agreement with the prominent privately-held legal publisher West, whose revenues will add $800m to Thomson. It is therefore likely that the Canadian-owned Thomson will report sales of $2.3bn in 1996 and will then be the largest publisher in the US, supplanting Simon & Schuster. The race to the top has become very competitive.

Of the twenty leaders, seven reported sales of over $1bn in 1994. Three more are well on the way to $1bn.The remarkably consistent position of Reader's Digest in book publishing shows how this global publisher of trade books is also the resident genius in direct mail selling of both fiction and non-fiction. In the period from 1980 to 1994, Reader's Digest increased its book sales fourfold.

Some of those who appear on the 1980 and 1985 lists, but not on the 1994 list, are still going strong, but are no longer visible. CBS Educational; Scott Foresman; World Book; Prentice Hall and Macmillan, for example, have been swallowed up. Doubleday, number five in 1980 and number eight in 1985, remains, combined with Bantam and Dell, at number nine on the 1994 list under the Bertelsmann flag.

Investors (on both sides of the Atlantic) still regard publishing as a growth industry. The major players and many smaller companies are listed on the stock exchanges. All of the top twenty except Random House, Bertelsmann, Rodale and Encyclopaedia Britannica are publicly held (see table on p. 235). However, in seven of the publicly held companies (Reader's Digest, Thomson, McGraw-Hill, HarperCollins, Times Mirror, Scholastic and Wiley) significant control rests in the hands of the founders' families, foundations or strong leaders. In this evolving drama, one wonders what will happen if and when this control passes into the hands of a wider class of shareholders. It is clear that there is still another act to be played.

*　*　*　*　*

A remarkable feature of the US book publishing scene in the mid-

1990s is the high percentage of foreign ownership. Seven of the top twenty are foreign-owned. Thomson (number three) is Canadian-owned. HarperCollins (number seven) belongs to Australia's News International. Addison Wesley/Penguin is part of the UK's Pearson. Bertelsmann, at number nine, is German. Harlequin belongs to Canada's Torstar and Grolier to France's Hachette. These seven represent over 25% of the total revenue of the top twenty (see table on p. 235).

Not yet in the top twenty, but not far behind, are Germany's Holtzbrinck, who, after acquiring Scientific American in 1986, bought Robert Worth, Farrar Straus and Giroux and St Martin's Press; Reed Elsevier, already owner of many US houses, who paid $1.5bn to acquire Lexis/Nexis from the Mead Paper Company; and Wolters Kluwer, the Dutch professional publishing group, who towards the end of 1995 acquired Commerce Clearing House, a major publisher of tax and business information whose revenues are over $400m annually. This one acquisition places Wolters Kluwer among the top twenty. Encyclopaedia Britannica is under contract to be sold to Jacob Safra, a private Swiss investor. The trend to foreign ownership is accelerating. It is likely that before long fully one-third of the US publishing revenues will be in the hands of foreign ownership.

Foreign acquirors have arrived in the US for a number of reasons, the most basic being that the US is the largest market in the world for English-language books. Secondly, this very factor of size, combined with the maturity of the US publishing industry, has made it difficult to start in the publishing business from scratch, except on a small scale. Thirdly, there are no barriers to the ownership of publishing companies, even in culturally-sensitive areas. Fourthly, privately-held US companies have proved to be amenable to being sold, provided the price is right. Fifthly, the strength of foreign currencies relative to the dollar has made acquisitions by immigrant companies attractive. Sixthly, the foreign publishing corporations who have established themselves as major presences in the US in the last fifteen years are themselves large, mature and well-funded. And, seventhly, there is an implicit element of reciprocity. US corporations have acquired substantial interests abroad, notably in Canada and the UK.

Publishers from countries such as Germany, France and the Netherlands have an additional reason for turning to the US – they

TABLE 2
Top 20 US Book Publishers

	Name	Ownership	National Origin
1.	Simon & Schuster	Viacom (public)	US
2.	Reader's Digest	Reader's Digest (public)	US
3.	Thomson Corporation	Thomson Corporation (public)	Canadian
4.	Random House	Advance Publications (Newhouse–independent)	US
5.	McGraw-Hill	McGraw-Hill (public)	US
6.	Time Warner	Time Warner (public)	US
7.	HarperCollins	News International (public)	Australian
8.	Addison Wesley, Penguin	Pearson (public)	UK
9.	Bantam Doubleday, Dell	Bertelsmann Foundation (independent)	German
10.	Harcourt General	Harcourt General (public)	US
11.	Times Mirror	Times Mirror (public)	US
12.	Scholastic	Scholastic (public)	US
13.	Houghton Mifflin	Houghton Mifflin (public)	US
14.	Harlequin	Torstar (public)	Canadian
15.	Encyclopædia Britannica	Jacob Safra (private)	Swiss
16.	Grolier	Hachette (public)	French
17.	John Wiley & Sons	(public)	US
18.	Putnam	Seagrams 80%; Mashusista 20% (public)	Canadian/Japanese
19.	Rodale Press	(private)	US
20.	Western Publishing	(public)	US

have limited room for growth in their domestic markets. Seeking to publish in English, these European companies have naturally turned their attention to the US market, which, according to Euromonitor, represents 32% of world revenue, with future sales projected at a compounded annual rate of increase of 7.3%. Those engaged in professional reference and journal publishing, such as Reed Elsevier, Wolters Kluwer or Thomson, no doubt also wish to be in the forefront in the application of the electronic technologies to book publishing, and this means being in the US.

So the phenomenon of concentration in book publishing in the US in the 1990s is not only a national phenomenon, but reflects a world trend in which the US is the leader. A major difference in the '90s, as compared with the '70s, is that most mega-publishers confine their activities to publishing or to businesses which are kindred with it. Most of the major transactions in the past ten years have been within what can loosely be called the publishing world, rather than between publishers and non-publishing entrepreneurs eager to enter into publishing. Before turning to an analysis of the merits or de-merits of this phenomenon, it is pertinent to examine what has happened to small publishers – the remaining 16% of the market.

*   *   *   *   *

Many industry experts felt that the extraordinary consolidation of publishing power would reduce the numbers of small publishers. Such data as we have do not support this. The Department of Commerce reports that the number of publishers with fewer than twenty employees grew from almost 1,400 in 1977 to 1,700 in 1982 and to almost 1,900 by 1987. This trend is confirmed by the numbers of exhibitors at the American Booksellers Association annual conventions. There were 1,600 publishers' displays at the ABA in 1994 and 1,800 in 1995. The additional 200 were all small publishers. Five years ago (LOGOS 1/1), Richard Abel drew attention to the growth of the small publisher by analyzing new ISBN numbers.

So small publishers are very much alive. Are they well? Endangered species do not multiply unless the environment favors them. Among factors working in the small publishers' favor is that they can get their books to market more effectively than ever before because, during the past decade, a number of national distributors have emerged. Small publishers can buy marketing services, sales representation, warehousing, billing and collection on a fee basis. Those who prefer to sell directly can contract with an army of independent sales representatives selling on a commission basis to the book trade and to schools and libraries. Ingram, for example, the premier US book wholesaler, stocks and sells books of all publishers large and small, affording small publishers as much access to chain and independent bookstores as their large competitors. Some of these competitors, eg, Simon & Schuster, Penguin, St Martin's Press or Little, Brown themselves act as distributors for small publishers.

We also have to ask: What is "small"? The top twenty publishers in 1994 had a cut-off of $175m. There is a sturdy group of publishers with sales from $25m to $175m who can be assumed to be flourishing, if only because they are acquisition targets for the top twenty.

At the bottom end of the scale there is a very large group of publishers with sales in the $1m to $5m range. *Publishers Weekly*, the US trade journal, runs an annual summary describing these small publishers, who generally serve niche markets. They are typically the brain children of creative entrepreneurs who have identified unexploited opportunities to create books that sell to discrete audiences. They are aggressive and represent a vital part of the industry.

While we have no surveys or analyses of publishers with less than $175m revenue, there is enough evidence to indicate that most small publishers are surviving and that most of those who survive manage to be profitable. The consumer is not interested in the publisher's imprint, but in the benefit he or she can get from the book. Successful small publishers have ready access to modern production technology, enabling them to create books which appeal to millions of bookbuyers.

The major deterrent to the smaller publisher is not competition from the big ones, but lack of financing and reduced government funding for libraries and schools. Small publishers find it difficult to obtain bank credit because bankers feel that their security (accounts receivable and inventory) is too ephemeral and their major asset (copyrights) too intangible. However, history has shown that small publishers are sturdy. They have survived recessions, interest rates as high as 17%, hard-hitting budget cuts and unfriendly banks.

Among the ranks of the so-called small publishers are the US's 114 university presses, pillars of scholarly publishing who also make a significant contribution to trade publishing. These subsidized presses, in order to reduce dependence on funds provided by their institutions, publish both non-fiction and fiction that appeal to the serious reader. They are, to an increasing degree, selling their books through trade outlets, a development pioneered by Arthur Rosenthal when he went to Harvard University Press from commercial publishing two decades ago. While continuing to fulfill their primary function as a publisher of scholarly books, Harvard enhanced its income by creating worthwhile and profitable trade books. Other university presses soon followed its example.

According to Peter Grenquist, Director of the Association of American University Presses, 16% of all titles published annually in the US (say roughly 8,000 out of 50,000) come from their members. The Association estimates that the 1995 sales of all university presses will exceed $400m, and increasing each year. Today's superstores, stocking 50,000 or more titles, attract many serious non-fiction readers, who bolster the growth of the sales of university press titles.

There are also many genuine and thriving small publishers hidden in the structure of big publishers, who are by no means as monolithic as they seem from the outside. Within some of the great marquees lie dozens of "publishing divisions" devoted to the creative processes of publishing. Sometimes, not always, their sales, warehouse and accounting are handled by a central corporate unit. International Thomson Publishing, with almost $1bn in revenue, is the most dramatic example of internal autonomy. It has 140 free-standing companies, some providing central services to smaller units, and all, Thomson claims, with their editorial and other creative functions as free as they were before they were acquired – and motivated by strong economic incentives to achieve superior performance.

Simon & Schuster is another example. At last count there were seventeen divisional presidents in that company, all with their own staffs and budgets. This decentralization is itself impelled by size. The larger the company, the greater is the need to decentralize decision-making. Small, creative, highly mobile, fully integrated publishing units within large enterprises are seen by most of the owners of the top twenty companies as the best models for success.

* * * * *

Another factor requires consideration. How do the mega-publishers relate to the electronic challenge to the book? There are now six million CD-ROM players in the US, and the number is growing exponentially. Using film, animation and sound, the wizardry of the computer has launched a totally new product in the art of publishing. What the large publishers are *not* doing is sitting on the sidelines. They are able to make the substantial investment required and to face the risks of uncertain success. Half of the top twenty have alliances of one kind or another with software developers. Generally, the publisher buys an equity interest in the technology firm and contracts for the conversion of books into CD-ROM. Only one major publisher – Pearson – has acquired a software developer. Software Toolworks, now renamed Mindscape, cost the Pearson shareholders a substantial $462m, 3.9 times the company's sales. Mindscape is now using the contents of Addison Wesley, Penguin and Longman books to develop CD-ROMs.

The Internet, the great leveller, is a separate but even more formidable challenge to any publisher's global ambitions. It is a leveller because even small publishers can use it to promote their books; to deliver content; or to sell books directly to consumers.

Another technology, online services, has been available to publishers since 1983. *CompuServe, America On Line, Dialog, Prodigy* and others license publishers' content for their subscribers, who reach their databases through home computers and modems. The publishers create the database; the online services load it onto their computers. The publishers receive income in the form of royalty when their material is used. The latest entry into the online market is Microsoft, the world leader in software, which plans to create a network and secure nine million users, about three times the size of the current market leader, America On Line.

The difference between the top twenty and the rest in relation to the electronic modes is that the former are investing heavily. The smaller publishers are content to license their rights and wait to see what, if anything, the new technologies mean to the growth of the publishing business.

* * * * *

To sum up, the US book publishing industry in the past fifty years has:
1.   grown and prospered dramatically;
2.   survived the threat of conglomeracy in the '60s and '70s;
3.   coalesced into large, mainly publicly-held, corporations in the '80s;
4.   attracted substantial foreign investment;
5.   spawned an increasing number of new small entrepreneurs; and
6.   is facing an unknown degree of mutation by the electronic modes.

How are we to assess the situation today in the light of this history?

Concern about the role of concentration has itself a considerable history. In 1979 and 1980, the US Senate's Committee on the Judiciary held hearings on the effect of concentration, not only in publishing, but in bookselling. Small publishers, authors and independent booksellers argued for legislation to inhibit growth. The larger publishers, represented by the Association of American Publishers, argued for laissez faire. The Senate deserves a vote of thanks for having taken no action as a result of these hearings, because the growth of publishing in the '80s and '90s has benefited all the players, not least the readers.

The critics predicted that:

1.   economic considerations would lead major publishers to act less responsibly, sacrificing quality for profit;
2.   larger publishers would crowd out smaller publishers, reducing the number of independents;
3.   publishers' revenues would decline and with that decline there would be a reduction in authors' income; and
4.   there would be fewer new titles, reducing consumer choice.

In brief, they predicted a slow meltdown. In fact, the opposite happened:

• *Quality or profit?* Publishing operates in a goldfish bowl. Reviewers pronounce publicly on the quality of each book published. University faculty members write critically about books in their fields. Editors who feel that their positions have been compromised as a result of their companies being taken over can and do move to other companies. Scores of awards identify the best and the most talented people. Other than complaints about the overwhelming importance of best-sellers and the excessive percentage of books returned, the US publishing industry today is awarded more than a passing grade by most observers. The most vocal and hardest to please are the booksellers, the ombudsmen who meet the public. With the exception of the recent case alleging discount discrimination by a number of publishers, the relationship between booksellers and publishers is one of respect and cooperation. Booksellers, like many publishers, are against the cult of the bestseller. They would like to see independent booksellers nurtured and strive to convince publishers of their responsibility in this direction. In the long list of booksellers' complaints about publishers, none has claimed that standards of quality have suffered as a result of concentration. William Jovanovich, engineer of many acquisitions of independent houses, who fell on his sword defending his own independence and commitment to quality, put it this way: "Editors and scholars are not votives who guard the truth against the black knights of capitalism .... Think not that publishing is the modern-day equivalent of the medieval monastery. It is a business. It is so purely a business that book publishing possesses all the characteristics of capitalism: central production, national distribution, routine wholesaling, retailing, price standardization and unmitigated speculation."

• *The large drive out the small?* The record shows that smaller publishers grow in number as larger publishers grow in size. In 1934, in the heart of the depression, there were only 410 publishers in the US. This number has increased every year since then. There are now more than 2,000 active publishers, and a net increase each year.

• *Lower revenues ?* Total sales of US books have grown from $1bn in 1960 to $19.4bn in 1994. During the period of greatest consolidation (1980 to 1990), revenues more than doubled – from $7bn to $15.4bn, a compounded growth rate of 8.75% per year. The projected growth rate for the next five years is 7.3%. To be sure, other factors contributed to this increase: population growth; demographic changes; increased prices; multiplication of retail outlets; and inflation. But the engine of expansion, responding to consumer surveys that the book as a form of entertainment and education would compete successfully with television and video, was the investment made by large publishers. Authors' income has also benefited.

• *Fewer titles published?* From 1960 to 1970, title production more than doubled; from 16,554 to 36,071. Growth thereafter was slower, reaching 50,070 new titles by 1985, and has remained steady since then, despite slight decreases in 1990 and 1993.

Those who have acquired, and who continue to acquire, publishing houses invest boldly in this unique and imperfect business. This investment has made it a better business for all. The challenges ahead are almost certainly greater than those that have so far been met. The serious-minded big players accept the burden of meeting these challenges for the simple reason that they have the most to gain or lose. Not only have entrepreneurial publishers not been snuffed out by the mega-publishers, but the latter, recognizing the uniqueness of each imprint, have fostered independence within their own structures, making publishing the best little "big business" in the world. Large-scale operations imply commitment.

It is a pity that there is no program in the US to encourage the formation of new innovative publishing businesses. Training facilities in publishing are limited. We can only hope that by some miracle talented young publishers will continue to start small businesses, a constant flow of which is needed to refresh the industry. The preservation of the spotted owl is a higher priority for government funding than the preservation of our publishing profession. The Small Business Administration, designed to assist the formation and growth of new businesses, is not permitted, by law, to furnish services to publishers.

The history of the past fifty years is an uncertain guide to the future. The old entrepreneurial class of publishers is gone. One of the few major family dynasties left in publishing is John Wiley & Sons. Such an exception only emphasizes the trend.

In putting the case for corporations, I have used events and statistics wherever possible to support my arguments. But I have also drawn on my thirty-four years as a publisher, much of it spent directing a large publishing enterprise. With eleven years behind me now as an attorney specializing in publishing mergers, I am conscious that my accumulated experience generates optimism, even when I cannot find facts to support it. There is magic in book publishing. Hi-tech products will find it difficult to compete with the simplicity, elegance, utility, portability and involvement of the book. This special indefinable quality has enabled the book to grow so far in a socially responsible manner. This augurs well for our future.

So I am ready for another public debate with Roger Straus, but I am not sure he will be ready to debate with me, since he recently sold his wonderful independent publishing business to Holtzbrinck. Maybe I won the debate after all.

A partner since 1984 in the intellectual property law firm of Cowan, Liebowitz and Latman in New York, Martin Levin has a very active practice in arranging publishing mergers, consulting with magazine and book publishers, teaching and writing professional articles and popular books. He began his publishing career in 1950 with Grosset and Dunlap, where he became Senior Vice President and Director. In 1966, he was appointed President of the newly formed Book Group of the Times Mirror Company. On retirement from this post in 1983, Levin fulfilled a long-nurtured desire to practice law.

20

An Independent Publisher Speaks His Mind

Donald S Lamm

The words can be faintly read on the old brick siding of the land-mark building on New York's Fifth Avenue at 48th Street: "Charles Scribner's Sons Publishers and Booksellers. Founded 1846." But Scribner's does not live there any more; in fact Scribner's hasn't lived there for nearly twenty years, ever since the venerable firm, publishers of Edith Wharton and Galsworthy and Hemingway, Fitzgerald and Thomas Wolfe, was sold by the third Scribner to inherit the business. The inscription on its sidewall notwithstanding, today the building is owned by an Italian sports clothes company.

The imprint "Scribner's" lives on, presumably lending a touch of class to the current owners of the Scribner's copyrights, the entertainment conglomerate known as Viacom. But the Scribner titles have endured heavy weather. Despite apparent pledges to the family to keep the list intact, many Scribner titles were transferred to the amorphous paperback line of the original acquiring firm (Macmillan, in its US incarnation). And while fitful efforts were made to keep a distinct Scribner's operation within the Macmillan complex, the publishing tradition represented by the fine old colophon became a trace memory.

What happened to Scribner's is emblematic of changes in American book publishing that began in the early 1960s and have continued to this day – the absorption of closely held firms, often family-owned, by large public corporations. Many attribute the waves of acquisitions and mergers over the past three decades to the inability of relatively small firms to compete against the bigger players. A slew of trendy terms have been trotted out as rationales for the relentless process of buying and selling: "synergy", "cradle-to-grave publishing", "full-service publishing". Not one of these terms reflects with any accuracy what the mergers actually have accomplished.

Worshipping the great idol synergy, for example, was a particularly telling case of misplaced zeal. By acquiring Simon & Schuster, the conglomerate Paramount, named after the Hollywood film company at its core, foresaw a natural progression within its corporate boundaries from the acquisition of a manuscript by its hardcover division, the Simon & Schuster trade department, to subsequent mass-market publication by its Pocket Books subsidiary, and ultimately to a blockbuster movie at your neighborhood theater. That simply did not happen. Decision-makers in diverse areas see their domains differently. The entertainment value of a book does not automatically translate onto the silver screen or the television tube.

The concept of cradle-to-grave publishing never has taken hold either. One need look no farther than the recent sale by the American branch of HarperCollins of their educational publishing division (itself an amalgam of two venerable imprints – Harper and Scott Foresman) for confirmation of the obvious fact that an imprint does not automatically transfer strength from one division to another. Reference books aside, brand-name loyalty in publishing exists mainly in the minds of public relations flacks. I can summon personal evidence from the behavior of my own children who, while at college, often purchased Norton books oblivious to the colophon (and heedless of the savings they might have realized by a mere glance down the spine of the book).

If sheer size is no guarantor of life everlasting for a publishing enterprise, why are independent publishers in such short supply in the United States? The answer once provided by Graef Crystal, a leading expert on executive compensation, is that the owners and managers of independent publishing houses suffer from a serious affliction, underdeveloped greed glands. Perhaps so.

There is, however, a more likely explanation. In my view, independence in publishing means having to report to no higher authority – other, that is, than the market. To achieve and maintain independence, a publisher must control all – or nearly all – the tools of the business. It is not enough to set up shop with an editor or two, a publicist and a sales manager, farming out copy-editing, design and production to freelancers. Even in the new age of desktop publishing, typesetting and manufacturing are not activities integral to my characterization of independent publishing. One could argue further that a publisher can hitchhike a ride with a larger firm when it comes to sales and distribution without threat to independence. (I am not completely persuaded on this point. "Low bag order" in a salesman's kit can be harmful unless there are very close personal ties with the firm providing the sales representation or with a regional commission-sales group. And more than one American publishing house has experienced rough patches when its surrogate's fulfillment operations went awry.) Over and beyond the controlling of the tools of the business, independence relies on something that I can only label a state of mind: an infatuation with books and the people who write them.

Hovering over all book publishing enterprises today is an economic imperative to channel resources in the direction likely to yield the highest returns on investment. The independent publisher who cares about insuring his business for the long run cannot ignore that imperative. But he has one distinct advantage over his conglomerate-owned competitors: time. The independent publisher, given a good credit rating and a friendly banker or two, is not the captive of forces that demand quick payoffs. Several lean years often must be endured before major new ventures come on stream, and the independent publisher, organizationally and temperamentally, stands a far better chance of maintaining equilibrium when profits fail to exceed a prior year's results.

*   *   *   *   *

The structure of publishing in the 1990s creates a danger for the book within the very industry that produces and disseminates it, in part because in the twilight of the independents, the heads of most publishing houses no longer are the driving editorial force in their companies. Management skills take precedence over the generation of book ideas: Aside from currying the most highly valued authors, publishing CEOs are left to crunch numbers and deal with their superiors at the corporate level.

Even more threatening to the literary endeavor is the bifurcated world of authors in which superstar novelists command advances in six and seven figures while most writers are left to settle for sums they cannot afford to live on.

The star system in fiction has its counterpart in non-fiction. Celebrity memoirs and accounts of out-of-body experiences, often written by people out of their minds, force serious biographies and books in history and current affairs off the bestseller charts.

Fiction and non-fiction combined, a few hundred titles a year do the heavy lifting for the trade, or retail, end of the book business. These titles greatly distort the image of publishing in the mirror presented to outsiders, a mirror that magnifies triumphs and diminishes disasters.

In the 1920s, publishing houses were started on the proverbial shoestring. Capital requirements were nominal. Today, what economists call barriers to entry make it hazardous, if not impossible, for new publishing ventures to survive for long. Very high hurdles must be cleared in an industry where twenty large companies account for over 80% of the total sales volume.

Still, I will go out on a long limb and forecast a change ahead. Before this decade ends, some book publishing companies that exist within giant conglomerates will be spun off, either to begin a new existence as independents or to serve as prongs of major European publishing cartels into the American market. For although book publishing units generate substantial income for their conglomerate owners, the annual return on investment in book publishing generally falls well below the 15% level that races pulses on Wall Street.

Something must be out of joint. In the American business scene, God is usually on the side of the biggest battalions. Why is size no guarantor of publishing profits? It turns out that in book publishing, size confers a warrant to overpay, time and again, for name-brand authors. Booksellers may expect the largest companies to produce the greatest number of bestsellers, and they do. But those same firms also produce the greatest numbers of substantial money losers, which is the reason no bookseller who expects to remain in business orders only from the largest two or three publishers.

In the face of uncertainty, publishers tend toward reactive decision-making, responding to the siren song of a literary agent or waiting for rumor of other publishers' interest before determining whether to make an offer of publication. The so-called auction in which a group of publishers enter a bidding contest for a given author's work (or works) may have been fostered by the invention of the copying machine, which made possible the submission of a manuscript or proposal simultaneously to many publishers. The auction has evolved into a substitute for independent judgment and discovery in a time when companies no longer are driven by a particular sense of identity.

Does this mean that big-money publishing denies acceptance to writers who fail to detect the way the wind blows? Not necessarily. Although the auction – or the threat of an auction – may drive the hot deals, as *Publishers Weekly* terms them, normal publishing still relies on the interest of an editor endorsed by the sales department and ratified by orders from the bookstores. For all their excessive spending, for all their oversights, publishers do bring some order to what otherwise would be the book equivalent of bedlam.

*   *   *   *   *

Still, I remain a publisher who is foolhardy enough to believe that the book will continue to enjoy a charmed existence. Few other tools of daily life have proved as resistant to the onward march of technology. The printing techniques developed in Mainz in the mid-15th century lasted with only minor modification for four centuries. Not until the 19th century could a line of type be set by a machine rather than by hand or printing presses be fed rolls of paper rather than a single sheet at a time.

Another century would pass before computer typesetting and printing plates made from film could telescope into a single day the entire process of translating an author's manuscript into a bound book. One-day publishing would now be the norm if publishers did not stand in technology's path. Instead, with their insistence on editing, copy-editing, design and other niceties that usually pass without the notice of readers, publishers manage to impede the rapid passage of the author's original work into the marketplace.

Here, then, is the easiest way to save the book from the encroachment of the electronic media: Get rid of publishers. More than a few authors would relish the prospect of a publisher-free culture. Examples abound of authors decrying the delays imposed by publishers who have adamantly refused to speed their manuscripts along to publication. Whether by phone, letter, fax or, now, e-mail, authors let publishers know what damage has been done to their careers, their psyches, their marriages and, most important, their incomes during the nine or ten months that elapse between the submission of a completed work and its appearance in the bookstores.

Skirmishes between author and publisher arise over much else besides schedules. Obviously, nothing has greater consequence to either party than the decision whether to publish in the first place. Books do occasionally get self-published and a handful of those succeed, thereby mocking the judgment of the professionals. But, with rare exceptions, the fate of a manuscript depends on a publisher from the moment it leaves the author's grasp.

On that single fact rests my primary defense of the book and of book publishing in an electronic age: The publisher serves as a gatekeeper to the print culture. No player remotely comparable to the publisher selects what goes out over the computer-based networks. The only constraints on posting material on the Internet are a modest entry fee and usage charges.

Given all the inane, witless, imitative, even socially derelict writing that can be found among the 50,000 or so new books that appear in this country each year, one might understandably wonder exactly what gates publishers are keeping. "How did *that* book ever get published?" is a familiar question lending itself to an easy answer: Some publisher thought that it might sell.

Neither a single success nor a single failure determines the viability of a publishing house. There are, of course, exceptions, unexpected outcomes as when a bestseller proves the undoing of a small publisher who expands operations to a size that can be sustained only by the steady production of more bestsellers. A half-dozen years ago, the runaway sales of *Son of the Morning Star*, Evan Connell's life of General Custer, prompted North Point Publishers to enlarge their staff and quarters. Soon, operating expenses wiped out income. A company that had almost reached the break-even point collapsed under the weight of its expectations. That is an ever-present threat for the independent publisher of any size. For a book publisher faces a market test not once, as does, say, the manufacturer of a new super-absorbent disposable diaper, but every time a book is launched. By misreading the public's taste consistently enough, the publisher earns a place for his company in the long line of publishing enterprises, many distinguished, that either have disappeared entirely or exist merely as fading imprints within the embrace of multimedia conglomerates.

The rise and fall of publishing tears to shreds any doctrine proclaiming publisher infallibility. And since, to the best of my knowledge, no econometric model has been invented that can be applied to editorial decision making, the defense of the publisher's role as gatekeeper must be mounted without either theological or statistical reasoning. Judgment in publishing ought, in my view, to reflect three factors: personal taste, intuition and experience. That is, some mix of these factors should guide decisions that in the aggregate define the character of the publishing company.

To speak of a company's character may seem anachronistic in an industry where most of the largest companies march to the beat of stock exchanges in New York, London and Frankfurt. But seven decades ago, during a remarkable flowering of new American publishing firms, taste and intuition, if not experience, bred character into the houses founded by Alfred Knopf, Warder Norton, Richard Simon, Max Schuster, Horace Liveright, Bennett Cerf, Donald Klopfer, Alfred Harcourt, Donald Brace, Pascal Covici, Harold Guinzbug and more. Many of the founders took the ultimate step in asserting personal control over their imprints: They put their own names on the companies. It is hard to find their match today.

They were apostles of the book. "Diversification" (another corporate buzz-word) never loosened their adherence to books. But many of them did expand on their pure trade beginnings. For then, as now, no publisher has a license to ignore an opportunity to expand into areas congruent with the strength of his list. Thus, a firm that has achieved success with trade books on politics and history might sensibly decide to test the waters for such books in the universities. But a move out of books even into kindred print formats such as periodicals or newspapers, could prove a distraction that would undermine the book operation. The temptation to follow trends to reassure stockholders that the firm is alive and well is one that independent publishers can resist. Especially in the case of today's non-print media, staying slightly behind the curve prevents whiplash.

*   *   *   *   *

Those who get wobbly about the future of the book fall into two principal camps: One group sees the computer sweeping away everything in its path, the book facing elimination along with other durable attributes of civilization. The other group argues that the book is a wasteful assemblage of atoms, an obsolete delivery system that in a short time will be transformed (or, should I say, blown) to bits.

Not all the doomsayers for the book set off alarms. Some toll a quieter bell, similar perhaps to the bell on a cart carrying away victims of the Black Death. Among them is the critic Sven Birkerts. In *The Gutenberg Elegies* he eloquently, despairingly subsumes the printed word under "that part of a vestigial order that we are moving away from – by choice and by societal compulsion". In a strange way Birkerts is cast under the spell of the very change he laments. "Next to the new technologies," he writes, "the scheme of things represented by print and the snail-paced linearity of the reading act look stodgy and dull." But he rallies later when he speaks of deep reading as "the slow and meditative possession of a book". There, I think, is the crux of the matter. The computer tends to force the reader's pace, much in the manner of the old reading machines that were treadmills for the eyes, designed to help sluggish readers by presenting lines of copy at rates that could be speeded up or slowed down by the operator.

A recent motto of the American Library Association, "Take Time to Read," inadvertently exposes the vulnerability of the book in an age when time is literally of the essence, when the millisecond separates the Olympic silver medalist from the gold. But there is more at stake than speed. At a deeper level the computer ushers in a change of mentality or, as Birkerts argues, we "are adapting ourselves to the ersatz security of a vast lateral connectedness ... giving up on wisdom ... and pledging instead to a faith in the web."

A pole apart from Birkerts is Nicholas Negroponte, founding director of the Media Lab at MIT. In his book *Being Digital*, Negroponte forthrightly identifies himself as "someone who does not like to read". His quarrel with the book might be hard-wired into his sensibility, but he makes a stab at a cognitive argument. Unlike the printed books, in which "sentences, paragraphs, pages and chapters follow in an order determined not only by the author but by the physical and sequential construct of the book itself", in hypermedia "chunks of information can be re-ordered, sentences expanded, and words given definitions on the spot." Every hypermedia thus has editorial license. The text is merely the starting point, something to be augmented by the user, mixed with pictures and sound, if desired. Literary theorists who conduct textual searches in order to unlock an author's intention might as well close shop, for in the digital future, change obliterates the past.

Negroponte, of course, puts this much more optimistically:

> The access, the mobility, and the ability to effect change are what will make the future so different from the present. The information superhighway may be mostly hype today, but it is an understatement about tomorrow. It will exist beyond people's wildest predictions. As children appropriate a global information resource, and as they discover that only adults need learner's permits, we are bound to find new hope and dignity in places where very little existed before.

Somehow I find this argument less than compelling. Is the revolution in technology going to be so stimulating to young minds that it will overcome what the Librarian of Congress refers to as *aliteracy* , that is, the ability to read without the desire to do so? And will the willful ignorance of history that courses like a polluting stream through American education somehow be more tolerable because only the present and future have meaning? The shade of Santayana cannot, I subject, be dispatched so conveniently. Those who do not remember the past may be able to manipulate everything but control nothing.

The debate over the future of the book echoes a controversy that was launched in 1959 when C P Snow delivered his Rede lectures on "The Two Cultures and the Scientific Revolution". The stakes were equally high, nothing less than the "intellectual life of the whole of Western society". Snow's definition of intellectual life included a large part of practical life because, he wrote, "I should be the last person to suggest that the two can at the deepest level be distinguished."

What were Snow's two cultures?

> Literary intellectuals at one pole – at the other scientists ... Between the two (exists) a gulf of mutual miscomprehension – sometimes (particularly among the young) hostility and dislike, but most of all a lack of understanding. They have a distorted image of each other. Their attitudes are so different that, even on the level of emotion, they can't find much common ground. The nonscientists have a rooted impression that the scientists are shallowly optimistic, unaware of man's condition.

On the other hand, scientists believe that literary intellectuals are totally lacking in foresight ... anxious to control both art and thought for the existential moment.

The cultural divide that C P Snow identified three-and-a-half decades ago was neither so deep nor so wide as he surmised. I'd like to believe that the two cultures that are the focal points of these remarks – the print culture and the electronic culture – can be reconciled despite the positions staked out by their most diehard adherents.

Yet casual empiricism suggests that the hour for the book is late. Ask a builder in Santa Fe, not exactly this nation's low-rent district, why he has designed a custom house without a single built-in bookshelf and he'll take you to the entertainment room, a mini-amphitheater, complete with a 10-foot-wide screen that descends with the touch of a button. What will people do in this inner sanctum? Select among 150 prospective channels of cable TV, play computer games, project their income tax calculations for the neighbors to view – the prospects, while almost endless, most assuredly do not include reading.

The scene from New Mexico is but one cameo of a larger society that increasingly seeks its entertainment from moving rather than fixed images, a society that listens to voices in Washington and elsewhere hell-bent on persuading us that information, uncontaminated by knowledge, will set us free. Amid these disturbing signs, I somehow do not fear that the book is in a duel to the death with the new electronic media, a duel that the book as the older, less versatile artifact inevitably must lose. Nor do I fear that the book will end up merely as a collection of data to be translated into digital form and then stored, a filling station, if you will, on the information superhighway.

The book will coexist with the computer, as it has had to coexist since far earlier in this century with movies and then television. Like symphony orchestras, however, books seem destined to move gradually – not today and not tomorrow – to the fringes of our culture. Their utility will not come to an end, even if books serve future generations mainly as beacons to the headlands of civilization.

College representative, editor, Vice President – Donald Lamm has been all of these in the independent (and employee-owned) publishing house of W W Norton, of which he has been President since 1976 and

Chairman since 1984. A graduate of Yale University, he includes among his many extra-curricular activities the presidency of the Board of Governors of Yale University Press and memberships on the Council on Foreign Relations and the Commission on Preservation and Access. Lamm is also a Senator of the Phi Beta Kappa Society.

Note

Parts of this chapter were delivered as a lecture at the New York Public Library and subsequently published in *Key Reporter*, the journal of Phi Beta Kappa.

Postscript

Gordon Graham

One of the defects of the US book industry today (and I dare say of other industries) is shortage of collective memory. This is partly because the industry is dominated by large agglomerations which have substantial holdings in media other than books; which don't have much interest in the past; and whose history is hard to delineate because it is scattered among companies which have been absorbed. Large corporations are self-sufficient and aim to serve primarily their shareholders. The common ground of the industry is seen in securing legal rights and political advantage, not in any ideological attachment to the shared product, its history or culture. Interest is concentrated on last year and next year. This absence of memory is aggravated by unease over the electronic onset, which claims that the past is irrelevant.

These two major phenomena – concentration into larger units and concern about the electronic future – are recurring themes in this collection of essays on "The Book in the United States Today". Concentration characterizes bookselling as much as publishing, and the electronic future preoccupies librarians even more than publishers.

Every one of our contributors has recognized the relevance of memory by recounting something of the histories of the fields in which they are expert, in order to put their analyses of the contemporary scene and their forecasts of the future into context. "What's past is prologue" indeed. But let's not forget to study the prologues, both those which we have personally experienced and those which we have been able to

257

reconstruct as we fashioned our professional lives in the templates bequeathed by our predecessors. Not to look for solutions; not to look for comfort; not to nod wisely and murmur *Plus ça change plus c'est la même chose* (a dangerous cliché when we all know the ground is moving under our feet); but to remind ourselves of the paths we trod to our present quandaries. In brief, for perspective.

My own prologue to the subject of this volume began in a cargo plane over Burma in 1944. A US sergeant and I (a British infantry officer who had thumbed a lift) were sprawled among sacks of supplies that would shortly be parachuted to some jungle outpost. Noticing that I had nothing to read, the sergeant tore his book in half and gave me the first half. I was both grateful and shocked. Was this any way to treat a book? Whether it was or not, it was countless casual discards like this (as Betty Ballantine and Dick Abel have pointed out in their essays) which, in the course of engendering a post-war home market when the GIs were demobilized, also initiated an export market which US paperback publishers are still enjoying. I might even have participated in that revolution, since Kurt Enoch of the New American Library, passing through Bombay in 1952, asked me to be his representative in India. But I was then, and have remained, a hardcover devotee.

Paperbacks were only one facet of the great American book explosion which started forty years ago and is still reverberating. There were parallel, differently impelled facets in children's books, in college and school textbooks, in reference books, in scholarly books and journals, in scientific, technical and medical books, in religious books and in many sectors of the book industry not covered in this volume – for example adult trade books, legal publications, engineering books, DIY and cook books, and computer books (what an explosion that has been).

In fact, we might well be challenged over calling this symposium "The Book in the United States Today" on the grounds that it is too narrow. It contains nothing from or about authors or printers. What about designers? Translators? Compositors? Illustrators? Paper makers? It contains no direct contributions from the great professional bodies – the American Library Association, the American Association of Publishers, the American Booksellers Association or the Association of

American University Presses, although among our distinguished contributors there are some who have served all of these. Our defense is that we had to draw the line somewhere. Our rationale has been to facilitate a view of the whole based on an intelligent sampling.

The resultant work, in the opinion of the editors, has messages not only for book people in the US, but for the world book community. Two characteristics of the US book trade which even its most ardent critics cannot deny is that it is vibrant and that it is large. Its size indeed is one of the factors which impelled this symposium. It is so large that its vital parts have become compartmented and hence ignorant of one another, thereby losing sight of their interdependence. The Cause of the Book is hard to articulate because "The Book" does not lend itself to compartmentalization. In its many forms it is a flexible technology serving the diverse wishes of innumerable groups, sectors, professions, organizations, which variously use books as tools of learning, vehicles of entertainment or channels of information.

The compartmentalization of the book market first came to my attention when I worked in the International Division of the McGraw-Hill Book Company. McGraw-Hill in those days (the '50s) had a sales policy called "across the board". Every division was expected to sell the publications of every other division in addition to its own. The concept didn't work very effectively, except in the International Division, which had no product of its own at that time. As International Sales Manager, I thus had a unique initiation into the universal utility and diverse uses of the book. It was an invigorating cross-cultural experience to sell shorthand books on one call, college textbooks on the next, engineering handbooks on the next, children's books on the next, a subscription to *Business Week* on the next, and so on. It was an education. I was even being paid. By contrast, the people working in the product divisions not only did not know the products of the others; more grievously, they did not want to know. They were too busy. Specialization – sharpened by divisional accounting – had taken them over.

This specialism extended into the marketplace. In India, where I first worked, I sold books not only to libraries, bookstores, teachers and industry, but to anyone whom I met. A generalist at large, I too became a specialist – in the Indian and South East Asian markets. In the scale of the US book industry, of course, specialism makes sense. One person covers only primary schools in Texas; one editor deals only with organic chemistry; one accountant is entirely devoted to the costing of books; and so on. Who then has the overview? It should be "management". But they too are busy. Some academics attempt the task, but, lacking the anvil of business practice on which to forge their theories, have difficulty in commanding an audience.

That was true in the '50s. It remains true today, except that the scale is larger than ever and there are ever more specializations. This fragmentation is the main reason why we have engineered this colloquium. Those friends with whom Dick Abel and I communed as we watched the fall colors begin to speckle the high Adirondack peaks in September 1994 (Donald Lamm of W W Norton; Dick Dougherty of the School of Library and Information Science at the University of Michigan; Mark Carroll, past Publisher of Princeton University Press; Ivan Kats of the Obor Foundation; and Ron Suleski, a US academic resident in Japan) were a compatible cross-section of different book cultures. If we could talk together about the overall picture, why could we not persuade a wider cadre of key book people to come together in print and address a concerned audience? And if we could, to what end? Nothing grandiose, but perhaps just to prove that a little cross-fertilization can enrich the future harvests, whatever they may be.

The specter at the feast of course is the electronic imperative, which has a curiously homogenizing effect on a scene so convincedly individual, partly because it makes all those raised in the print culture apprehensive, and partly because the electronic culture is a business of large and (so far) long investment, well suited to the global ambitions and deep pockets of the large corporations.

There are, I think, deeper reasons why the electronic modes have a homogenizing effect. Global and instantaneous they may be, but they are not tactile. Unlike the book, they are spineless. Gone is the tingle of first picking up a book and reading on its spine the title, the author and the publisher. Gone are the proclamation and sometimes good design of the dust jacket. Gone are the blandishments of the blurb and the titillation of the title page. Gone is the verso with its vital statistics discreetly stated and its copyright notice convoluted by the threat of electronic theft. Gone is the list of contents like the movements of a symphony scanned before a concert. Gone are the dedication, the preface, the foreword. Gone is the moment when the reader settles back sensuously with the first page of the first chapter to a duologue with the author.

Certainly, the Internet is instantaneous. World Wide Web is wonderful. CD-ROM is remarkable. But individual and sensuous they are not. I know that some who read this will say, and many who don't read it would say, "Goodbye Grandpa." But when the aficionados of the keyboard, the screen and satellite tire of their endless, unedited, uncontrolled, verbal interaction, I expect to be around to hear these electronic apostles say, "Well, thank goodness that's over." It was only, after all, the development of a new format, and once this fact was recognized, the author, the publisher, the librarian and the bookseller were still around, performing their essential roles.

I began to nurture these views with some pretence to authority eighteen years ago when I was involved in persuading my employers (Reed International, now Reed Elsevier) to make a major move into electronic publishing. In the late 1970s, Butterworths licensed the LEXIS system and wired the by no means willing English legal profession into Dayton, Ohio. It worked fine, after a time. I saw lawyers weaned from their bookish habits to keyboard and terminal. I saw them search, and find in minutes, citations that would have taken days to locate in print sources. But I also saw them continuing to turn to their books, not to search, but to read and to ponder. That was when it became clear to me that the book and the non-print media would cohabit. The author remained crucial; the publisher was still useful; and the library was still necessary. And now booksellers (what shall we call them in future?) are seating their customers in front of terminals.

Naturally, I have sought confirmation in these twenty essays of this eighteen-year-old vision. I think I found it, but have diplomatically deferred any such claim to the tail end of this epilogic essay, knowing that, like all readers, I nod vigorously over, and remember vividly, the statements of those who agree with me. I might even sideline and annotate such passages. That's something which can't be done on a terminal. Please pass me my pencil sharpener.

A graduate of Glasgow University, Gordon Graham was gathered into the international book business in India, where he was trying to make a living as a newspaper correspondent in the late '40s and early

'50s. After seven years in the United States as International Sales Manager of the McGraw-Hill Book Company, he returned to the UK as Vice President for McGraw-Hill's book business in Europe and the Middle East. In 1974, Graham was appointed Chairman and Chief Executive of Butterworths, a post from which he graduated in 1990. Since then, he has edited LOGOS.

Index

ABC, 228
Abel, Richard, 25, 98, 184, 236, 260
Academic Press, 89, 150, 155, 162;
    Print and Electronic Access
    License, 162
Addison-Wesley, 144, 148
Advertising in journals: medical, 149,
    150–51; society, 193
Agency for International
    Development, 89–90
Agents, literary, 93
American Association for the
    Advancement of Science, 151
American Astronomical Society, 220
American Book Publishers Council,
    26
American Bookseller, 50, 51, 57, 60
American Booksellers Association
    (ABA), 51, 54; Convention, 13,
    236
American Educational Publishers
    Institute, 26
American Geophysical Union, 220
American Heritage Dictionary, 135
American Institute of Physics, 162,
    220
American Library Association (ALA),
    37, 38, 185, 252
American Meteorological Society, 220
American News Company, 105
American Physical Society, 159, 161,
    162
American Psychiatric Association, 221
American Society for Microbiology,
    221
American Textbook Publishers
    Institute, 26, 28
American Wholesale Booksellers
    Association, 81
Apartheid, 95

Applied Physics Letters, 162, 220, 222
Archives, 199; e-print, 159–61
Armed Services Editions, 103–104
Artandi, George, 119, 120, 123–4
Asia, 89
Aspen, 149
Association for Computing Machinery
    (ACM), 161
Association of American Geographers,
    220
Association of American Publishers
    (AAP), 240; Higher Education
    Division, 178, 180; School
    Division, 28; textbooks, 26, 167
Association of American University
    Presses (AAUP), 59, 202–203,
    208–209, 238; Book Show, 208;
    membership, 202; World Wide
    Web, 209
Astrophysical Journal Letters, 220,
    222
Auctions, 93, 248–249
Authority, 133–6
Authors: medical, 145; relations with
    publishers, 249–50; research jour-
    nals, 192; for schools, 31; society
    members, 194; star, 247–8; of text-
    books, 172, 174–5
Avon Books, 102, 108

Ballantine, Betty, viii, 101–112
Ballantine, Ian, viii, 101–112
Ballantine Books, 108–11, 112
Ballantine Sierra Club Series, 110
Banks, Russell, 52, 56
Bantam Books, 91, 105, 106, 112
Barnes and Noble (chain stores), 49,
    52, 58, 64–71, 111
Bellow, Adam, 56, 60
Bellow, Saul, 122